STRATEGIES
FOR TEACHERS

second edition

STRATEGIES
FOR TEACHERS

Teaching Content
and
Thinking Skills

PAUL D. EGGEN

University of North Florida

DONALD P. KAUCHAK

University of Utah

PRENTICE HALL, ENGLEWOOD CLIFFS, NEW JERSEY 07632

Library of Congress Cataloging-in-Publication Data

EGGEN, PAUL D.
  Strategies for teachers.

  Includes bibliographies and index.
  1. Teaching. 2. Education—Experimental methods.
3. Thought and thinking—Study and teaching. 4. Learning,
Psychology of. I. Kauchak, Donald P.
II. Title.
LB1027.3.S77 1988   371.1'02   87-14382
ISBN 0-13-851577-8

Editorial/production supervision
  and interior design: Sue Dib
Cover design: Lundgren Graphics, Ltd.
Manufacturing buyer: Carol Bystrom

This book was formerly published under the title
*Strategies for Teachers: Information Processing Models
in the Classroom*

Printed in the United States of America

10 9 8 7 6 5 4 3 2 1

ISBN 0-13-851577-8 01

Prentice-Hall International (UK) Limited, *London*
Prentice-Hall of Australia Pty. Limited, *Sydney*
Prentice-Hall Canada Inc., *Toronto*
Prentice-Hall Hispanoamericana, S.A., *Mexico*
Prentice-Hall of India Private Limited, *New Delhi*
Prentice-Hall of Japan, Inc., *Tokyo*
Prentice-Hall of Southeast Asia Pte. Ltd., *Singapore*
Editora Prentice-Hall do Brasil, Ltda., *Rio de Janeiro*

We want to dedicate this book to our parents, Clifton and Evelyn Eggen, the late Martin Kauchak, and Eleanor Kauchak for helping us to persevere in the face of difficulty and to experience the joy that can come from learning for its own sake. They gave us security to grow by providing love in the way only parents can, and this dedication is but a tiny measure of the gratitude we feel for all they've done for us.

CONTENTS

PREFACE

Major changes have occurred since the first edition of *Strategies for Teachers* was published, and we're now immersed in one of the most exciting periods in the recent history of education. Research has identified a number of links between effective teaching and improved learning. Public interest has focused, as perhaps never before, on the important role that schools serve in educating students for a technological world. Increased emphasis is being placed on the development of critical thinking skills. And, cognitive psychologists continue to unravel the mysteries of learning and memory through the use of research focusing on the information processing strategies of learners.

These advances in education serve to reinforce and embellish the ideas presented in the first edition. The teacher's central role in learning is continually verified; the need for variety and a repertoire of skills and abilities is now thoroughly documented; and the importance of students' active involvement in the learning process is increasingly apparent.

In writing the second edition we relied heavily on three sources. The first is the research on effective teaching which provided us with both a framework for the development of the models and a source for documenting their effectiveness. The second is the growing field of cognitive psychology, which served as the foundation and frame of reference as the text content was prepared. Major advances in problem-solving, schema theory, and generative learning have all provided new insights into students' thinking and learning. Work in the area of thinking skills has also helped teachers understand ways to assist students in developing their cognitive potential.

The third source is experience. Since the first edition was published, we have spent literally hundreds of hours in schools working directly with teachers and students. Because of this experience, we believe we've been able to reach our overriding goal for the second edition—a readable, practical, and useful source of staff development for teachers and supervisors that is thoroughly grounded in theory and research. We believe this combination is much improved compared to the first edition.

Like the first edition, the organization of this book is centered around teaching models. It is designed to meet the need for variety that teachers encounter in order to work most effectively with their students. Our book is different from other methods texts in that teaching strategies are not presented as cure-alls or general approaches for all teaching situations, but rather as prescriptive teaching techniques designed to accomplish specific goals. We believe that this specificity in matching strategies to goals, called a *models approach to teaching,* marks a significant step forward in pedagogical thinking. At the same time we've consciously avoided giving superficial coverage to every popular topic in education. We've attempted to present and illustrate our topics with enough depth to help readers master the techniques and comprehend the useful ideas.

The book consists of two main parts. The first three chapters provide the conceptual background needed to understand and apply the models. The remaining chapters are devoted to an in-depth presentation of the individual models including suggestions for modifications to help teachers better adapt the procedures to a variety of learning situations.

The chapters describing the specific models have been refocused to place more emphasis on the development of student thinking skills. Evidence indicates that thinking skills *can* be taught, and direct, conscious efforts by teachers facilitate this process. Accordingly, we have included sections in each chapter designed to help teachers include the development of thinking as an integral part of their teaching.

In attempting to illustrate the models in classroom settings we have used many scenarios and classroom dialogues. In each case they are based on actual classroom lessons that we have taught or observed. We hope this enhances the practical nature of the text. Our only concession to authenticity has been to reduce the length and to eliminate extraneous occurrences in the actual lessons for the sake of brevity and clarity in our written presentations. As educators, we realize that lessons do not always run smoothly, interruptions occur, and discussions often get sidetracked. We hope the value of the dialogues as clear examples will offset any compromises we've made.

Major changes have been made in the presentation of each model. The Inductive Model and the Deductive Model are now presented in separate chapters. Chapter Six, "The Integrative Model" is new and designed to help students acquire integrated bodies of knowledge in an inductively oriented procedure. Chapter Seven, "Developing Thinking Skills Through Inquiry" has been broadened to include alternate models of the inquiry process and refocused to help students develop their thinking skills through inquiry. Chapter Nine, "The Interactive Model" is also new and combines schema theory and the theory of meaningful verbal learning in a deductively oriented teaching strategy designed to help students learn and retain integrated bodies of information. The information in each chapter is thoroughly documented with research and theory, and extensive reference lists are included, which will allow readers to pursue the topics in greater depth.

A final new feature of the text is included. In addition to the exercises found throughout the text, discussion questions appear at the end of each chapter. These are designed to stimulate readers' thinking about the topics and to help internalize some of the major issues. In the final analysis, teaching is a very personal and ideosyncratic process, and we have attempted to consciously acknowledge that notion with the discussion questions.

We have tried to make this second edition one of the most up-to-date and conceptually sound teaching methods texts available today. The content is based on the best that researchers know about the teaching-learning process. We hope it provides you with the opportunity for professional growth that we all find rewarding.

STRATEGIES
FOR TEACHERS

1

INFORMATION PROCESSING MODELS AND THE DEVELOPMENT OF THINKING SKILLS

INTRODUCTION

This is a book about teaching strategy. As you study the text, you will be exposed to a variety of thematically related techniques designed to help your students learn more effectively. Effective learning occurs when students are actively involved in organizing and finding relationships in the information they encounter rather than being the passive recipients of teacher-delivered bodies of knowledge. This activity results not only in increased learning and retention of content but also in improved thinking skills.

To accomplish the goals of the text, the strategies will be described using the planning, implementation, and evaluation of teaching as organizing threads.

To introduce the techniques, let's look at two teachers involved in learning activities with their students.

Mrs. Rand began her junior high language arts class by welcoming them and saying, "Today we're going to learn a new way to think about the stories we've been reading. To do this, look at the screen and describe the two passages that you see."

She then displayed the following information on the overhead projector:

> On Friday, September 13, 1973, I was gratefully born to JoAnn and Bob Cheever. My mother said I smiled soon after arriving.

> As I place the carefully wrapped package on the park bench, I look up and see Molly walking across the street. I hope that she doesn't see me.

After the class briefly discussed the material, she put the following examples on the overhead and asked the students to compare them with the previous ones.

> Robert H. Cheever, Jr. was born to JoAnn and Bob Cheever on Friday, September 13, 1973. The nurse told his mother that he smiled after making a hesitant cry.

> As George placed the carefully wrapped package on the park bench, he looked up and saw Molly walking across the street. Her head was facing forward.

As the class proceeded, Mrs. Rand presented several additional examples of first and third person perspective in writing. After the students appeared to be comfortable with these two concepts, she asked each one to write a short narrative paragraph in both the first and third person.

Let's turn now to another teacher involved in a different subject matter area and topic. As you read the second example, consider what the two lessons have in common.

Mr. Harris was ready to begin a unit on immigration and its effect on America's development. He remembered from past experiences with this topic that it was sometimes hard to get his history class to appreciate and understand that immigration is a dynamic process shaping the American experience. To try to capture its dynamic nature, he began the first lesson of the unit by saying, "Class, I thought we might try a slightly different approach to begin our unit on immigration in America. Rather than just reading about the different immigrant groups, I'd like each of you to go out into your neighborhoods and interview someone who has actually immigrated. If you have trouble finding someone, I'll help. When you locate this person, ask the following questions:

1. Why did you decide to come to America?
2. What were the major problems that you encountered?
3. What was the biggest difference between this country and the one that you left?

Write down the responses that you get and summarize them, and then bring them to class and we'll put them on the chart that I've attached to the board."
The chart appeared as follows:

	REASONS	HARDSHIPS	DIFFERENCES
European Immigrants			
Central and South American Immigrants			
Asian Immigrants			

He went on, "When we have all the information on the chart, we will analyze the data for any similarities or differences among the groups."

What common features did you notice between the two teaching episodes? We'll examine the lessons now and see how they relate to the themes of the text.

First, the teaching in each case was based on information processing theory in psychology which views learners as active investigators of their environment (Wingfield & Byrnes, 1981). This theory is grounded in the premise that people innately strive to make sense of the world around them. In an effort to achieve the order they instinctively need, they investigate and structure the experiences they have. Teaching strategies based on this theory require that learners become active participants in the learning process. These strategies ask students to observe, compare, find similarities and differences and to form concepts and generalizations based on the similarities.

If students are to be drawn into and involved in information processing strategies, they must be provided with data to process. They cannot think in a vacuum. A second characteristic of this approach to teaching is the providing of materials which serve as the focal point for the thinking and interaction in the lesson. The teachers in the two episodes arranged to have information displayed for the students which was subsequently analyzed.

Third, the activities were thoroughly grounded in research. Mrs. Rand used examples to illustrate first and third person points of view, which are potentially difficult ideas for junior high students to understand. She dealt with the problem by first providing her examples of these ideas and then asking students to provide their own. The value of this practice in student learning is well documented in research literature (Klausmeier, 1976; Tennyson, 1978). Mr. Harris dealt with the need for illustrations by asking the members of the class to bring in individual case study data to analyze. These case studies then served as the basis for further information processing.

Fourth, Mrs. Rand and Mr. Harris were both actively involved in directing and guiding the students' analysis of the information. Good (1983) coined the term *active teaching* to provide a label for teachers with this philosophical and behavioral orientation, and the professional literature clearly documents the effectiveness of this approach.

An orientation toward problem solving is a fifth characteristic that the episodes have in common. In each instance students were asked to find patterns in the information through their own investigation and analysis. With continued practice in these processes, students learn not only the content of the lesson but also develop their thinking skills.

Finally, while the lessons were related in many ways, the specific technique each teacher used was different. The goals of the lesson were not the same, and each teacher chose the method most appropriate to reach the goal. This text is developed around the stance that there is no single most appropriate method for reaching every educational goal, and the techniques we present in the following chapters are developed with that premise as a framework.

To this point we have suggested that the text is developed from a foundation of information processing theory which is research based and requires a direct and active teacher guiding the learning activities. Through the activities, students learn content at the same time that they develop their own thinking skills. However, the specific techniques vary according to the goals and style of the teacher. Let's look now at each of these themes in more detail.

RESEARCH AND THE TEACHER'S ROLE IN LEARNING

After reading this section of the chapter, you should be able to meet the following goals.

1. You will understand design issues in the teacher effectiveness research.
2. You will understand the concept of active teaching.

The emerging body of educational research underscores the importance of the teacher in producing learning in the classroom (Brophy, 1979; Good, 1983; Gage, 1985; Brophy & Good, 1986). The findings consistently indicate that the teacher is the single most important factor outside the home environment in affecting student development. Teachers who purposely plan and actively strive for learning using effective methods produce results. The research has also reinforced the idea that classrooms are enormously complex arenas requiring vast teacher knowledge and understanding as well as skill and expertise (Dunkin & Biddle, 1974; Good & Brophy, 1984). In this section of the chapter we explore this research, place it in an historical perspective and discuss its implications for the types of teaching strategies that can be most effectively used.

Educators have not always been optimistic about the ability of research to guide practice in the classroom. In fact, there was a period during the 1960s and 1970s when teachers as well as researchers wondered not only if research caused any change, but if teachers themselves made a difference. This pessimism arose from a number of factors including faulty research designs as well as inefficient research procedures (Rosenshine, 1979; Gage & Giaconia, 1981).

One of the oldest traditions in research on teaching focused on teacher characteristics. The theme was based on the implicit assumption that teachers were "born and not made" and this idea is not completely dead today. The strategy that followed from the assumption was to look at teacher characteristics, such as warmth and humor, and to investigate whether the presence or absence of these characteristics made any differences in student learning. Unfortunately from a methodological perspective, the researchers often failed to investigate whether these traits or characteristics, typically measured on paper and pencil tests, first produced any differences in actual teaching behaviors in the classroom, let alone differences in student achievement. As we would expect, this approach proved unproductive and was ultimately abandoned.

Another line of research originating in the 1960s and extending into the 1970s focused on the relationship between home and school related factors and student learning (Coleman, Campbell, Hobson, McPortland, Mood, Weinfield, & York, 1966; Jencks, Smith, Acland, Bane, Cohen, Gintis, Heyns, & Michelson, 1972). Basically refinements of earlier work, these studies attempted to identify factors that correlated with student achievement. These studies indicated that the most important determinants of school learning were outside the classroom and even outside the school, including variables such as parents' income and educational background which were unalterable and outside education's sphere of influence. Needless to say, researchers as well as teachers were discouraged by the results. The trends seemed to suggest that the most important variables in learning were beyond anyone's control. An additional ramification of these results was a sharply reduced national and state level allocation of funds for conducting educational research. With reduced economic support, research efforts were made even more difficult.

However, from this discouragement a new and productive paradigm emerged which focused on teacher actions in the classroom. It resulted from the convergence of two separate lines of research. One of these was a re-analysis of the Coleman (1966) data mentioned earlier. This re-analysis focused on individual schools and individual teachers and found that there were large differences in the effectiveness of both. When the effects of home variables were held statistically constant, the researchers found striking differences in student achievement at both the school and teacher levels. Certain schools and teachers were much more effective in producing student learning than were others (Brophy & Good, 1986; Good & Brophy, 1986). The next questions to be asked were "Why?" and "How?".

Answers came from research methodology that focused on teacher behaviors. These observational studies took investigators into classrooms and attempted to link teacher actions to student learning. Unfortunately, the first studies were guided by speculative researcher beliefs and hunches about what *they thought* constituted good teaching. For example, a theme that generated literally hundreds of studies was based on the idea that the more indirect a teacher was in asking questions and using student ideas the more students would learn (Dunkin & Biddle, 1974). However, the realities of the classroom as measured by the data collected did not match the beliefs of the investigators.

It was not until the observational studies were combined with an additional model that the efforts became productive. This research model which attempts to document the effects of teacher behaviors on student learning is called *effectiveness research,* and it has become an important focus of attention in education. A major factor setting the effectiveness paradigm apart from the earlier efforts was the lack of any predisposition on the part of the researchers as they conducted their investigations.

The process was begun when the investigators identified samples of teachers whose students scored higher than expected for their grade and ability levels on standardized achievement measures as compared to teachers whose students scored as expected or below. They then analyzed the teachers' classroom behaviors in both groups to see if any differences existed. The results were striking. Investigators found wide variation in the behavioral patterns of the two groups, and a description of these patterns makes up the expanding body of knowledge that we now call the *teacher effectiveness research.*

Although initially correlational in nature, the model was later advanced to include experimental investigations in which effective teaching behaviors identified by the correlational studies were then taught to new groups of teachers and their effects measured (Gage & Giaconia, 1981; Gage, 1985). The actions of these teachers, and more importantly, the learning gains of their students were compared to control groups of teachers and students with positive results; the effective teachers acted differently and the students learned more. These teacher-effectiveness studies have focused on a diverse spectrum of behaviors ranging from classroom management strategies to homework and seatwork practices. The overriding conclusion from this research is that teachers do indeed make a difference.

One of the most important concepts generated by this research and an idea central to this book is called *active teaching.* We turn to it now.

ACTIVE TEACHING

The term *active teaching* was formulated by Good (1983) to refer not only to a category of teaching behaviors but also a philosophical orientation to teaching. As the name implies, active teaching places the teacher in a proactive rather than a reactive stance. It is based on the documented premise that teachers do indeed make a difference and this difference occurs when the teacher takes a positive stance toward learning and translates this position into teaching behaviors that produce improved student outcomes.

Good operationalized the concept of active teaching by describing teachers who implement the idea. These teachers

> . . . were much more active in presenting concepts, explaining the meanings of those concepts, providing appropriate practice activities, and monitoring those activities prior to assigning seatwork (1983, p. 61).

To this list we would add the following:

ACTIVE TEACHING:

1. requires that teachers purposefully plan for student learning;
2. involves the careful analysis of goals and the selection of teaching strategies that are congruent with those goals;
3. places heavy responsibility on the teacher for the presentation of content in a form that is comprehensible to students;
4. stresses the importance of teaching strategies that actively involve students in the learning process.

A thread that runs through all of these characteristics is the central involvement of the teacher in the learning process. In the pursuit of active instruction, teachers must roll up their sleeves and through their planned interactions with students help them learn.

A repertoire of effective instructional strategies that allows interaction with students is essential for active teachers. This is the topic of the next section of the chapter and the primary theme of this text. If teachers are to help students learn, they must be able to select and use teaching strategies that produce learning. In doing this, the inevitable question concerning the best way to teach arises.

THE MODELS APPROACH: A NEED FOR INSTRUCTIONAL ALTERNATIVES

After reading this section of the chapter, you should be able to meet the following goals:

1. You will understand the models approach to instruction and how it differs from other approaches.
2. You will understand the three major factors influencing the choice of a particular teaching model.

Arguments over the question about the best way to teach have absorbed educators' energies since the beginning of formal education. Attempts to answer this question have focused on authoritarian versus democratic techniques (Anderson, 1959), discovery-oriented versus explository approaches (Keislar & Schulman, 1966), teacher versus student-centeredness (Dunkin & Biddle,

1974) and direct versus indirect approaches to teaching (Peterson & Walberg, 1979). Thousands of studies have been conducted in an attempt to answer this question in its various forms and the overriding conclusion from this research is that *there is no one best way to teach.* To put these ideas into perspective, let's look now at the teaching act and some historical foundations for teaching models.

Joyce and Weil first formalized the notion of varying procedures for different teaching situations when *Models of Teaching* was published in 1972. At that time the idea was quite new and perhaps even somewhat controversial. However, since then the efficacy of teachers being able to add variety to their instruction has become so widely accepted that it is no longer an issue. At this point we are accepting the value of alternative strategies and the idea is one of the major themes of the text.

Teaching can be viewed as a task in which someone (the teacher) attempts to help one or more persons (the students) learn knowledge, skills, or attitudes (the subject matter). Each of the components influences the form or shape of the teaching act. The models approach to teaching recognizes the importance of these components and integrates them into a decision-making framework based on the three factors. It is grounded in the premise that an optimal strategy can be selected only when each is considered. They will be discussed in the following paragraphs.

Teachers are probably the most important factors influencing the question of how to teach. Directing student learning at any level is a very personal and idiosyncratic enterprise. How we teach depends to a large extent on who we are. The goals that we select, the strategies we employ and the way that we relate to students all depend on what we bring to the classroom as human beings.

Attempts to identify an ideal teacher type have proved fruitless. Hundreds of research studies investigating typology have indicated that there is no best personality pattern. Our own experiences in the schools confirm these findings. Energetic, thoughtful, humorous, serious, typical and unorthodox teachers have all proven effective in various situations. Much of teachers' effectiveness lies in understanding their own personal strengths and preferences and adopting compatible teaching strategies.

The students are a second factor influencing the choice of a teaching method. Individual students respond differently to various instructional strategies (Corno & Snow, 1986). This differential effect has been called by some researchers an aptitude-treatment interaction (Cronbach & Snow, 1977). Additional studies indicate that practices found effective with one type of student are actually ineffective with others (Coker, Medley, & Soar, 1980). Researchers in this area have shown that what a student brings to the classroom may be as important as any other factor in determining the effectiveness of a given method. Aptitude in these studies was defined in a number of ways, varying from academic abilities and background to the various kinds of interests and motivations students bring to the learning task. Each of these has been found to influence the effectiveness of a particular instructional strategy.

A third factor influencing a teacher's choice of technique is the content being taught. For example, a social studies teacher may want the class to remember basic facts concerning the American Revolution in one lesson, to understand the assimilation problems encountered by immigrants to a country in a later unit, and to analyze the strengths of a democracy compared to a communist society in a third case. Though these tasks are similar in that they all involve American history, the goal differs in each case because the content changes. The teacher is trying to deliver factual information to one class, have the students understand the process of assimilation in the second, and develop analytical skills in the third. In each of these cases, the goals of instruction change with the type of content, and the teaching strategy must match the goal.

The problem of differentiating dissimilar goals is not unique to different classes. Even within a single class period, they will vary considerably. For example, a literature teacher discussing the poem, *The Raven* might want the students to remember the poem's author, to relate it to his life, and to learn the concepts of meter, rhyme and imagery. All of these goals are related but different, and they require different teaching strategies.

As another example, consider an elementary teacher in a reading class. Here the teacher will want students to be able to correctly pronounce words, identify the major theme of a story, explain cause-and-effect relationships and predict the consequences of certain events in the story. In this case, as with the others, the teacher's goals are related but different. Trying to reach each of the goals in the same way would not only be ineffective but potentially counterproductive.

This text is based on the premise that no single approach to teaching is appropriate in all situations, and consequently, effective teaching requires alternative strategies to accomplish different goals. The best technique is the one which is most effective for reaching a particular goal in a given situation. Only when teachers are aware of different types of content can they think in terms of a "best" technique. In addition, the actual selection and use of a procedure can occur only if the teacher possesses a repertoire of techniques. The use of optimal strategies in teaching demands knowledge of alternatives. This book is designed to provide the alternatives in the form of teaching models.

Models are prescriptive teaching strategies designed to accomplish particular instructional goals. They are prescriptive in that the teacher's responsibilities during the planning, implementing and evaluating stages are clearly defined. The models described in this book are oriented toward teachers who are interested in increasing their instructional effectiveness in an active mode. However, the same models could also be used in the improvement of a curriculum or in choosing and constructing instructional materials.

Models differ from general teaching strategies in that models are designed to reach specific goals. The use of models requires an ability to specify precise learner outcomes so that a specific model can be selected to match a particular goal.

To better understand this selection process and how a teaching model relates to it, let us compare the role of a teacher using a model to that of an engineer. In considering a project, an engineer first identifies the type of structure to be built, such as a building, a bridge, or a road. Having done so, an appropriate design or blueprint to follow in building that structure is selected. The specifications of the blueprint determine the actions the builder takes and the kind of building that will result. The type of blueprint depends on the type of structure to be built. Similarly, teachers considering a model first identify what is to be taught and then make a selection in accordance with that goal. The model is specifically designed to achieve a specified set of objectives and will determine in large part the actions of the teacher.

A teaching model, then, is a type of blueprint for teaching. Extending this analogy, other similarities between a teaching model and a blueprint can be seen. Several disciplines, such as physics, structural engineering, and architecture, influence the design of a building. Similarly, many disciplines influence the design of teaching models. Anthropology, sociology, and psychology have all impacted the models currently used in the schools. Psychology is probably the most significant of these influences.

Each of the models discussed in this text is based on a particular learning theory. Various theories focus on different aspects of the learner, and as a result, their implications for teaching procedure vary. The implications are then translated to the teacher through the teaching model. In a similar manner, the procedures to be followed in building a structure are translated to the engineer through the blueprint based upon architectural theories of design.

The teacher is analogous to the builder, and just as the builder is ultimately responsible for the structure, the teacher is ultimately responsible for accomplishing the goals of a lesson. Further, just as a blueprint provides structure and direction for the builder, the model provides structure and direction for the teacher. However, a blueprint does not dictate all the actions of a builder, and a model cannot dictate all the actions taken by a teacher.

A blueprint is not a substitute for basic engineering skill, and a teaching model is not a substitute for teaching skill. A model cannot take the place of fundamental qualities in a teacher, such as knowledge of subject matter, creativity, and sensitivity to people. It is instead a tool to help good teachers teach more effectively by making their teaching more systematic and efficient. Models provide the flexibility allowing teachers to use their own creativity, just as the builder uses creativity in the act of construction. As with a blueprint, a teaching model is a design for teaching within which the teacher uses all the skill and insights at his or her command.

The number of possible teaching goals is so large and diverse that it would be impossible to consider them all in one book. As indicated in the introductory section of this chapter, this text will focus on one set of related tasks called *information processing*. We will turn now to this discussion.

INFORMATION PROCESSING

After reading this section of the chapter, you should be able to meet the following goals:

1. You will understand the differences between a behaviorist and information processing approach to learning.
2. You will understand the two major approaches to organizing internal knowledge.

Educational goals are typically divided into three families or domains: cognitive, affective and psychomotor. Cognitive goals address the development of the student's intellect; emotional and social development goals are in the affective domain; and the acquisition of manipulative and movement skills is classified as psychomotor. Each will be described briefly in the paragraphs that follow.

The affective domain considers a student's self-concept, personal growth and emotional development. Teachers who work in this area need skill in helping students diagnose and find solutions to personal and social problems. Goals such as "ability to work with peers," "consideration of the elderly" or "willingness to listen to other people's ideas" all fall within this domain. They are attitudinal in nature and do not have students' intellectual growth as their primary focus.

The psychomotor family, on the other hand, is concerned with the development of muscular skill and coordination. This area includes goals such as "learning how to sew a buttonhole," "developing a good tennis serve" or "learning to operate a wood lathe." While intellectual skills enter into each of the psychomotor tasks, the primary focus is on the development of manipulative skills rather than the growth of intellectual capability.

Cognitive goals center on the intellectual growth of the individual. Growth in this area includes the acquisition of basic skills such as reading and the ability to add and subtract as well as the learning of facts, concepts and generalizations. The explicit focus in the schools is primarily in this domain.

Within the cognitive family is an important set of goals called information processing. While admittedly oversimplified, information processing can be thought of as *the way people gather and organize information from the environment in order to form useful patterns, which can be used to explain and predict events in their experience.* Information processing goals focus on the acquisition of knowledge through an analysis of data from the world around us. They are aimed at intellectual growth achieved by students' active investigation of their environment rather than the emotional or social development of the individual.

Teachers who focus on information processing goals have dual sets of objectives. One helps students acquire bodies of useful information; the other set helps them develop the thinking skills that will allow them to learn on their own. Information processing strategies designed to teach both content and thinking skills help teachers reach both sets of objectives.

Information processing teaching strategies are based on a movement in psychological thinking which views the learner as an active investigator of the environment rather than a passive recipient of stimuli and rewards. Bruner described this emphasis as " . . . a view that treats man as a searcher after, processor of, and indeed, creator of, information" (Farnham-Diggory, 1972, p. xiii). An information processing approach to learning stresses the importance of meaningful, purposeful learning versus rote memorization of content. The brain is considered to be an organ whose primary function is "to actively seek, select, acquire, organize, store, and, at appropriate times, retrieve and utilize information about the world" (Smith, 1975, p. 2).

Information processing psychology developed from a dissatisfaction with behaviorism (Calfee, 1981; Floden, 1981). The behaviorist approach describes learning in terms of conditioning and stimulus-response pairing. For example, a teacher question is a stimulus and a memorized answer is the response. A common procedure in investigating learning within the behaviorist tradition was the serial learning task (Wickelgren, 1977). As an example of serial learning, consider the following:

Examine the following list for about three seconds each and then cover the words with a piece of paper. Now count backwards from twenty by twos.* When you've finished counting, try to recall the words in any order and compare your list with the original one.

SERIAL LEARNING LIST

Apple
Cat
Shovel
Dog
Hammer
Pear
Parrot
Saw
Banana

*Note: In formal learning studies the words would be presented one at a time for a fixed period of time. Other aspects of the study such as the distraction task designed to keep you from rehearsing and the recall task itself would be more tightly controlled.

Hamster
Vice
Orange

In the behaviorist learning paradigm, the serial list that you encountered was the stimulus (or stimuli) and the list that you remembered was the response.

However, as researchers studied the serial learning process they encountered something unanticipated; learners did not reproduce the lists in the way they were presented. Instead, when given the freedom to recall these lists in any form they preferred, they would often produce lists that appeared as follows:

Apple
Pear
Banana
Orange
Shovel
Hammer
Saw
Vice
Cat
Dog
Parrot
Hamster

It was obvious from these recall lists that something was going on in the learners' heads while they were attempting to memorize these words. They were employing a memorization strategy that linked the new material to existing cognitive structure or schemes. Learners grouped words into categories, such as fruits or animals, and use these categories to retrieve the information. Rather than facing the learning tasks passively, learners actively restructured the information to take advantage of existing categories of knowledge.

These experiments led psychologists to believe that the most interesting components in a learning experiment were not the stimuli or the responses, but rather what was going on in learners' heads when they were faced with the tasks. This emphasis on mental processes and cognitive structures stressed the importance of the way people process information. The central goal of this processing is to make the world more comprehensible or understandable.

Information processing psychologists think about the cognitive structure in learners' minds in one of two major ways. The first is as an organized and interconnected network of ideas. For example, the network of ideas surrounding a child's concept of dog might be represented as follows in Figure 1.1:

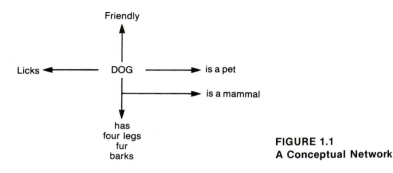

FIGURE 1.1
A Conceptual Network

Each person's conceptual network around an idea is personal and idiosyncratic and reflects that person's exposure to the concept. The structure for a child who has or raises dogs is going to be quite different from that of a child who has not been around them. More importantly, each person's conceptual framework determines how new information will be encoded. As a result, an elaborate structure based on numerous experiences allows for the ready integration of new material. The patterns we see in schools support this notion. Students who come to us with a wealth of past experiences typically learn more and faster than those who have not had such experiences. This premise is a fundamental principle that undergirds early enrichment programs for disadvantaged students.

A second way of thinking about cognitive structures is to describe them as scripts or schemas. This view emphasizes the dynamic and utilitarian aspects of knowledge. Schemas not only organize information and tell us what to expect from the world; they also tell us how it operates and what we need to do to function within it. Each of us has a schema for driving cars in general as well as one for driving our own particular car. Our schemas allow us to get into a strange car, put the key in, and with a minimum of fuss, start it and drive away. Schemas allow us to store past information in usable forms and to integrate new information into existing ones.

Anderson (1984) provided a good example of how people integrate new information into presently existing schemas. Consider the following phrase:

eat steak

As you think about these words, they evoke other thoughts and images that are clustered around your schemas for "eating steak." These typically include a plate, a knife and fork and probably a table and chair. As new information is added, our schemas change to accommodate the new information. Again, consider the following:

The baby ate the steak
The dog ate the steak   (Anderson, p. 7)

We create additional schemas to help us integrate the new information as it is encountered, and make it meaningful. No longer are knives and forks essential components of our schemas; instead, images of dog food dishes and ground-up steak are activated.

As information is integrated into our cognitive structures, whether viewed as networks or schemas, psychologists emphasize the difference between short-term and long-term memory. Short-term memory functions, for example, when someone gives you a telephone number to dial; it has limited duration and its capacity is limited. By contrast, long-term memory is virtually unlimited in capacity and duration; through it we are able to remember things that occurred years ago (Wingfield & Byrnes, 1981). In making the transition from short-term to long-term memory, information processing occurs. The quality of that processing determines the length of the memory trace and its accessibility at a later time.

To illustrate the interaction between cognitive structure and the environment and to show how information processing operates in this interaction, consider the young child as the concept of food is developed. Initially, the child's cognitive structure for food consists of a bottle or the mother's breast. This concept has been formed through interaction with the world, that is, by processing the data that come through the senses. Eventually the mother introduces solid food. At first the baby is hesitant, as the cognitive structure for food does not include concepts to help comprehend this new experience. Eventually, however, the child comes to recognize the new stimulus and no longer registers puzzlement and surprise when fed solid food. The child's cognitive structure has changed through learning that food can also exist in solid forms. The concept of food has been influenced by sensory impressions which the child has processed in an attempt to make the world more comprehensible.

This process continues with experience, each new food changing the cognitive structure and each familiar food being assimilated by the same structure. This process extends throughout life with the concept of food as well as with other concepts, and this interaction between the learner and the environment is the basis for cognitive growth. The strategies described in this text are designed to take advantage of our ability as learners to actively investigate the environment and structure our experiences.

In general, processing that emphasizes the meaningfulness of the material being learned and the integration of new material into presently existing schemas is superior to rote approaches to learning (Gage & Berliner, 1984; Rosenshine & Stevens, 1986). While *meaningful* is one of the most overused terms in the educational literature, it does, however, have a reasonably well-defined meaning. An idea is considered meaningful to the extent that associations can be made with it and other ideas (Gage & Berliner, 1984). The more associations that can be made, the more meaningful the idea is. For example, we have made an effort to make the concept of teaching model more meaningful for you by associating it with engineering. As you continue the study of this text, we hope the meaningfulness will increase when you begin to make associations between the models and various forms of content, thinking skills, types of reasoning, and modifications.

As noted earlier in this section, information processing involves a dual and inextricable relationship that involves the acquisition of organized bodies of knowledge and the intellectual skills necessary to learn independently. We turn now to a discussion of these skills.

THINKING SKILLS IN THE CLASSROOM

In recent years considerable emphasis has been placed on the school's role in the development of students' thinking skills (Link, 1985; Costa, 1985). Educators are recognizing that it is no longer sufficient to simply teach students what they should know, but in addition they must be taught *how* to know. Psychology in general and information processing specifically provide one valuable framework for addressing the development of students' thinking skills and abilities (Steinberg, 1985; Rosenshine & Stevens, 1986).

Optimal development of students' intellectual abilities occurs in the classroom when learners are provided ongoing opportunities to practice these skills across diverse areas of curriculum. As illustrations of activities which develop thinking skills, consider the following:

1. A teacher wants her class to understand the concept of participatory democracy. She teaches the lesson by providing the students with descriptions that range from their student government to the United Nations. She also includes cases of nonparticipatory governments for contrast. The students examine and discuss the similarities in the examples and identify the ways they are different from those that are nonparticipatory. They continue until they can specify the features of participatory democracy that are consistent with the examples.
2. A field trip to the zoo is followed by the teacher asking the class to list all the animals they saw. The class then groups the members of the list in terms of similarities, and they discuss the basis for the groups.
3. A biology teacher wants students to know how the human circulatory system operates. To reinforce the idea students are asked to form an analogy with the sanitary system of a city. Students make comparisons between the analogous parts such as large water mains, pumping stations, and sewage treatment plants.
4. As an introductory activity in the reading of *Silas Marner*, a freshman literature class is given a handout describing two seemingly dissimilar characters. When told the descriptions are of the same person, the students attempt to explain the disparity. The teacher uses these explanations as a basis for discussing the book.

Let's look now at the similarities in the examples.

First, each teacher was trying to communicate some type of knowledge. The content ranged from understanding participatory democracy and the circulatory system to identifying the similarities among zoo animals and characters within a novel. Attainment of knowledge was a central goal in each of the lessons. The development of thinking skills was not pursued at the expense of content.

Second, as the students were learning the content, they were presented with information and were involved in making comparisons, finding patterns, forming and documenting conclusions and developing generalizations. Rather than being passive listeners, they found their own relationships in the content they were learning with active guidance from the teacher.

It is our opinion, as well as the opinion of others working in the area (Beyer, 1983, 1984), that the most logical and productive way to teach students thinking skills is to provide them with ongoing and continual opportunities for direct practice. Students are given enormous amounts of experience in developing the basic skills of reading, writing, and various components of math. It should be no less the case with thinking skills.

The most efficient way to provide the needed experience is by integrating the skills into the regular curriculum. This is important for several reasons. First, this approach allows teachers to help students develop their thinking skills without sacrificing content. This not only allows teachers to develop both important goals but also insures ample opportunities for ongoing practice.

An alternate approach is to deal with thinking as a separate part of the curriculum, such as a course in "thinking." This approach has several drawbacks. First, thinking and content are literally inseparable. When students practice the skills, they must practice them on some form of knowledge. As we stated earlier, thinking is not done in a vacuum. A separate approach to thinking skills also is less likely to succeed. Because thinking skills compete with other areas for time, a win-lose relationship develops. As more time is devoted to one area, less time is devoted to the other.

SUMMARY

In this chapter we discussed four separate but interrelated themes. Perhaps the most important of these is the idea developed from the teacher effectiveness research that teachers make a difference. The entirety of this book is based on the idea that an *active* teacher is the primary factor that influences learning in classrooms. A major goal of the text is to empower teachers with the knowledge, understanding and strategies that will allow them to become more effective.

Two additional themes of information processing and thinking skills were also introduced in the chapter. Information processing as a major school of psychology provides the framework for the design of the effective teaching strategies described in Part II.

Thinking skills, the ability to use information to find order in the world and solve problems, are an important part of the school curriculum. Information processing teaching strategies provide an effective means of teaching thinking skills without sacrificing content.

The fourth theme was the models approach to instruction. Models are alternative teaching strategies designed to achieve specific goals. The models described in this text were developed to help students learn content while they practice thinking skills. These two goals are the focus of Chapter 2.

The themes and organization of the text can be represented with the following outline. We will develop this material as the content evolves.

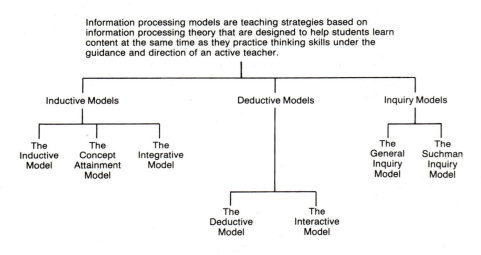

Information processing models are teaching strategies based on information processing theory that are designed to help students learn content at the same time as they practice thinking skills under the guidance and direction of an active teacher.

- Inductive Models
  - The Inductive Model
  - The Concept Attainment Model
  - The Integrative Model
- Deductive Models
  - The Deductive Model
  - The Interactive Model
- Inquiry Models
  - The General Inquiry Model
  - The Suchman Inquiry Model

DISCUSSION QUESTIONS

1.   Refer to the short teaching episodes at the beginning of the chapter. How might the same content have been taught differently? What would be the advantages and disadvantages of the alternative approaches?

2.   Describe a specific class you've been in that used an information processing approach. In your description explain how the three characteristics of information processing discussed in the first section of the chapter were either present or missing.

3.   One criticism made of the effectiveness research is that teaching effectiveness was defined in terms of student performance on standardized achievement tests. What other important school outcomes might be missed or ignored by these tests?

4.   Describe a particularly effective teacher that you've had in terms of the characteristics of active teaching described in this chapter. Do all of these characteristics apply? Are there some behaviors displayed by this teacher that were not described by the definition of active teaching?

5.   Are there some times when a teacher doesn't want to take an active teaching role? If so, when would this be and what would this role be?

6.   Choose two different content areas of the curriculum (e.g., science versus language arts). Discuss how the content in each area might influence the choice of teaching methods.

7.   Briefly describe your own personal goals for teaching and discuss how these might influence your choice of teaching methods.

8.   How does the age or ability of a student influence the choice of a teaching strategy? Imagine that you are responsible for teaching the same basic content to three different classes ranging from remedial to accelerated. How would your teaching methods differ? (See Corno & Snow, 1986, and Rosenshine, 1986, for excellent discussions of this problem.)

9.   Describe a thinking skill that you believe is important at your level or in your area of the curriculum. How would you go about teaching this thinking skill? How would you measure whether students learned it?

REFERENCES

ANDERSON, R. (1984). Some reflections on the acquisition of knowledge. *Educational Researcher, 13,* 5–10.

ANDERSON, R. (1959). Learning in discussions: A resume/the authoritarian-democratic studies. *Harvard Educational Review, 29,* 201–216.

BEYER, B. (1983). Common sense about teaching thinking skills. *Educational Leadership, 41,* pp. 44–49.

BEYER, B. (1984). Improving thinking skills—practical approaches. *Phi Delta Kappan, 65,* pp. 556–560.

BROPHY, J. (1979). Teacher behavior and its effects. *Journal of Educational Psychology, 71,* 733–750.

BROPHY, J. & GOOD, T. (1986). Teacher behavior and student achievement. In M. Wittrock, ed., *Third handbook of research on teaching.* (New York: McMillan), pp. 328–375.

CALFEE, R. (1981). Cognitive psychology and educational practice. In D. Berliner, ed., *Review of research in education,* 9th ed. (Washington D.C.: AERA), pp. 13–73.

COKER, H., MEDLEY, D., & SOAR, R. (1980). How valid are expert opinions about effectiveness teaching? *Phi Delta Kappan, 62,* 131–134, 149.

COLEMAN, J., CAMPBELL, E., HOBSON, C., MCPORTLAND, J., MOOD, A., WINFIELD, F., & YORK, R. (1966). *Equality of educational opportunity.* (Washington, D. C.: Government Printing Office).

CORNO, L. & SNOW, R. (1986). Adapting teaching to individual differences among learners. In M. Wittrock, ed., *Third handbook of research on teaching* (New York: McMillan), pp. 570–604.

COSTA, A., ed. (1985). *Developing minds* (Alexandria, Va.: Association for Supervision and Curriculum Development).

CRONBACH, L. & SNOW, R., eds. (1977). *Aptitudes and instructional methods.* (New York: Irvington/Naiburg).

DUNKIN, M. & BIDDLE, B. (1974). *The study of teaching.* (New York: Holt, Rinehart and Winston).

FARNHAM-DIGGORY, S. (1972). *Cognitive processes in education: A psychological preparation for teaching and curriculum development* (New York: Harper and Row).

FLODEN, R. (1981). The logic of information-processing psychology in education. In D. Berliner, ed., *Review of research in education,* 9th ed. (Washington D.C.: AERA), pp. 75–109.

GAGE, N. (1985). *Hard gains in the soft sciences.* (Bloomington, Ind.: Phi Delta Kappa).

GAGE, N. & BERLINER, D. (1984). *Educational psychology,* 3rd ed. (Boston: Houghton Mifflin).

GAGE, N. & GIACONIA, R. (1981). Teaching practices and student achievement: Causal connections. *New York University Education Quarterly,* XII, pp. 2–9.

GOOD, T. (1983). Research on classroom teaching. In L. Shulman and G. Sykes, eds., *Handbook of teaching and policy* (New York: Longman), pp. 42–80.

GOOD, T. & BROPHY, J. (1984). *Looking in classrooms,* 3rd ed. (New York: Harper & Row).

GOOD, T. & BROPHY, J. (1986). School effects. In M. Wittrock, ed., *Third handbook of research on teaching* (New York: McMillan), pp. 570–604.

JENCKS, C., SMITH, M., ACLAND, H., BANE, M., COHEN, D., GINTIS, H., HEYNS, B., & MICHELSON, S. (1972). *Inequality: A reassessment of the effect of family and schooling in America* (New York: Basic Books).

JOYCE, B. & WEIL, M. (1972). *Models of teaching* (Englewood Cliffs, N.J.: Prentice-Hall, Inc.).

KEISLAR, E. & SHULMAN, L., eds. (1966). *Learning by discovery: A critical appraisal* (Chicago: Rand McNally).

KLAUSMEIER, H. (1976). Instructional design and the teaching of concepts. In J. Levin and V. Allen, eds. *Cognitive learning in children* (New York: Academic Press).

LINK, F., ed. (1985). *Essays on the intellect* (Alexandria, Va.: Association for Supervision and Curriculum Development).

PETERSON, P. & Walberg, H. (1979). *Research on teaching* (Berkeley, Ca.: McCutchan).

ROSENSHINE, B. (1979). Content, time and direct instruction. In P. Peterson and H. Walberg, eds. *Research on Teaching* (Berkeley, Ca.: McCutchan).

ROSENSHINE, B. & STEVENS, R. (1986). Teaching functions. In M. Wittrock, ed., *Third handbook of research on teaching,* 3rd ed. (New York: MacMillan).

SMITH, F. (1975). *Comprehension and learning.* New York: Holt, Rinehart & Winston.

STEINBERG, R. (1985). Critical thinking: Its nature, measurement and improvement. In F. Link, ed., *Essays on the intellect* (Alexandria Va.: Association for Supervision and Curriculum Development).

TENNYSON, R. (1978, January). *Content, structure, and instruction control strategies on concept acquisition.* Paper presented at the meeting of the American Psychological Association, Toronto.

WICKELGREN, W. (1977). *Learning and memory.* (Englewood Cliffs, N.J.: Prentice Hall, Inc.).

WINGFIELD, A. & BYRNES, D. (1981). *The psychology of human memory* (New York: Academic Press).

2

CONTENT
AND
THINKING SKILLS
goals in the cognitive domain

THINKING SKILLS

Introduction

Chapter 1 introduced the themes around which the remainder of the text is developed. They are: (1) the central role active teachers play in student learning, (2) the need for different teaching methods to reach specific goals, (3) information processing as the theory on which the methods are based, and (4) thinking skills to provide students with the foundation for learning on their own. We now want to further develop the discussion of thinking to include specific skills, the reasoning involved, and the products that result from the processing.

Thinking skills are an issue of major concern to educators in our country and around the world (Beyer, 1984a; Costa, 1985; Link, 1985; Carnegie Forum Task Force on Teaching as a Profession, 1986) perhaps in response to the long-standing emphasis on basic skills, the need for people to cope with techno-logical change, the increasing information orientation of our society, and the world's ever expanding body of knowledge.

Nickerson (1984) explains the increased interest more succinctly by stating, "The increasing interest in the teaching of thinking skills and in particular in the desirability of teaching them explicitly, stems in large part from concerns about such documented failings of the current system." (p. 29)

The evidence from a number of sources suggests that the development of thinking skills is not given high priority in our schools. Research on textbook questions (Davis & Hunkins, 1966), study and test questions (Trachtenberg, 1974) as well as teacher oral questions all support the idea that the vast majority of classroom time and energy is devoted to memorization and relatively low-level thinking activities (Gall, 1970; Daines, 1982).

A more recent comprehensive study by Goodlad (1984) further supports this general conclusion. In this study, which included 38 schools, 8,624 parents, 1,350 teachers and 17,163 students, researchers observed in over 1,000 classrooms. They found

> Only *rarely* did we find evidence to suggest instruction (in reading and math) likely to go much beyond mere possession of information to a level of understanding its implications and either applying it or exploring its possible applications. Nor did we see activities likely to arouse students' curiosity or to involve them in seeking solution to some problem not already laid bare by teacher or textbook.
>
> And it appears that this preoccupation with the lower intellectual processes pervades social studies and sciences as well. An analysis of topics studied and materials used gives not an impression of student studying human adaptations and exploration but of facts to be learned. (p. 236)

Paul (1984) summarizes the evidence by stating, "Everyone with any claim to knowledge of critical thinking skills seems to agree, however, that most school systems and most teachers are not well prepared for this transformation of emphasis." (p. 5)

If we accept the conclusion that thinking skills do not presently occupy a central role in the curriculum, "why" is an important question. Beyer (1984a) in an analysis of the problem suggested several reasons, many of them outside the individual teacher's control. According to Beyer, among them are the lack of agreement among educators as to what skills should be taught, lack of precise definition of the skills, skills overload in the schools meaning that students are bombarded with one-shot exposure to dozens of skills without adequate practice, and the failure of presently used achievement tests' ability to evaluate the students' competence in the skills.

This is not to suggest that thinking skills are never taught in the schools; good teachers have always taught their students to think. However, in view of the evidence it is likely that the process is generally not systematic, and the teaching of thinking has not been a central, explicit goal of most learning activities. Rather, instruction in thinking is usually an implicit concomitant of the content being taught. Our goal is to reverse this tendency and help teachers to systematically focus on thinking at the same time as they teach their content.

Another question facing educators is whether thinking skills should be taught as separate curricula or as conscious goals within the context of existing content. Some experts (deBono, 1984; Lipman, 1984) argue the former. However, several factors support an argument against this approach. Among them is a lack of evidence that they do indeed work. Nickerson (1984) in reviewing several of these programs states, "Evidence regarding the effectiveness of specific programs for teaching thinking is sparse." (p. 36)

In addition to this lack of evidence other arguments against the creation of separate thinking skills curricula include duplication of effort, lack of training, and the problems involved in asking students to think in a content vacuum. The duplication of effort argument contends that thinking can be taught in presently existing courses, and that creating new ones is not necessary. The training argument pertains to the way teachers are prepared at the middle, junior high, and high school levels. At these levels they have a strong content orientation and a primary allegiance to some organized body of knowledge such as science, math, or social studies. To try to produce teachers without this academic background robs them of all the advantages of in-depth study in a discipline (Holmes Group, 1986).

Finally, content and thinking skills literally cannot be separated. Learners must "think" about something. Because they are inextricable the most appropriate approach is to teach thinking as a formal and explicit concomitant of the content being considered.

Further, and perhaps more pragmatically, few public schools across the nation have separate thinking skills curricula. Not many students in our country have the opportunity to be exposed to specific thinking skills instruction and materials, and it is unlikely that there will be a national trend in this direction in the near future. In order to meet the expressed need for the development of thinking skills, students need practice throughout their schooling, just as much practice is required to learn any skill. They will only get this practice if thinking skills are identified as a goal within the framework of the content being taught, so they may practice in a learning environment that is thorough, ongoing, and systematic. This is one of the themes we identified in Chapter 1.

Thinking Skills: What Function Do They Perform?

Before beginning our discussion of thinking skills and the content that results from their use, let us consider two philosophical questions which pertain to both the acquisition of knowledge and the learning of intellectual skills. The questions are: How do humans acquire knowledge, and even more basically, why do they go through the effort?

In order to begin to answer these questions, let's compare humans to other animals. They are less strong than many and they are certainly less fleet-footed than most. Their senses of smell, sight, and hearing are less developed, and yet they are not only able to control most animals but are fully capable of exterminating entire species including their own.

As Bronowski (1974) has suggested, humans are different from the lower animals in that they are capable of rational thought. Lower animals progress little past instinct and automatic responses to certain stimuli and must, therefore, live within the confines of a certain habitat. Humans, on the other hand, because of their ability to think rationally are capable of controlling their environment. One major example is the control of disease. At one time in our history the plague and more recently smallpox and polio were feared elements of our environment. Because of our ability to identify patterns in the causes and effects of the diseases, they are not only controlled but have been virtually eliminated from existence. Other animals have no such ability.

This ability to comprehend appears to extend well beyond events of necessity such as the control of disease, however. Rather it is motivated by or has its origins in a fundamental need to understand and explain the world; that is, the need to comprehend appears to be a basic intellectual drive in humankind. This need explains why small children "get into everything," why they want the same story read over and over (correcting the most minute miscue) and why they will repeatedly button and unbutton a coat long after they are fully capable of accomplishing the task. It also explains why scientists live in their laboratories, sacrificing sleep or perhaps even health in the pursuit of a new discovery. The scientist like the child is searching for order and predictability. The child corrects the miscue because the order is disrupted, and continues to button and unbutton the coat to reinforce the sense of order. The scientist is doing essentially the same thing at a more intellectually advanced stage.

On a slightly different level these same ideas explain why people are uncomfortable when the unexpected or unpredictable happens or when change is too rapid. The drive for order and predictability is an interesting idea to consider. We live in a world of patterns and routines and many people do not like their routines broken. They often go through the same ritual in the morning, travel the same route to work, park in the same place if possible, and begin their work in the same way. Most married couples have their own side of the bed, and when sleeping away from home, consciously consider the orientation of the different bed so they will be able to remain on "their own side." The least comfortable people to be around are those who are moody or inconsistent. A commonly heard remark is "I don't know how to take her. One day she is your best friend and the next day she doesn't know you," or even "I would like it better if he was a jerk all the time. At least I would know how to react." In essence the person is saying that the other individual is unpredictable. Middle school or junior high students are often considered to be the most difficult to teach, significantly because their behavior seems to vacillate so capriciously.

All these examples relate to the same idea of our need for order. Thinking skills provide us with strategies that enable us to make sense of, or to order the events in the world. The development of thinking skills give students the necessary tools to understand the content being taught as well as the larger world around them.

As teachers, we often complain that our students do not want to think, that they merely want to be told what to do. The reason for this is simple. Being told is a more ordered and less demanding state than being forced to make decisions and conclusions. Further, once made, we tend to stick with our original conclusions, sometimes in the face of added information. We have all heard the joke "Don't confuse me with the facts. My mind is made up." Paul (1984) goes further in stating, "Open-mindedness may be the proper, but is not the 'natural' disposition of the human mind" (p. 7). Open-mindedness may simply be thought of as the tendency to alter a view or conclusion in the face of new evidence. This is one of the goals of thinking skills training.

Specific Thinking Skills

What are these skills that allow us to order our environment? How can we tell if our descriptions of the order are accurate? How do we know if the conclusions we have drawn are the best ones? How can we remain open-minded? We will try to answer these questions as we develop this chapter.

Beyer (1984b) describes thinking skills as existing in three major categories: (1) the broad skills such as problem solving, (2) discrete and basic operations or processes, sometimes called microskills, and (3) a combination of the two resulting in critical thinking. Our focus will be on Beyer's second category. The reason for this emphasis is that these skills can be integrated with most content at most grade levels, and, when mastered, result in the ability to solve problems and think critically. In a sense this is where all thinking skills begin. They can, therefore, be systematically practiced throughout an entire school career.

Let us turn now to a description of the specific skills. Upon completion of this section of the text you will be able to meet the following objectives:

1. You will understand the difference between observation and inference so when given a series of statements, you will identify each as based on observation or based on inference.
2. You will understand the different forms of inference so when given a series of statements, you will identify each as based on explanatory, predictive, or generalizing inference.
3. You will demonstrate thinking skills so when given unfamiliar information, you will identify the best available conclusion based on the information.

We will begin our discussion with observation, the most fundamental of the thinking skills.

Observation

Our contact with the external world is through our senses. We are deluged with a variety of stimuli from the day we are born until the day we die. We are continually bombarded on all sides by sights, sounds, tastes, tactile sensations and smells. Our senses are our first and most basic mechanism for gathering information. Items of information acquired in this way are called *observations*.

The process of observation is common in our everyday experiences. When children recall the sequence of activities in a story, they are attempting to recall observations in the same order in which they were made. A musician plucking the strings of a guitar is making observations through the sense of hearing. The detective in mystery stories is considered to be brilliant because he is capable of making sensitive observations often missed by the untrained observer. For example, in a recent thriller, the detective walked around the swimming pool in which a body had been found, sniffing the air and tasting the water from the garden hose as well as the pool. He ultimately concluded that the body found in the pool and presumed drowned had actually died in some other way. He found out from lab tests that there was chlorine in the victim's lungs but the pool was unchlorinated. The detective, through the process of observation, was able to determine that the death was not as simple as it was made to appear.

Every time a person makes an observation, an item of information is acquired. When we read that George Washington was the first president of the United States, we are observing the words in the statement, and we vicariously experience historical events through the observations of those who had the sensory experience directly. When a boy says to his mother, "The dog is wagging his tail," the child is making observations and has acquired information about the world around him.

Observation can be defined as any information gathered through the senses alone. The reason we say "alone" is that making conclusions, finding patterns, and predicting future events all involve observation but go beyond observation to involve additional mental processing. Our experience and expectations among other things affect what we "see," but these influences do not change the fact that we are nevertheless making observations. They merely suggest that the process is not as simple as it appears on the surface.

Because of the apparent ease with which people make observations, teachers sometimes assume that the process comes naturally. It would be more accurate to say that the capacity to make observations comes naturally, but that this capacity must be developed to reach its full potential. For example, the very young child works hard at focusing and differentiating shapes. This skill becomes developed over the years until the child can observe small scribblings on the printed page and differentiate between *dog* and *god* and *dab* and *bad*. Anyone who has tried to teach a child to read will attest to the fact that the process of observation is alterable through training. Many of our preschool programs have the improvement of observational skills as one of their primary curriculum goals. Teachers at all grade levels must be sensitive to the fact that the process of observation, while naturally occurring, needs to be developed.

Even as adults our powers of observation are not always what we would like them to be. For instance, we have all heard that eyewitness accounts of an incident may vary so widely that it hardly seems like they are all talking about the same event, or we ask someone about an event that occurred an instant before and the response is, "I'm not sure, I didn't notice."

As another example, read the following phrase:

How did you read the statement? Did you miss the second "the" in it? If so, your response was very typical. Because we do not *expect* to see the word repeated, if asked what we saw, we usually say, "Tall in the saddle," and not Tall in the the saddle."

Unquestionably our observations are screened through our experience, our emotional and intellectual orientation, and our expectations. While observation seems very straightforward and simple at first glance, if considered more carefully, we see it is a very complex process. The role of experience and inclination in influencing perception is beyond the scope of this text. However, we want to emphasize the importance of observation as the fundamental thinking skill and the foundation on which all other thinking skills are based.

Inference

To begin this section let us start with three examples, the first of which is a true anecdote involving one of the authors. He was riding with a friend in the friend's Volkswagen and the car had a terrible vibration in it. His friend somewhat embarrassedly commented that he had owned the car for two years and it had been in the repair shop six times already. The author, involved in a discussion with a second friend, commented on the repair record of the VW. The second friend, an owner of a Toyota remarked, "I have 60,000 miles on my car and have never had it in the shop." The author then, almost without realizing it, concluded that the repair record of Japanese cars is better than the repair record of German cars.

Now let's consider a second illustration. While you are teaching a lesson, you see a child with his head down on his desk. You react, perhaps with irritation, at the notion that the child would be so bored that he would fall asleep during your lesson.

In another case imagine you are discussing an upcoming test and as you describe to the students what will be on it, you notice that an individual is looking out the window. You probably say wryly to yourself, "He isn't going to do very well on the exam."

Let's look briefly at the three illustrations. In each case one or more observations were made, and in each case a conclusion was drawn from the observations. Conclusions formed in this way are called inferences. The form is slightly different in each but they were inferences nevertheless.

An inference can be defined as a conclusion that is based on and extends an observation. We want to consider inferences in more detail now and also examine the thinking in the three illustrations.

Generalizing inference.   Let's now look at the first illustration in a bit more detail. The author had the repair record of the two cars described for him. This is a form of vicarious observation, information gathered through the observations of others. Based on the two observations, a pattern relating repair record to country of manufacture was suggested. The conclusion was that in general the repair records of Japanese cars are better than German cars. This is an inference because a conclusion was formed on the basis of observation, and it is a generalizing inference because the conclusion suggests that other, as yet unmade, observations would fit the pattern. In other words, the author generalized from observations that were made.

Generalizing inferences can be defined as *conclusions that summarize a series of observations to suggest a pattern, on which explanations and predictions can be based.* A generalizing inference is used to condense a set of observations into usable form and extend this summary to other, unmade observations.

Consider now another example. A small boy having just fed his dog exclaims, "Look, Dad, he likes the food. See him wag his tail." In noticing other dogs wagging their tails he first (perhaps subconsciously) summarizes the information by noting that the dogs all wagged their tails when they ate (first function). Finally he concludes, "Dogs wag their tails when they eat." From a number of discrete observations he has generalized to all classes of those observations (second function). In other words, from observing a number of dogs wag their tails while they eat, he has inferred that *all* dogs wag their tails while they eat. This is represented in Figure 2.1.

Because the boy generalized from a few observations to all members of the class, we call this a generalizing inference. We use the term to refer to the process of extending observations of events or characteristics to include those which have not yet been observed. As with all types of inference, our confidence in any generalizing inference is dependent upon the number and con-

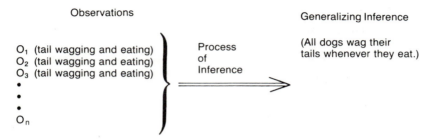

FIGURE 2.1   Generalizing from observations

sistency of the observations that we have to support it. As the number of supporting observations increases, our confidence in the generalization grows.

The process of generalizing (forming generalizing inferences) is common in our everyday life, and is a critical skill because it is through this process that we form our concepts about the world. In forming concepts we infer characteristics about a total category on the basis of our observation of a subset of that category. For example, the small boy who encounters his and other children's dogs observes characteristics such as fur, four legs, tail wagging, barking, and hand licking. His concept of *dog* then includes those characteristics, and he will expect other dogs that he encounters to also wag their tails, bark, and lick his hand, i.e., he has inferred the existence of these characteristics in dogs he has not observed.

Now, let's return to the original illustration involving the two automobiles and examine the thinking involved. Based on the repair record of one and only one observation of each auto, the author generalized in a most sweeping way. To suggest that all Japanese cars have a better repair record than all German cars is obviously ridiculous. However, unfortunately, this type of thinking is very common. We as human beings tend to form patterns on the most skimpy sets of observations. As we noted earlier in this chapter, we desire order, structure and predictability. Suggesting a pattern that applies to all cars is a more ordered state than considering individual instances. Therefore, we tend to do this, and for the most part, do it subconsciously.

Consider a second, amusing illustration involving professional tennis players Pam Shriver and Ann White. Ms. Shriver accused Ms. White of publicity seeking by wearing a somewhat provocative outfit in a tournament and was quoted as saying, "She is one of my friends, sure, one of my weirder ones. She's a California girl you know. They do anything."

In this instance Ms. Shriver is generalizing from her observation of Ms. White—and presumably a few other California girls—by suggesting that California girls as a group and as a pattern will do anything. This form of generalizing is stereotyping, and while essentially harmless in this case, it can be very destructive and dangerous when applied to racial, religious, or socioeconomic groups. The purpose of thinking skills instruction is to increase students' awareness of and sensitivity to this type of thinking, which in turn will hopefully reduce its occurrence.

We have presented examples of generalizing as a form of inference that is used inappropriately. However, generalizing is an extremely important part of learning and thinking, and when used appropriately it is an enormous aid in helping students simplify the topics they study through finding patterns and relationships. We will develop this idea more fully in the following sections, but let's examine a case taken from actual experience.

A sixth grade math student learns that the distributive law states:

$$a(b + c) = ab + ac$$

Suppose the student is now asked to respond to the following:

$$a(b + c + d) = ?$$

Many students studying this material cannot comfortably state $a(b + c + d) = ab + ac + ad$. However, by having it demonstrated and seeing the beginning of the pattern, they have little difficulty extending the relationship to as many terms as desired. Here they have generalized, so that ultimately seeing an algebraic expression such as $2(x + 2a + 3b + 5p)$ will not be a bewildering experience for them.

Further, the grammar, punctuation, and pronunciation rules that students learn are nothing more than patterns which keep students from having to memorize each instance separately and in isolation.

We can see from this discussion that generalizing is a double-edged sword. While in one sense it can be amusing at best and destructive at worst, in another sense it is a powerful tool in learning and thinking. The ability to find patterns and relationships is one of the most fundamental thinking skills.

Explanatory inferences.   Let's look now at the illustration involving the child with his head on his desk. In this case, just as with the first example, the person has made a conclusion based on observation. However, in this instance instead of suggesting a pattern based on the observations, the person is providing an explanation for the observation. For example, being bored would explain why the child has his head down.

We call inferences that tell *why*, or *explain* observations *explanatory inferences*. An explanatory inference is a conclusion that explains a single observation or a limited set of observations. Unlike generalizing inference, it does not suggest a pattern but the conclusion is based on a pattern. We will use the term "explain" in lieu of "explanatory inference" for the sake of simplicity and brevity as we develop this material.

Let's consider now other simple examples. We observe a small child watching *Sesame Street* on television every afternoon. Based on the observation of the child, we infer that she *likes* the program. *Liking* it would explain *why* she watches it. In another case we notice two men smiling and nodding, and we infer that they are enjoying themselves. Enjoying the experience would explain their smiling and nodding.

Explanatory inferences are based on previously formed generalizing inferences. For example, the conclusion that the child likes *Sesame Street* would be based on the pattern, "People tend to watch television shows that they like." "People smile when they enjoy themselves" would lead to the conclusion that the two men were having a good time.

As we did with the discussion of generalizing inferences, let's examine the thinking in the example where the student's head was on his desk. Being bored would indeed explain why the child has his head down. However, being ill would also explain the behavior, and as with generalizing, we must be cautious about the inferences we make when we explain events, particularly when we try to explain human behavior. As another example, we have all probably experienced meeting a person in the hall or on the street, speaking to the person, and having them not return the greeting. Our instant reaction might be, "Stuck up," "Snob," "Unfriendly," or some similar assessment. On the other hand, the person may have just experienced a personal crisis, or possibly was simply preoccupied at the moment. Our natural tendency is to "jump to conclusions" or "overreact" as we are sometimes accused of doing.

As a final illustration, consider a social event such as a party. We probably have all had the experience of talking to someone and getting the feeling that the person wants to leave or move. This feeling is inferential and would explain why the person is not making eye contact, is turning away, or acting restless. The process of inference is the primary mechanism that exists for explaining the events of the world, and the ability to make and assess the validity of inferences is an extremely important thinking skill.

The reasons for our tendency as human beings to "jump to conclusions" or "overreact" are complex and beyond the scope of this text. Our focus is on the examination of the thinking involved and on the effort to raise the level of sensitivity to the thinking. We will not attempt to address any moral or psychological issues involved in the process.

The process of making explanatory inferences is an important and useful one in teaching as well as life in general. For instance, as we teach we watch our students and based on their body language and facial expressions we gauge whether or not they seem to be with us. We are inferring when we do this. We watch a student, we see a frown on his face and we infer that he is confused. Being confused would explain the existence of the frown. However, obviously he could be frowning for some other reason. The tenuousness of the inferring process is one of the reasons we strongly encourage teachers to establish open communication with their students to help validate the inferences they make about their students' understanding and emotional reaction to the situation at hand.

The ability to make explanatory inferences is also a critical thinking skill for students. For example, suppose students are shown two cups of clear liquid and as two ice cubes are taken from a tray, one is dropped into each liquid. The liquids with the ice then appear as follows:

Now what might the students conclude and which of the conclusions is the most valid? Three possibilities among a variety of others might be:

"Magic."
"The ice cubes came from two different materials."
"The two liquids are not the same."

Each of the conclusions would explain why the ice cube floated in one liquid and not in the other. The teacher's goal, of course, is to encourage thinking on the part of the students that will lead to the most valid conclusion. This might involve an examination of the ice cubes or smelling the liquids. Noting that the ice cubes came from the same tray tends to detract from, although not completely eliminate, the conclusion that the ice cubes came from two different materials. A more valid conclusion would probably be the suggestion that the two liquids are different. Both of these conclusions could be easily assessed through additional observations.

The notion of magic as a reason seems silly, but we present it as a reminder that small children often find magic a very acceptable explanation for a variety of events. We should also keep in mind that the greatest intellectuals of their age once believed that everything that existed was made of earth, air, fire, and water, and within many of our lifetimes parents were discouraged from stimulating the minds of their children. We then may be less apt to react to the absurdity of small children's thinking. We need only to be a bit introspective to find some absurdity in us all.

Predictive inferences.   The third type of inference is called predictive inference or simply prediction. A predictive inference is a conclusion that suggests what a future observation will be. As with explanatory inference, it is limited to a single occurrence or a limited set.

Prediction is very common in our lives. We see a traffic light turn yellow as we approach and we begin to slow down because of the unconscious prediction that it will turn red. Signal lights on cars are designed specifically for the purpose of allowing fellow drivers to predict the behavior of the one signalling. Meteorologists predict the weather to allow us to better plan a day's events. In the case of very severe weather, such as hurricanes or tornadoes, reliable predictions can literally become a matter of life and death.

The third example described earlier illustrates this process in a school environment. In this case, based on the observation of the student looking out the window, the teacher predicted that the student would not do well in the upcoming exam.

As with explanatory inferences, predictive inferences depend on generalizing inferences. For example, the teacher's prediction that the student looking out the window would do poorly on the exam would be based on a pattern such as, "Students who don't pay attention do less well than those who do."

In the case of the turn signal, we base our prediction on the unconscious pattern, "Drivers turn in the direction indicated by the turn signal." If the driver signals and then does not turn, we typically react and in some cases are slightly irritated by the driver's behavior. This irritation is a response to the driver not following the pattern, which is a slight disruption of our *structure* for driving, a topic we discussed in the first section of this chapter.

The extent to which generalizing, explanatory, and predictive inferences impact our lives is difficult to overstate. For instance, if you are reading the material in this chapter as background material for a course, you are tacitly predicting that your achievement will be higher as a result, and that prediction would be based on the generalization, "Study enhances learning." The number of examples could go on and on.

Derived Thinking Skills

Observing, explaining, predicting, and generalizing are the foundation on which thinking is based. However, there are other important skills that derive from those fundamental ones. We want to describe them briefly now.

Comparing.   Comparing is the skill that asks learners to identify similarities and differences in information. It derives directly from observation but is an important extension, for without the ability to make comparisons, finding patterns would be impossible and generalizing depends on the identification of a pattern. We will discuss comparing in more detail as we describe the Inductive and Integrative models.

Hypothesizing.   The ability to consider a question such as "What if . . . " is a form of hypothetical reasoning. Hypothesizing is an extension of the process of generalizing, and allows learners to extend their thinking to another as yet unconsidered level. For example, in the case with the ice cubes and the fluids, students might ask or be asked, "What if the fluids were something other than water and alcohol? What might happen then?" The process of hypothetical reasoning can be applied to almost any circumstance as we will see when we discuss the Integrative model.

Critical thinking.   Critical thinking can be viewed as a derived skill that results from the ability to form valid generalizations, explanations, predictions, hypotheses, and comparisons, or the ability to assess the validity of existing statements. Recognizing irrelevant information is also a critical thinking skill. A number of other related thinking skills can be identified and defined. However, they are in essence further derivations of the skills we have discussed here. We will discuss these more specifically in later chapters. We are purposely choosing to keep the set of skills quite focused here for the purposes of brevity and clarity.

The skills discussed can be represented diagrammatically in Figure 2.2 as follows:

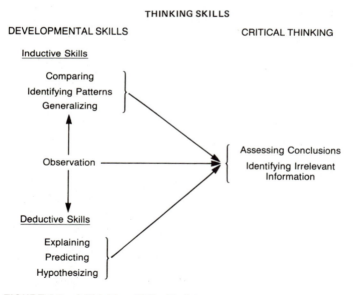

THINKING SKILLS

DEVELOPMENTAL SKILLS   CRITICAL THINKING

Inductive Skills

Comparing
Identifying Patterns
Generalizing

Observation

Assessing Conclusions
Identifying Irrelevant Information

Deductive Skills

Explaining
Predicting
Hypothesizing

FIGURE 2.2   A Thinking Skills Model

Please turn now to the exercises designed to reinforce your understanding of the material in this section.

EXERCISES

The following statements were made by a child while watching some people at a dinner party given by the child's parents. For the items numbered 1–12, identify each statement that is an observation with an O, an explanatory inference with an EI, a predictive inference with a PI, and a generalizing inference with a GI. Read item 13 and follow the directions as given.

1. Mr. Johnson is still eating.
2. The people in the room are happy.
3. There are eighteen people in the room.
4. Mrs. Jones's eyes are closed.
5. People get sleepy after they eat.
6. Some of the people are smiling.
7. Mr. Smith is taller than Mrs. Smith.
8. Mrs. Jones is asleep.
9. If Mr. Jones sees Mrs. Jones, he'll be upset.
10. Adults laugh a lot at parties.
11. My mother will be tired tomorrow.
12. Mr. Johnson must be really hungry.
13. This item is designed to measure your ability to identify a pattern and then predict on the basis of it. In later chapters we will discuss the measurement of thinking skills in more detail. At this point we want to encourage your thinking and introduce you to the measurement of it.

The following represents an animal population over a period of years.

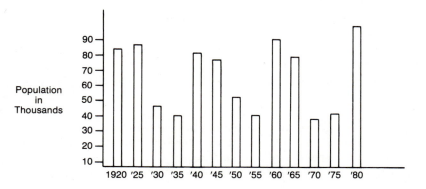

Based on this information, the best estimate of the population in 1990 would be:
   a. 10,000
   b. 40,000
   c. 80,000
   d. 130,000

FEEDBACK

O	1. Mr. Johnson is still eating.
EI	2. The people in the room are happy.
O	3. There are eighteen people in the room.
O	4. Mrs. Jones's eyes are closed.
GI	5. People get sleepy after they eat.
O	6. Some of the people are smiling.
O	7. Mr. Smith is taller than Mrs. Smith.
EI	8. Mrs. Jones is asleep.
PI	9. If Mr. Jones sees Mrs. Jones, he'll be upset.
GI	10. Adults laugh a lot at parties.
PI	11. My mother will be tired tomorrow.
EI	12. Mr. Johnson must be really hungry.

Let's look at each item briefly.

1.   This can be observed.

2.   This may appear to be a generalizing inference, but the statement is limited to the people in the room as opposed to people in general and would serve to explain some observations, such as laughter and smiles.

3.   This is an observation of the number of people in the room.

4.   Again, this could be directly observed.

5.   This is an inference about people in general. This statement could also be used to explain the observation in item 4.

6.   This is an observation which might be explained by the inference, "The people in the room are happy."

7.   This is another observation involving numbers.

8.   Mrs. Jones being asleep would explain why her eyes are closed. Sleep cannot be observed but rather must be inferred from observations such as regular breathing, snoring, body position, unresponsive behavior and so on.

9.   This statement refers to a specific person rather than people in general and suggests what a future observation will be.

10.   The statement refers to *all* adults and is therefore an inference.

11.   This refers specifically to the boy's mother and suggests a future observation.

12.   Mr. Johnson's hunger would explain why he's still eating (the observation in item 1).

13.   The best choice in the example is (b). Let's first look at each of the other choices.

The population has never been as high as 130,000 nor as low as 10,000, so these choices can be eliminated immediately. The pattern demonstrates ten years of relatively high population followed by ten years of relatively low population. The population was high in 1980, would presumably still be high in 1985, and would then be lower in 1990.

Now let's examine the thinking involved. You first had to observe. Without careful observation you might be inclined to only extend the pattern five years to 1985 instead of ten as the quesiton directs. In that case you would probably have chosen (c). Second, you had to identify a pattern in your observations and generalize from the pattern to suggest that it would continue into the future. Finally, you had to predict the population based on your generaliztion. This is a brief illustration of the type of thinking we are encouraging you to provide for your students. We will continue to illustrate these skills throughout the remainder of the text.

INDUCTIVE AND DEDUCTIVE REASONING

We have introduced the topic of thinking skills and have discussed observations and inferences in some detail. We now want to carry the analysis a step further and examine the reasoning involved in making inferences. The combination of the two is the essence of thinking skills. We will then combine the specific processes with reasoning in the final section of this chapter to see how we acquire knowledge in the form of abstractions.

Upon completion of this section you will be able to meet the following objectives:

1. You will understand inductive and deductive reasoning so when given vignettes illustrating each you will identify the process in each case.
2. You will understand the deductive syllogism so when given examples of deductive reasoning you will identify the parts of the syllogism in each case.

Reasoning can be described as proceeding in one of two ways. We either summarize a series of observations to form a pattern, or we use a pattern to explain or predict a particular event. The former is called inductive reasoning, which is the process involved in making generalizing inferences, and the latter is called deductive reasoning which is the way explanatory and predictive inferences are made. These are the reciprocal processes around which the study of logic is built.

Let's examine a simple example from common experience. You leave home at 7:30 a.m. and notice as you arrive at work that it is 8:05. The next day you leave at 7:30, arriving at 8:00 exactly. The third day you have extra work to do so you leave at 7:00 and notice that you arrive at 7:15. The same thing happens on the fourth day. You then conclude, perhaps, that leaving at 7:00 allows you to get to work in only half the time, or more formally "Leaving at 7:00 a.m. rather than 7:30 a.m. cuts the driving time to work in half."

You have identified a pattern in the observations of leaving and arrival times and have summarized the pattern into a generalizing inference. This process is an example of inductive reasoning, which can be defined as *a reasoning process that summarizes a series of specific items into a more general conclusion.* It is typically described as moving from specific to general. For instance, the reasoning process moved from the specific leaving and arrival times to the general conclusion that leaving at 7:00 results in less driving time than leaving at 7:30.

Let's look back at the example with the German and Japanese cars. The author had two observations and based on these two induced the general conclusion, "Japanese cars have a better service record than do German cars." The number of observations was clearly inadequate as a basis for forming a conclusion, but he generalized from them anyway. This is very common practice in everyday experience, and we are all guilty of it at one time or another. Interestingly, generalizing from a single example is very typical. In fact, the most common number of examples we use in generalizing is *one*!

As another example, imagine that you decide in good faith to give a friend a suggestion about how she should handle a child-rearing issue with one of her children, and your friend reacts very negatively to the advice. You are likely to conclude that "People don't want advice when it comes to their own kids." On the basis of a single example you infer that a pattern exists related to advising people about their offspring. This is another example of inductive reasoning, again with an obviously inadequate number of experiences from which to generalize, but also very common in our daily living.

The ability to assess the validity of a particular generalizing inference is an important critical thinking skill. We should be saying, "Wait, you can't generalize from only one or two examples like that." Another way of saying it might be, "Stop jumping to conclusions," which we referred to in the previous section, and have all heard and probably said. One form of "jumping to conclusions" is inappropriately generalizing.

Deductive reasoning is the counterpart of inductive reasoning. For instance, consider again the example of the social event and the conclusion that the individual was no longer interested in talking. You notice the person periodically glancing away during your conversation. You subconsciously draw from a pattern which says "Disinterested people look away during conversation," or "People trying to leave no longer make eye contact." Based on this subliminal pattern and the observation of periodic glances away, you conclude that this person wants to leave.

Let's consider now some other examples. As a parent you see your small child rubbing his eyes. You conclude that he is tired and then probably prepare him for bed. We see a person yawn and conclude that they did not get enough sleep the night before. We see students look at their watches in class and conclude that they are waiting for the class to end. Each of these is an illustration of making inferences through the process of deductive reasoning.

While inductive reasoning proceeds from a series of specific events to a general conclusion (or perhaps from one specific event to a general conclusion in many cases, which we have suggested has questionable validity), deductive reasoning begins with a general pattern and moves to a specific conclusion. Look at the process in the examples from the last paragraph. In each case it can be described in a three-part sequence as follows:

People stop making eye contact when they become disinterested.
This person is not making eye contact.
This person is not interested in continuing the conversation with me.

Children rub their eyes when they are tired.
Billy is rubbing his eyes.
Billy is tired.

The examples illustrate the three-part reasoning sequence or classification scheme, which is called the *deductive syllogism.* The first part is called the major premise, the minor premise is the second, and the last statement is called the conclusion. The deductive syllogism has no counterpart in inductive reasoning, that is, there is no inductive syllogism.

As an illustration to reinforce these ideas, consider the third example mentioned. We tacitly decide that students are waiting for class to end (conclusion) when we see them look at their watches. Observing them look at their watches is the minor premise and the conclusion is based on a pattern, probably subconscious, that would be approximately stated as, "Students look at their watches when they are waiting for classes to end" (the major premise).

There are several important features of this discussion that should be mentioned. First, the preceding example shows that the reasoning process in the real world rarely proceeds in an ordered sequence beginning with the major premise, continuing with a minor premise, and following to a conclusion. Second, many or perhaps most of the major premises we use to form our conclusions about the world are subconscious, particularly until we are forced to think about them. Third, we see how easy it is for our reasoning to be flawed, or in other words to form invalid conclusions. This may result from generalizing on too few examples, generalizing inappropriately from the examples we do have, or forming a deductive conclusion that does not follow from the major premise, the minor premise, or neither of the two. Often the examples we have presented fall into this trap. We have purposely presented them in this way for sake of illustration and to show how our thinking operates in daily living. Entire courses in logic are built around the assessment of the validity of inductive and deductive conclusions. Readers interested in a further discussion of the topic are referred to Ennis (1969), Belth (1977) or other texts on the subject.

Finally, we see how forming inferences and inductive and deductive reasoning are inextricably intertwined. Simply stated, generalizing inferences are formed inductively, and predictive and explanatory inferences are formed deductively. A discussion of making inferences necessarily requires an examination of inductive and deductive reasoning and vice versa. We will return to the topic of inductive and deductive reasoning when we consider alternative teaching methods.

To complete this section let's look at one more example of classroom practice and examine the thinking involved. Researchers have gone into classrooms and made many observations of teachers and teaching practice. Based on these observations they have concluded that teachers call on perceived high achievers significantly more often than perceived low achievers (Good & Brophy, 1984). This conclusion is a generalizing inference based on inductive reasoning. Because the number of observations was large and the observations were consistent, the conclusions appear valid. Consequently, this is an example of appropriate inductive reasoning.

The researchers found other interesting patterns as well. For instance, perceived high achievers are not only called on more often, but they are given more time to respond, receive more praise and feedback, are prompted more and are the recipients of more positive teacher nonverbal behavior. Each of these patterns has been formed inductively and is based on large numbers of consistent observations. The conclusions have a high level of validity.

On the other hand let's see how the discriminatory practice may come to happen in the first place. Consider a hypothetical teaching situation. A teacher having worked with a class for a period of time identifies students who typically do well and those who do less well. These are inductively formed patterns. The teacher then calls on one of the low achievers. The student hesitates. The teacher then goes through a subconscious reasoning process that could be described as follows:

> Low achievers typically cannot answer questions.
> This student is a low achiever.
> He is not going to be able to answer.

On the other hand the teacher calls on the perceived high achiever who is also unable to answer and the reasoning process would be something such as:

> High achievers typically can answer questions.
> This student is a high achiever.
> She will be able to answer the question.

Based on the expectation of the student not being able to answer in the first instance the teacher quickly leaves the student in favor of someone more likely to respond, while in the second case based on the opposite expectation the teacher waits longer or prompts the student. The interesting feature of all this is how the reasoning processes and the resulting inferences impact our behavior. Expectations are important inferential notions. This further illustrates how careful we must be in our thinking to avoid invalid, or in the preceding case destructive conclusions. The deductive reasoning processes in the last two instances were essentially valid, but the behaviors that result from the outcomes can have far-reaching, unfortunate consequences.

Encouragingly, this is not a problem that defies solution. Kerman (1979) describes a program that produced startling results when teachers were trained to avoid subconscious discriminatory practice. When teachers changed their expectations and began to treat students equitably, not only did overall student achievement go up, but absenteeism went down and the number of discipline referrals was reduced.

The implications of inductive and deductive reasoning processes extend well beyond the classroom. For example, we see a rugged male in mountain climbing gear staring intently across a vast wilderness holding a cigarette and we are encouraged to subconsciously think: "Rugged men smoke cigarettes."

This is the conclusion the advertisers want us to make. It could simply be described as being encouraged to induce the generalization based on the example we see in the magazine or paper.

The effort on the part of the advertiser goes further, however. For instance, we see an ad involving a romantic couple, and a female television viewer is encouraged to conclude, "If I wear the fragrance they're advertising, I will be involved in a scene like that." This is a deduced conclusion that is based on a major premise such as, "Women in romantic interludes are wearing 'Essence de Fluff.'"

Even casual thought would force us to conclude that smoking 'Old Charcoal' will not make us more rugged nor will wearing 'Essence de Fluff' appreciably increase the likelihood of us having a dazzling romantic encounter. However, the advertisers rely on our tendency to react emotionally to what we see rather than think critically about it. This is a human tendency, and none of us including your authors are immune from it. In many cases, such as the perfume advertising example, the results are essentially harmless. Our effort in writing this material is to hopefully raise the consciousness of our readers and increase their sensitivity, so they might catch themselves when invalid reasoning has the potential for harm.

Hopefully, the contents of this section illustrate the processes of inductive and deductive reasoning, show how they relate to the inferential thinking skills and further how they both are common and fundamental processes in our daily existence. We will continue to develop these themes as the rest of the text unfolds.

EXERCISES

In each of the following examples consider the conclusions made and decide if the conclusion was derived inductively or deductively. The conclusion is identified for you in parentheses.

For each of the conclusions that were derived deductively, identify the major premise and the minor premise that led to the conclusion. One or both of the premises may not be written in the example in some cases.

1. Two children were looking at the sky on a clear, moonless night.
    "What's that bright star up there?" Jimmy asked.
    "It's not a star, it's a planet," Susan responded.
    "How do you know?" Jimmy wondered.
    "It isn't twinkling," Sue said.
    (It's not a star, it's a planet.)

2. (This example is an actual incident with only a change in people's names.)
    Two people, Tom and Bill, were discussing their friend, Mike.
    "Why does Mike behave that way? I just don't understand it," Bill asked, bewildered.
    With some conviction Tom said, "Aw, it's his background, He's from New York. They're all weird."
    (Mike's behavior is weird.)

3. David and Nikki were playing with a toy ukelele one day.
    "Hey," David said. "When I make the string shorter the sound goes up."
    "What do you mean?" Nikki asked.
    "Listen," David directed. He then plucked several strings as they both listened. "Hear that? That's how it sounded before too," David concluded.
    (The sound goes up when the string is shortened.)

4. A small boy was looking at pictures of animals with his dad.
    "This is a cheetah," his dad pointed out. "And this is a leopard."
    "They're all kitties," Mikey pointed out.
    "That's right, son. They're all in the cat family." His dad then showed a picture of a hyena.
    "He's not in the cat family," Mikey concluded.
    (He's not in the cat family.)

5. A math teacher was drilling his third grade class on the "9s" multiplication tables. He put the following problems on the board:

    $9 \times 3 =$ $7 \times 9 =$
    $4 \times 9 =$ $2 \times 9 =$

    After the students had answered the problems, one raised her hand and said, "Hey, the individual digits in the products all add up to 9."
    (The individual digits all add up to 9.)

FEEDBACK

1. Susan deduced her conclusion. The syllogism would appear as follows:

    Stars twinkle but planets do not.
    This point of light is not twinkling.
    Therefore, it is not a star.

Note that Susan had learned the generalization that was the major premise some time prior to the conversation with Jimmy.

2.   Tom deduced his conclusion. The syllogism in this case would appear as follows:

People from New York act weird.
Mike is from New York.
Therefore, Mike acts weird.

When reading an example like this it appears preposterous that anyone would make a conclusion such as illustrated here. However, this type of reasoning is surprisingly common. Look for examples of invalid conclusions as you interact with people. You will probably be amazed by the number of conclusions that you will now react to as being anywhere from marginally valid to utterly ridiculous.

3.   David induced his conclusion from the individual sounds he heard when he plucked the strings of the ukelele.

4.   Mikey deduced his conclusion. The syllogism would be:

Members of the cat family have short snouts, whiskers, large feet, etc.
(or whatever characteristics the child used to form the concept).
The hyena does not have these characteristics.
Therefore, the hyena is not in the cat family.

5.   The student induced the conclusion from the pattern she found in the individual examples.

CONTENT

Introduction

In the preceding sections we have discussed thinking skills and the processes of inductive and deductive reasoning. We have also made the point that these processes can be and often are used with invalid or even dangerous conclusions, such as their role in teacher expectations. However, these processes have the potential for powerful and positive impact on learning. In fact, without them the vast storehouse of knowledge we know as classroom content would have been impossible to acquire. In this section we examine the relationship between thinking skills, reasoning, and knowledge, and we discuss the forms of knowledge in detail.

Thinking is not done in a vaccum. When we practice thinking skills we think about *something* and the thinking process usually produces a mentally tangible outcome. These results of the thinking process, or the products if you will, are called *knowledge* or *content*.

Everything we teach in schools or everything we know can be described in terms of fundamental forms of knowledge. These forms are facts, concepts, and generalizations. As you read you will undoubtedly think that some of the topics that you teach do not fit neatly into one of these classes and your reaction will be accurate. However, on closer examination you will see that the larger body of information is made up of combinations of these forms of knowledge and, therefore, this classification is a convenient and appropriate means for describing the information. We illustrate this idea as the forms of knowledge are developed.

After completing this section of the chapter you should be able to meet the following objectives.

1. You will understand the three main forms of content so when given a series of statements you will identify each as a fact, definition, or generalization.
2. You will understand the structure of generalizations so when given a series of generalizations you will identify each as a simple generalization, a rule, or a principle identifying the related concepts in each.
3. You will understand the structure of concepts so when given a list you will identify the superordinate, subordinate, and coordinate concepts, and characteristics of each.

Facts

Facts are the building blocks of all the more advanced forms of knowledge, and enormous numbers of facts are learned in school. Children must learn addition, subtraction, multiplication, and division facts. They are asked to know the names of countries and the capitals of states. They memorize scientific and technical terms. They learn times, dates and places. These are all examples of fact learning.

Facts can be defined as *forms of content that are singular in occurrence, which occur in the past or present, and which have no predictive value.* For instance when students learn that the first Crusade began in 1095 AD, that DNA stands for deoxy-ribonucleic acid, or that $5 \times 7 = 35$, they have learned facts. Notice that each case describes a single event as opposed to a pattern, that none of the three have an element of the future about them, and there is nothing that can be predicted from any of the examples. In the section on thinking skills we saw how patterns are inferred from observations and how these patterns can serve as a basis for explaining and predicting. We examine this process further when we discuss the product outcomes of fact learning.

In the section on thinking skills we identified observation as the foundation from which other skills are developed. Facts are observations' counterparts and are the product or content outcomes of observing. For example, we are essentially observing when we read or are told that the first Crusade began in 1095. This might be called a vicarious observation or indirect observation based on the original observations of others, but it is an observation nevertheless. In the case of DNA we are observing what amounts to a defined convention in the naming process. We observe directly when we feel the exoskeleton of a crab compared to the soft warmth of a dog, cat, or human. Vicarious or direct, however, we are observing in each case.

When events are observed, they are stored in memory until they are recalled, processed further, or forgotten. This means that facts are acquired through memory, or simply, they are memorized. In terms of learning theory, they are acquired through the process of contiguity, which is the pairing of two sensations until the existence of one sensation results in the other. (Woolfolk & McCune-Nicolich, 1984). In more common terms we can describe this as stimulus-response learning.

This has significant implications for teaching. If we have a fact that we want the students to know, we simply tell them or have them read it. The students must memorize the fact and you as the teacher can help them through the drill and practice using various memory strategies. This is not the case with the learning of abstractions, the topic of the next section.

Concepts

Let's now apply the information we have developed to this point. Imagine that a student is in an English class and sees the following statement written on the chalkboard.

1.   Kathy's glasses are her windows to the world.

The student can make a number of observations about the statement. Some of the following could be examples.

It is a complete sentence.
There is a possessive illustrated.
There are four nouns in the sentence.
A comparison is being made between glasses and windows.
The comparison between glasses and windows is not literal.

Notice that each of these observations is singular. There is no pattern suggested in any of them, and they are all stated in the present. Each of these is a factual statement. Obviously, there are many more observations that could be made about the sentence, but we stop at those listed for the sake of brevity.

Now imagine the student sees the following sentence.

2.   Kathy is the sunshine of Don's life.

In this case we may again observe and identify facts about the sentence such as:

There are two nouns in the sentence.
It is a complete sentence.
Kathy is being compared to sunshine.
We are not saying that she is literally sunshine.

Again note that each of the statements is singular and that nothing could be predicted from them alone. However, we are beginning to see a pattern develop between the two statements. We see that there is a comparison in each case and that the comparison is not literal.

Let's consider one more example.

3.   Judy's limpid green eyes are like pools of emeralds.

We observe and see that this statement does not quite fit the pattern because the word *like* appears in the sentence. It does not say that Judy's eyes *are* pools of emeralds but rather they are *like* emerald pools.

Consider one more statement.

4.   Tom is as strong as an ox.

As with the previous example, this one also does not quite fit the pattern because the world *as* appears in the statement.

Finally, consider a last example.

5.   His mind is a steel trap.

We examine this statement and again see that among other observations a nonliteral comparison is being made. We now can classify the statements. Statements one, two, and five have a common feature which is: A nonliteral comparison that does not use the word *like* or *as*. We then generalize about statements that are nonliteral comparisons that do not use the word *like* or *as*. Statements of this form are identified for us as metaphors. We have learned a *concept*.

Let's examine this process in a bit more detail. We were presented with a series of statements. We made observations about the statements and from the observations we found a pattern. We made a generalizing inference on the basis of the pattern to include any and all examples that had those characteristics. This is an example of inductive reasoning where we went from the specific examples of metaphors to the general notion. Finally, we were presented with the label *metaphor*. Notice that the label could be essentially anything we wanted it to be, but convention has chosen to attach the pattern to the symbols m e t a p h o r. This is a form of fact learning, that is, we simply memorize the label that goes with the generalized pattern.

In the previous paragraph we use the term "notion." Keep this in mind as we define a concept. A concept is *an abstracted notion that is based on a class of objects, events, or ideas with common characteristics*. For instance, in the example with metaphor we found a class of three members that had the common characteristics *nonliteral comparison without the words like or as*. We then generalized from this class to include all examples of nonliteral comparisons without the words *like* or *as*. From this we can see how the thinking skills of observing and generalizing with inductive reasoning are used to form concepts, which is a form of content learned in schools.

The number of concepts that students of all ages learn is virtually infinite. For example, all of the following are concepts:

mammal	community helper	fraction
addition	body system	major chord
digestion	force	red
longitude	socialism	verb
symmetry	bias	honesty
holiday	square	ion
quadratic	monocot	density
war	empathy	noun
miscible fluids	internal conflict	soft

As you can see, the list could go on and on. Some of the concepts are very simple such as *square,* and others are very abstract, such as *honesty.* However, they are all concepts.

Consider again the example with metaphors, and while it may seem a bit backward, let's begin with what the concept is not. It is not the *word* metaphor. It is not any of the sentences that served as examples nor is it the combination of those examples. Further, it is not a form of "average" of those examples. Instead it is a mental construct abstracted from the experience with the examples, or simply it is an abstraction we hold in our minds that is formed from the examples. Keep this in mind as we turn to a discussion of the different features of concepts.

Characteristics.   In the example with metaphors we found that the examples had the features "nonliteral comparison without the words *like* or *as*" in common. We then generalized to include all cases that had those features and called the general class *metaphors.* These common features that describe the concept are called the concept's characteristics or attributes. They are extremely important because they are the essence of the concept. It is from them that the concept is formed.

The ease or difficulty of learning a concept depends on the characteristics. For instance consider the concept *square.* It has two characteristics: four equal sides and four equal angles. These characteristics are first very tangible, that is, they are readily observed in any example of a square, and second, there are only two. Therefore, the concept is very easy to learn. Its ease is evidenced by the age at which children typically learn the concept. Most preschoolers understand and can identify examples of squares. By contrast, a concept such as *socialism* is much more difficult to learn because its characteristics are more abstract or intangible and the number of characteristics is greater. Consequently, a concept such as socialism is typically taught at the ninth grade or perhaps even later. From this we see that the ease or difficulty of learning a concept depends on the number of characteristics a concept has and how tangible or concrete those characteristics are (Stanley & Mathews, 1985; Tennyson & Cocchiarella, 1986).

In acquiring any concept, the learner must identify the essential from the nonessential characteristics. For instance, with squares the child must learn that such features as size or color or spacial orientation are not important. In learning a concept such as *fish,* the learner typically would attach to it the characteristic "lives in water." However, this feature would not discriminate fish from other aquatic animals that are not fish such as whales or sea turtles. As we pick up concepts in our everyday living, we must learn to do this on our own. In formal educational settings, the teacher can contribute greatly to the process by identifying explicitly which characteristics are essential and which are not.

Concept name.   In a previous paragraph we provided what we called a list of concepts. Technically, we provided a list of labels or terms used to name concepts. In practice no harm comes from simply calling the labels concepts as long as we keep in mind that the labels themselves are not the concepts but are in fact the concept names. The concept name is the label attached to the mental construct, and that name is used for the purposes of communication. If two people have a concept of *metaphor,* they can use the name and each knows what the other means. Using the name greatly simplifies the communication process. Instead of discussing statements of nonliteral comparisons that do not use *like* or *as,* we merely identify them as metaphors and the communication process is easy and smooth.

The problem with labels is that in some instances the label becomes the concept. This happens when the characteristics of the concept are not identified by the learners, so they have no generalized pattern into which additional examples can be classified.

Examples and nonexamples.   We said earlier that the concept is learned through generalizing from the common features in an observed class. The opportunity to make these observations comes from encountering examples and nonexamples of the concept. In the case of the illustration with metaphor, the examples were three metaphorical statements and the nonexamples were two statements of simile. As simple as it seems, this is how concept learning in general takes place. The learner is exposed to examples and nonexamples of the concept, identifies the features common to the examples that are not found in the nonexamples and generalizes from those features. As teachers, our task is to provide examples of the concept that illustrate the characteristics. This is the reason we make an effort to liberally illustrate the concepts presented in this text. We are trying to model the desirable practices we encourage you to use with your own students.

We all assess the quality of our examples in the same way. We simply ask ourselves, "Are the characteristics observable in the examples?" The role of quality examples is difficult to overstate!

Interestingly, the number of examples does not have to be extremely large. Frayer (1970) found that students learned as much from three or four well-chosen examples as they did from eight examples. We readdress this issue when we discuss the specific models later in the text.

The role of nonexamples is also important and is often overlooked. For instance, unless a learner is exposed to similes in the process of learning the concept *metaphor* the natural tendency would be to overgeneralize and include any instance of a nonliteral comparison in the class *metaphor*. Also, and particularly with young children, there might be a tendency to include any comparison as a metaphor. This suggests that a nonexample such as, "Jim is taller than Tony," be included. In this case a comparison is made, but it is a literal or real comparison. This helps the learners identify the boundaries of the concept.

The importance of nonexamples varies somewhat with the nature of the concept. Again in the case of the concept *metaphor*, nonexamples are very important because a learner could easily confuse metaphor and simile. Another situation where this could arise would be in learning the concept *reptile* or *insect*. Reptiles are often confused with amphibians, so a salamander which is an amphibian would be an important nonexample. Likewise, a spider which is an arachnid and not an insect would be an important nonexample in learning the concept *insect*. In general, the more closely related and easily confused two concepts might be, the more important nonexamples are. In these cases examples of one concept serve as nonexamples for the other. In fact the research literature suggests in the case of two closely related concepts it is often most effective to teach them together (Markle, 1980).

There is an interesting paradox in the selection of examples and nonexamples. On the one hand assessing the quality of examples is quite simple. Teachers must merely ask themselves, "Does this example illustrate the characteristics of the concept I'm trying to reach?" or "Can the kids see the characteristics of the concept in this example?" On the other hand, actually finding or creating the examples can be something else again. In a sense it's somewhat like learning to hit a forehand correctly in tennis. We know that we should get the racquet back early, keep the face vertical and watch the ball. Simple. As evidenced by the number of balls that go into the net or hit the back fence, doing it is somewhat more difficult.

The same is true for concept learning. The problem is that the concepts that are easiest to learn are those that are easiest to illustrate, such as *square, mammal, work,* or *noun*. We have little difficulty teaching these concepts and examples can be found with ease. On the other hand, many concepts are much harder to illustrate and consequently much harder to learn (Stanley, 1985). For instance consider concepts such as *inner conflict, apathy, republican,* or *so-*

cialism. They are certainly important for our learning, and in spite of common use in the media and considerable emphasis in the schools, these concepts are often poorly understood. Rather, they are often symbolic, being represented by a person with that label or a vague notion such as "socialism means high taxes," or "inner conflict means a person is unhappy."

The reason these concepts are hard to learn is that they are hard to illustrate in a concise way. Herein lies the irony in concept learning. The concepts that are easiest to learn are those easiest to teach and the reason for both is that they are easiest to illustrate. The exact opposite is true for those most difficult to learn. Creativity in teaching is related to the ability to generate examples for concepts most difficult to learn. A powerful technique in illustrating concepts such as *inner conflict* is the use of short anecdotes or vignettes in which the concept is embedded. We discuss this process in the section titled "Case Studies" in the following material. We now examine this process in a bit more detail.

As discussed earlier, a learner acquires any concept by being exposed to examples that illustrate its characteristics. The quality and form of examples is so important that it warrants a more complete discussion at this point.

We have all been exposed to different experiences in teaching, for example, we have seen case studies, simulations, pictures, role playing, and models. In general, these experiences are examples used to illustrate concepts that cannot be demonstrated directly. They are powerful tools that can be employed to help our students learn those concepts that are otherwise difficult to acquire. Let's examine the form that examples can take in teaching.

Realia. Realia is nothing more than a substitute word for "the real thing." This is the most fundamental form of example and of course the most desirable form if possible. For instance, an ideal example of a mammal would be a child's guinea pig brought into class. The children could see and touch the animal, feel its warmth, notice its hairy covering and feel its soft body. Combined with another animal such as a live lobster, which would serve as a nonexample with its hard, cold covering the teacher has a simple but very effective means of illustrating for the students concepts such as mammal, warm-blooded animal, and internal skeleton.

Demonstrations are another form of realia. When a book is pushed across a table, we are seeing an *actual* example of work being done—not a simulation, model, role play, or other indirect method of illustrating the concept. When children connect two wires to a battery and make a bulb light up, they are seeing an *actual* complete circuit.

As we said earier, realia is the ideal and should always be used if possible. You would never choose to use a picture of an animal if you could conveniently bring the guinea pig into class. However, obviously this is not always possible.

Pictures. When realia is impossible, pictures are often a good compromise. In that it would be hard to bring the Taj Mahal into the classroom, pictures of South Asian architecture would be a totally appropriate means for illustrating this concept. The key is to come as close as possible to reality. Detailed colored slides or photographs are better than black and white pictures, which are in turn better than outline drawings.

Models. Instances exist where not only is the real thing impossible but pictures and drawings are not available either. In these cases, models are valuable aids in helping students acquire concepts. A model is a description or analogy that is used to help us visualize something that cannot be observed directly. The most common examples of this occur in science where, for example, styrofoam balls and toothpicks can be used to help students form concepts. Consider the following model.

While the model is obviously not reality, it does illustrate accepted characteristics of the water molecule. One atom (the oxygen) is larger than the other two (the hydrogens), they are both equidistant from the oxygen, and the shape is accurate. From this we can see that while models do not actually illustrate reality, they can help us identify some of the characteristics of reality. It is important, however, to help students understand that the model is a device to help them visualize the concept. The model does not suggest that the concept actually appears as represented in the model. This is particulary the case in models of atomic structure, an instance where they are commonly used.

Case Studies. Case studies, particularly mini-case studies, can be powerful tools in illustrating otherwise difficult to illustrate concepts. For example consider the following statements:

> Mary's dream had come true. John, the captain of the basketball team, had asked her to go to the movies. However, as she thought about her homework assignments for that night, she remembered the term paper that was due on Friday. She had been putting off work on the paper until the last moment, and now she didn't know what to do.

> Johnny knew if he cheated off Bill's paper, he'd pass the test, but he also knew if he got caught cheating, he'd be suspended.

> Although Mary hated to leave her hometown friends and family and even her red teddy bear she had as a child, she wanted to go to college in Boston 500 miles away.

Notice that in each of the three anecdotes, the character is faced with two alternatives that are antagonistic to each other. The brief case studies illustrate the concept *internal conflict*. In considering a concept such as this we see how hard it would be to describe, and a definition such as ''To come into collision, clash, or be at variance within oneself,'' would also do little to clarify the concept for the learner. However, the brief scenarios provide a clear picture of the characteristics of the concept. Skill in developing case studies of this sort can help teachers communicate many difficult concepts to their learners. Case studies can be a powerful teaching aid in areas such as social studies or literature where other forms of illustration are often difficult to find.

To reinforce this idea, let's consider the following scenarios.

> Jim and Sally were honeymooning at Niagara Falls and reached an overlook in full view of the falls at sunset. "Oh, how beautiful!" Sally exclaimed as she was moved nearly to tears by the beauty of it all. "Yes, it is," Jim said flatly, glancing briefly at the sight and then back to the paper he had been sporadically reading as they walked to the overlook.

> Jose and Jaunita also were honeymooning in the same area and came upon the same scene described in the previous example. Jaunita was overcome. Jose, his voice shaking with emotion at the beautiful scene, embraced his new wife and said, "May all our times be as beautiful as this one."

The first example illustrates the concept *apathy,* and the second is a nonexample of the same concept. A teacher planning to teach the concept would, of course, provide more than a single example and nonexample, but they demonstrate how case studies can be used as effective examples for concepts that are otherwise hard to illustrate.

Simulation and Role Play. Simulation and role play are another means of indirectly illustrating concepts that are otherwise hard to show. Because they are often found together, we discuss them at the same time. For instance, consider a concept such as *relative deprivation* in social studies. The concept is very hard to directly illustrate and even a case study does not quite present the important characteristics. However, by placing certain conditions on different students and having them role play the effects, they experience the characteristics and thereby acquire the concept. A complete discussion of simulation is beyond the scope of this text, and interested readers are referred to Cline (1979), Sisk (1975), or other sources in the field.

We have devoted this space to a discussion of the various forms of examples because they are critical to the entire process of concept learning. Without examples, the learner has no chance to observe the concept's characteristics and as a result the concept is reduced to the symbolic or fact level. Further, the more abstract or elusive the characteristics, the more essential it is that they are illustrated. Models, case studies, simulations, and role playing can be powerful aids to learning in these instances.

The impact of these aids has been documented in research literature (Hintzman & Ludlam, 1982; Tennyson & Cocchiarella, 1986). Their studies indicate that learners often remember an idealized prototypical example from a concept learning experience. This prototype is a composite picture of the concept which is distilled from the positive examples (Tennyson, Younger, & Suebsonthi, 1980).

Concept definition. A concept definition is a statement that summarizes the description of the concept and helps a learner achieve a form of closure related to it. For instance, the definition of metaphor would be: "Metaphors are figures of speech that describe a nonliteral comparison without the words *like* or *as*." Notice that in the definition the concept name is provided, a larger class (figures of speech) into which the concept fits is stated and the essential characteristics are identified. The same three features should exist in any definition.

The role of examples and definitions in learning concepts is well documented. Tennyson (1978) and Feldman (1980) found in studies of college students and sixth graders respectively that examples combined with definitions resulted in greater learning than either alone.

Conceptual hierarchies. We suggested earlier that we form concepts in our efforts to structure and understand the world. However, each concept is not formed in isolation from, but rather in relation to, other concepts. Smith (1975) described this process of forming new concepts as one of partitioning or breaking down old categories into smaller and more specialized ones. To illustrate this process he cited the example of the child who initially sees all drinking utensils as a unitary category and later, after experiences with each, comes to differentiate bottles from cups and cups from glasses. This process would be represented as follows in Figure 2.3:

FIGURE 2.3
Drinking Utensils Hierarchy

One way of describing the relationship is in terms of superordinate, coordinate and subordinate concepts. These terms refer not only to the scope or inclusiveness but also to its relationship to other concepts. For example, *animal* is more inclusive and also subsumes the concept *mammal* which, in turn, subsumes *dog*. Dog is described as a type of animal. Related concepts such as these form a hierarchy, or ordered arrangement. This relationship can be depicted by a diagram or outline such as the following in Figure 2.4.

In this example, the concept *animal* is superordinate to *sponges, protozoans,* and *vertebrates.* Conversely, these concepts (*sponges,* etc.) are sub-

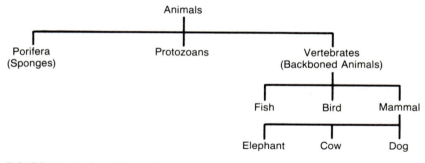

FIGURE 2.4   Animal Hierarchy

ordinate to *animals.* In a similar fashion, *elephant, cow,* and *dog* are all sub-ordinate to the superordinate concept *mammal.*

Smith explained the utility of superordinate and subordinate relation-ships in the following manner.

> Usually when we are asked to explain what something is, we begin by giving it another name. If asked to explain what a trout is, for example, we describe it as a fish. A finch would be described as a bird, the Boy Scouts as a youth organization. Each time we put the object into a broader category: there are more fish than there are trout; more birds than finches; more youth organizations than the Boy Scouts. The effect of such a description is to point to the similarities between the object being "explained" and other objects that fall within the same larger category. Thus, by saying trout are fish we are saying that trout have something in common with salmon, mackerel and marlin. (1975, pp. 17–18)

The connection between trout, salmon, mackerel and marlin is called a coordinate relationship. Trout, salmon, mackerel and marlin are all types of fish. Because of this similarity, we call them coordinate concepts. They are coordinate in the respect that all are fish.

A coordinate relationship among concepts has meaning only when a frame of reference is assumed. This frame of reference becomes the continuum or dimension on which the concepts are compared. To illustrate with an example (which, again, is one of the most effective ways of teaching a concept), let us consider the concept *cat.* Can you name a coordinate concept for the concept *cat?* There are at least three possible dimensions that might have been chosen for the coordinate concept. One dimension is "mammalness." In this case, the coordinate concepts would be *cow, horse,* etc. Another possible dimension could be that of "felineness." Here the coordinate concepts would be *tiger, lion, jaguar,* etc. A third possible dimension is that of "pets." In this case, the concepts coordinate to cat would be *bird, fish, dog,* etc.

Diagrammatically, these relationships might appear in the following way in Figure 2.5.

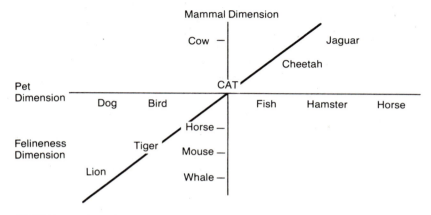

FIGURE 2.5   Coordinate Dimensions

Coordinate concepts have a particular role in helping the teacher select examples and nonexamples of the concept. For instance, using the previous illustration with the concept *metaphor,* we see that *simile* is a coordinate concept, and a consideration of the coordinate concepts helps the teacher identify the nonexamples. The same process was applied in the selection of the salamander as a nonexample for reptile, in that salamander is an example of the coordinate concept *amphibian.*

Subordinate concepts also have a practical role in helping us think about the concepts we teach. While coordinate concepts help us think about nonexamples, subordinate concepts help us think about the examples. For instance the subordinate concept *whale* is an important example to be used in teaching the concept *mammal* to prevent the learner from undergeneralizing and excluding aquatic mammals from the concept.

Concept analysis.   In preparing to teach a concept, a thorough understanding of that concept is essential. A planning tool which has proved valuable to teachers in the structuring of their concept-learning activities is a concept analysis. A concept analysis is a thorough examination of the different aspects of a concept, as described in previous sections. As such, concept analysis involves a description of the following:

1. Concept name
2. Definition
3. Characteristics
4. Examples
5. Superordinate concepts
6. Subordinate concepts
7. Coordinate concepts

Each of these dimensions of concept learning describes a different and unique aspect of the concept. An analysis such as this not only serves to provide the teacher with a thorough understanding of the concept to be taught but also can serve as a basis for instruction.

An example of a concept analysis of the concept *parallelogram* would consist of the following:

1. Concept name: *parallelogram*
2. Definition: A parallelogram is a four-sided geometric figure whose opposite sides are parallel.
3. Characteristics: four-sided, opposite sides parallel, opposite angles equal
4. Examples:

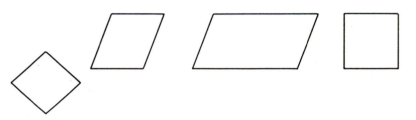

5. Superordinate concept: geometric shapes, or quadrilaterals
6. Subordinate concept: rhombus, square
7. Coordinate concept: trapezoid

In summary, concepts are abstractions which people form to comprehend the world around them. Doing so allows people to organize the immense number of facts they receive into a workable number of categories. Concepts, then, are one product of information processing.

In completing this section we want to briefly consider two more general facets of concept learning and teaching—the dynamic nature of concepts and creativity in teaching.

The dynamic nature of concepts.   In order to accurately portray the essential nature of concepts, we must briefly consider their dynamic nature.

Because a concept is an abstracted notion that we acquire from our individual experiences, no two people have exactly the same concept of anything. Consider the example with South Asian architecture. An individual who has seen the Taj Mahal and has walked on its decks has a different concept as a result of that experience than does a person who has only seen pictures of it. A child who has seen and ridden on an elephant has a different concept than a child without the experience. In some cases this different experience is more important than others. For instance, in the case of South Asian architecture or elephants the essential characteristics of the concepts are probably obtainable with either experience. On the other hand, people who have never been near or touched a snake often think of them as slimy, dirty, evil animals. In reality they are not the least bit slimy, they are very clean, and are more afraid of us than we are of them. In this instance the lack of experience results in us forming misconceptions or invalid concepts.

Concept validity is an important aspect of concept learning. In that no two people hold exactly the same concept, it is important that there be a form of agreement about concepts or the communication process breaks down. Concept validity is defined as *the extent to which the characteristics we attach to a concept agree with the generally accepted characteristics of the concept.* In the case of snakes we see that many people have invalid concepts. In another case with animals, wolves were once viewed as bloodthirsty, wanton killers, when in reality we have later found that they kill only what they eat, mate for life and are doting parents. Research in recent years has demonstrated that our original concept was completely invalid. We will see another example of invalid concepts in the next section when we discuss generalizations.

Finally, the dynamic nature of concept learning suggests that our concepts change. For a kindergarten child the concept mammal may be essentially limited to the characteristics: furry, warm, and nurses young. For a small child this concept is valid. On the other hand a biologist would attach to the concept characteristics such as four-chambered heart, seven cervical vertebrae, and advanced nervous system. This concept too is valid, but is dramatically different from that held by a kindergarten child. By the same token a person who says ''Anna Karenina served as a metaphor for Tolstoy's life,'' has a much different, and valid, concept of metaphor than a fifth grader who may have acquired an essentially valid concept of metaphor, appropriate to the age of the student, from the examples we used earlier in this section.

Creativity in teaching. We want at this point to briefly consider the notion of creativity with respect to teaching concepts. While this discussion will be admittedly somewhat simplistic, it will provide a reference frame for your consideration.

Creativity can be viewed simply as how attractive, eye catching or unique the examples are that you choose for illustrating a concept. For instance, much of *Sesame Street* is devoted to teaching children concepts. The people of the Children's Television Workshop have no fundamental secrets that we do not know. They simply use examples to teach the concepts. However, they embed the examples in musical themes, use muppets, role play the examples, and generally employ the techniques discussed in this section. Their use of music, the muppets, and other techniques are examples of creativity. Their motive is simple. They want the children viewing the shows to pay attention.

While competing with television is tough, we as teachers can at least periodically increase the attractiveness of our examples if we think about it and continually watch for the opportunity. For instance, pulling a child across the room in chair is a more attractive example of the concept work than merely pushing a book across a desk. "At night I think you are the moonlight drifting through my window lifting the curtain," is a more attractive metaphor than "Stars are the windows of heaven." Often with a little effort we can improve our examples if we try to remain alert to the possibility. The result will be more fun and increased learning because of increased attention of the students.

Generalizations

We said that concepts are categories that have common characteristics. When we find an object, event, or idea that fits the category, we classify the single instance into the overall class. This helps us simplify our experience by allowing us to remember the large categories instead of each particular instance. Imagine how bewildering the world would be if we had to try to identify and understand each individual insect among the billions rather than understand the broad classes. Some very practical aspects of our lives, such as pest control, would be literally impossible.

We also said we form the concepts through the process of generalizing. We see patterns among the characteristics in the specific examples and we generalize on those patterns.

The process of generalizing can be even more powerful, however. Individual concepts can be linked to each other through this process to find broader patterns than the concepts themselves.

These broad patterns are called generalizations which are defined as *relationships between two or more concepts that usually can be described in cause-effect terms, describe patterns, and have explanatory and predictive value.*

To illustrate the definition consider the generalization, "People who smoke have a higher incidence of lung cancer than those who do not." In this generalization there is a relationship between smoking (a concept) and cancer (another concept). Look now at the characteristics of the statement. It applies to more than one event in that it collectively describes people who smoke. In other words, it describes a pattern among smokers rather than referring to a single case of smoking. Each single instance of a smoker who has cancer is a fact, and further, a number of observed cases of cancer in smokers is still a fact. However, when the statement is extended to unobserved cases it becomes a generalization.

Examine the relationship again. While it can be appropriately argued that the statement only suggests a correlational rather than a causal relationship, it can be put in the form of a causal statement, such as "*If* people smoke, *then* they are more likely to get lung cancer (than if they do not). Note, too, that the statement, like all inferences, affords the opportunity for prediction and explanation. For instance, we would predict that the chances of a smoker getting lung cancer are higher than those of a nonsmoker. Generalizations also allow us to explain phenomena or events. For example, in the case of smokers and lung cancer, we might attribute a high incidence of lung cancer in a given population to smoking.

Let's look now at some further examples illustrating the relationship between facts and generalizations. Consider the two statements "F.D.R. was reelected several times while in office" and "Incumbent American presidents usually win reelections." The former statement is a fact which is based upon observation and refers to the occurrence of a specific event. The second statement is a generalization. It not only summarizes data but can also be used to predict the outcome of future presidential elections. The concepts included in the generalization (*incumbent presidents* and *reelection*) refer to categories, and the generalization describes the relationships between these categories. Again, it should be noted that the generalization was based upon facts but extended these facts to include situations not yet encountered.

Generalizations vary in terms of the amount of information that supports them and the amount of information that contradicts them. For example, in the previous illustration of incumbent presidents, it is obvious from our past experiences that incumbent presidents are not always reelected. Thus, we would say that the generalization made from these data usually holds true, but there are some exceptions. However, there are other generalizations which are based upon large amounts of supporting data with little or no contradictory evidence. A previously mentioned example of this type of generalization is "Like magnetic poles repel and unlike poles attract."

Principles.   Statements such as these are called laws or principles. The idea of principle or law in this context is simple and directly related to generalizations. We can simply say that a law is a generalization which we accept as true, or for which there are no common exceptions. In the case of smokers, we all know examples of smokers who live perfectly healthy lives and by contrast we know unfortunate nonsmokers with lung cancer. The statement relating cancer and smoking is appropriately called a generalization. On the other hand the statement, "Like poles of magnets repel and unlike poles attract," has no known exceptions. We accept it as true. However, the statement does describe a pattern rather than a single instance, and we can predict and explain on the basis of it. It is therefore a generalization and not a fact. Further, it is what we would commonly call a principle or law.

The statement is also readily amenable to a causal description as well, such as, "*If* the poles of magnets are alike, *then* the magnets will repel," and we see that the statement has all the characteristics of a generalization.

Other examples of principles would be:

1. The acceleration of a body is in direct proportion to the unbalanced force acting on it.

2. All persons must someday die.
3. $P_1V_1 = P_2V_2$ (Boyle's Law)
4. Change is inevitable.

Again, these statements describe patterns without common exceptions, and they serve as a basis for explaining and predicting.

In the previous section we said we would again address the notion of concept validity. We have here described the difference between facts and generalizations because people typically have an invalid concept of *fact*. They attach the characteristic of truth to *fact* and then classify any statements considered to be true as facts. In these cases the persons' concepts are not valid. Consider the definitions of fact and generalization again. Notice that truth does not appear as a characteristic in either of the definitions.

Academic rules.   Consider statements such as the following:

1. When punctuating a quote the punctuation mark goes inside the quotation mark.
2. When simplifying an expression involving the four arithmetic operations, you multiply, divide, add, and subtract in that order.
3. The square of the hypotenuse of a right triangle is equal to the sum of the squares of the other two sides.
4. In pronouncing a word with two vowels the first vowel is silent and the second is long.
5. The area of a triangle is one half the base times the height.

Each of the above statements could be called an academic rule. In example five you would write the expression algebraically $A = 1/2 (b) (h)$ and the result is commonly called a formula.

Rules are typically presented to students to be memorized and then applied when the situation warrants. We discuss the presentation of rules in more detail in Section II, but let's examine for a moment the characteristics of each of the examples just mentioned.

Notice in each case that a relationship is described. Also, each example describes a pattern and the example could be used as a basis for explanation or prediction. Therefore, each has the characteristics of a generalization.

Examples.   Generalizations and their subsets, principles and academic rules, are—as with concepts—abstracted mental constructs that learners hold in their minds. These abstracted ideas are based on the examples the learners encounter in a related way to the formation of concepts. The difference between the two is that learners form concepts by generalizing from the observed characteristics in the examples, and learners form generalizations from observing a relationship in the examples they encounter. This is a subtle but important difference. Just as a child must see the characteristics, "four equal sides and four equal angles" in the concept *square,* he must see the relationship *attraction together with like magnetic poles and repulsion with unlike magnetic poles* in order to learn the principle "Like magnetic poles repel and unlike poles attract." Just as teachers ask themselves, "Can the kids see the characteristics of the concept in this example?" They also ask themselves "Can the kids see the relationship between the concepts in the example?"

To reinforce the point, consider the following illustration. A teacher wanted his students to learn the generalization "Aerobic exercise lowers the resting pulse rate." However, the illustrations he used were pictures of people doing aerobic exercise. While the pictures in themselves may have been acceptable for illustrating exercise, they did nothing to illustrate the *relationship* between exercise and heart rate. The learners then were told about the relationship, which they accepted essentially "on faith," and the learning experience was reduced to a form of fact learning in that the relationship was memorized rather than derived through the thinking of the learners.

The role of examples in learning generalizations as with learning concepts is critical, which is the reason for our emphasis on this topic. Further, examples are also critical in learning principles and academic rules, and for this reason together with the similarity in their characteristics we have discussed them together in this section.

Diagrammatically, we can represent the forms of content as follows in Figure 2.6.

FIGURE 2.6   Content Forms

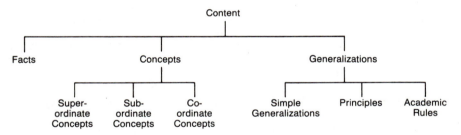

This completes our development of thinking skills, reasoning, and content. Turn now to the exercises in this section to reinforce your understanding of these topics.

SUMMARY

In this chapter we have discussed thinking skills, inductive and deductive reasoning, and the products of thinking skills which we call *content.* The particular thinking skills covered were observation and explanatory, predictive, and generalizing inferences. Thinking skills and reasoning are closely interrelated. In fact it could be argued that all thinking is an application of valid inductive and deductive reasoning. We have chosen to discuss the more specific thinking skills for sake of reader comprehension and application to classroom environments.

Explanatory and predictive inferences are formed through the process of deductive reasoning and generalizing inferences are formed through the process of inductive reasoning.

The outcomes of the thinking and reasoning process are the forms of content students encounter in school curricula. Facts result from observation, and concepts and generalizations result from a process of observing patterns and inducing a concept based on the pattern found in the characteristics, or inducing a generalization based on the pattern observed in the relationships.

Principles and academic rules have the characteristics of generalizations and are treated as subsets of generalizations in this chapter.

EXERCISES

1.   We have discussed the three main types of content that students learn in schools and that people acquire through ordinary experience. Consider each of the following statements and identify them as facts, definitions, or generalizations. Keep in mind that definitions always define concepts.

   A. The radius of the earth at the equator is 6,387,160 meters.
   B. A quadrilateral with two parallel sides is called a trapezoid.
   C. Russia lost more men in World War II than did any other country.
   D. Water boils at a lower temperature in the mountains than it does at sea level.
   E. Tall people have more back trouble than do short people.
   F. In Spanish the adjective must agree with the subject in number and gender.
   G. Mercantilism is an economic policy that requires a colony to trade only with the mother country.
   H. The area of a triangle is equal to one-half the base times the height.
   I. The acceleration of gravity in a vacuum is the same for all objects regardless of weight.
   J. The chemical symbol for sodium is Na.
   K. Wars are the result of economic factors.
   L. Mass is a physical property that describes the total amount of matter in an object.
   M. Above is a spacial relation that identifies one object as being higher in physical space than another object.
   N. Words with a consonant-vowel-consonant pattern are pronounced with the vowel long when an e is added to the word.

2.   Consider the examples on the previous list that are generalizations. In each case identify the two or more key concepts that are being related in the generalization.

3.   Again consider the examples in item one that are generalizations. Identify each as a simple generalization, a principle, or an academic rule.

4.   Consider the examples in item one that were definitions. For each identify (a) the concept being defined, (b) the superordinate concept, and (c) the characteristics of the concept. After having analyzed the definitions select (d) a concept coordinate to the defined concept and (e) a concept subordinate to the defined concept.

5.   Consider again the statements in item one that are definitions. Assess the quality of the definition in each case, that is, how good a definition is each, and explain why.

6.   Consider again the concepts that were defined by the statements in item one. Decide which of the concepts would likely be most difficult to teach, which would likely be least difficult to teach and explain why.

7.   A first grade teacher wanted to teach the concept of plant. To do so, she listed the following words on the board.

carrot   lettuce   onion   cabbage

At this point, she said, "These are examples of plants." Analyze the quality of her examples for purposes of teaching the concept.

FEEDBACK

1.   Items A, C, and J are facts. The statements are all singular, describe no pattern, are essentially observed, and have no predictive or explanatory value. The symbol for sodium is an agreed upon convention, and as such is a form of fact.

Items D, E, F, H, I, K, and N are generalizations, and the remaining statements are definitions.

2.   The concepts being related in each generalization are as follows:

D. Boiling temperature	Elevation
E. Height	Back trouble
F. Prefix and spelling	Number and gender
H. Area	Base and height
I. Acceleration	Object weight
K. War	Economics
N. Word pronunciation	Word spelling

Notice that in some generalizations the key concepts appear directly in the statement while in others the concepts are implicit rather than explicitly stated. A good example of this is item D. Boiling point is not related to sea level, nor is temperature related to sea level. More careful examination tells us that the concepts being related in this case are boiling temperature and elevation.

3.   Statements that would be classified as principles are D and I. They have all the characteristics of a generalization, and in addition, we accept them as true, that is, there are no exceptions we can identify under ordinary conditions.

Statements F, H, and N are rules. They fit the characteristics of a generalization in that they describe patterns and have both predictive and explanatory value. Items

F and N vary from simple generalizations and principles, however, in that they do not attempt to describe a form of physical or social reality in our world, but instead they are conventions adopted for the purposes of consistency. H does describe a form of reality, but is typically taught as a rule rather than a generalization, and for this reason we are classifying it under rules at this point in the development of our content.

Items E and K are generalizations that people typically identify intuitively. In each case patterns are described and the statements have predictive value, but there are obvious exceptions to each pattern. Because of these exceptions they cannot be classified as laws or principles.

4.   The analysis of the definitions can be described as follows:

B.	Concept name	Trapezoid
	Superordinate	Quadrilateral
	Characteristics	Two parallel sides
	Coordinate	Any quadrilateral with no parallel sides
	Subordinate	Any parallelogram
G.	Concept name	Mercantilism
	Superordinate	Economic system
	Characteristics	Colony must trade only with mother country
	Coordinate	Socialism
	Subordinate	British mercantilism
L.	Concept name	Mass
	Superordinate	Physical property
	Characteristics	Describes the total matter in the object
	Coordinate	Density
	Subordinate	Mass of solids, mass of any unique materal
M.	Concept name	Above
	Superordinate	Spacial relation
	Characteristics	Higher in physical space than another object
	Coordinate	Behind, below, any other spacial relation
	Subordinate	Any example of 'above'

Notice that in each of the examples the superordinate concept is a larger set into which the concept fits. For instance, *trapezoid* is a subset of *quadrilateral*. Notice also in this example that parallelogram is not coordinate to trapezoid. It is in fact a subset. It includes the characteristic 'two parallel sides' but goes further to also include the other pair of sides as parallel.

Consider also the concept *above*. This concept is typically taught to small children, and it is easily acquired. However, it is not often defined for the children, which is totally appropriate because the language used to define it is quite abstract. Here the value in the concept analysis is for the teacher in planning for teaching the concept.

5.   The quality of a definition is determined by the extent to which the statement describes a complete set of characteristics and separates the concept from other closely related concepts. For example, defining a metaphor as: "A figure of speech that makes a nonliteral comparison between two dissimilar ideas" does not separate the concept from the closely related concept *simile*. Also, defining noun as a person, place, or thing does not account for nouns that are abstract ideas, such as honesty, so the definition is incomplete in this case.

In the exercises the definitions of trapezoid, mass, and above are quite good. The definition of mercantilism is not as good, however, because the concept has the following additional characteristics that do not appear in the definition:

> Belief that a country's wealth was determined by its store of gold and other precious metals, and
> Increased exportation of goods and establishment of colonies should be encouraged.

Without inclusion of the additional characteristics the learners' concept would be incomplete, and therefore, not completely valid.

6.   The most difficult of the concepts to teach would be *mercantilism*. The concept's characteristics are somewhat abstract, and it is not an easy concept to illustrate. For this reason students are typically expected to learn the concept from the definition alone. This partially explains why very few people have a valid concept of mercentilism. (There are, of course, other explanations such as the extent to which the concept is used and how it impacts daily living.)

Trapezoid is a very easy concept to teach, and while small children are not typically taught the concept, they could easily learn it. It has only one essential characteristic which is readily observable.

Above is also very easy to teach as evidenced by the fact that it is taught to young children. It also has only one essential characteristic which is readily observable. Above, as we noted earlier, is interesting in that while it is easy to teach and learn, it is quite difficult to describe in words, and a stated definition for young children would be inappropriate in this case.

Mass is a bit more difficult to teach because the characteristic is quite abstract and difficult to "grab onto" for learners. This is evidenced by the amount of difficulty teachers have in helping students understand the difference between mass and weight—a coordinate concept—and mass and density.

7.   There are two primary problems with this lesson. The first is that students would acquire an incomplete and, therefore, invalid idea of the concept. With just the examples provided, students could come away with the idea that all plants are vegetables. The teacher needed to include a more complete selection of examples, such as ivy, palm tree, grass, rose bush, pine tree, weeds, and so on. A second potential problem with this lesson is that the teacher assumed that the verbal symbols used had physical referents. In other words, she assumed that all of her students had had experiences with these plants and knew what the words meant. However, there is a good chance that

students' experiences with onions had taken place in supermarkets or kitchens; consequently, their idea of an onion was something round and dry on the outside rather than something that grows in the ground and has roots and leaves.

The problem in the preceding paragraph points out the need for presenting examples in such a way that the important *characteristics* of the concept can be observed. The value of using examples in teaching derives, in large part, from their ability to transmit or convey the important characteristics of a concept.

ADVANCED EXERCISES

The following exercises are designed to help you synthesize the information from all three sections of the chapter.

1.   Look at the following statements and answer the questions that follow:
      a. I was struck by the cruel kindness of a mother-in-law's kiss.
      b. And I am dumb to tell the crooked rose my youth is bent by the same wintry fever and I cannot leave.
      c. Duley Bensel, Harry's accountant, studies the added deductions, hoping to find the error soon and escape from the stifled heat in the room.
      d. Marsha touched the many features of her face. They said she was the original imitation of her grandmother and she wished she could see it.
      e. Anise struggled in his drunken stupor and as he fought for consciousness, he tasted the sweet bitterness of the stale room.

a) Identify a pattern in the statements. b) When you formed a conclusion based on the pattern, was your conclusion formed inductively or deductively? c) What intellectual skill (process) did you use in forming the pattern? d) What form of content did you learn? e) You may not be familiar with the name of this particular piece of content. When you learn the name, which of the three—fact, concept, or generalization—are you learning?

2.   Consider exercise 1 on page 62 again for a moment. You concluded that item A in exercise 1 was a fact. You deduced this conclusion. Write an appropriate major premise, minor premise, and conclusion in a syllogism.

3.   a) Consider the major premise in exercise 2. Based on this and other examples of major premises make a statement about the forms of content that make up major premises. b) Did you use inductive or deductive reasoning to make the statement in part a? c) Consider minor premises. Make a statement about the form of content that typically make up minor premises. d) Did you use inductive or deductive reasoning to make the statement in part c? e) What form of content is the statement you made in part d?

FEEDBACK

1.   You looked at a series of statements and found a pattern among them. There were a number of characteristics illustrated in the examples, but the critical one was the use of contradictory or incongruous terms in proximity with each other. b) When

you identified this pattern and formed a conclusion you were using inductive reasoning. c) The inductive reasoning process involved generalizing inference, and d) resulted in a concept. The name of the concept is 'oxymoron.' e) When you learn that the name is oxymoron you are learning a fact. The particular symbols o x y m o r o n have no meaning in themselves. The meaning exists in the mental construct and the label or name merely exists for communication.

2.   The deductive syllogism would appear as follows:

Facts are forms of content that are singular in occurrence, exist in the past or present, and have no predictive or explanatory value.

The statement 'The radius of the earth at the equator is 6,387,160 meters' is singular in occurrence, exists in the present, and it has no predictive or explanatory value.

Therefore, the statement is a fact.

3.   Based on the example and the others in this chapter we would conclude that major premises exist as either definitions or generalizations. b) We would have induced the statement from the examples seen. c) Minor premises are primarily observations, d) which we also induced from the examples seen in the chapter. e) The statement 'Minor premises are observations' is a generalization. It describes the relationship between 'minor premise' and 'form of content.'

DISCUSSION QUESTIONS

1.   Consider all the concepts our students encounter in their curriculum materials. Obviously, there is too much material to cover in formal lessons. How do we decide which of the concepts are the ones we should build formal lessons around, and which we hope the students pick up on their own?

2.   We have emphasized the idea that examples are critical in learning concepts. Consider the circumstances when concepts might be learned from words alone, such as being presented a definition without examples.

3.   Identify a list of concepts and then decide what form of example, such as case study, simulation, model, or demonstration would be best suited for illustrating the concept.

4.   Consider again the list you prepared in question three. Actually generate an example in each case.

5.   We have emphasized the difference between definitions, facts and generalizations. Why is it important to know the differences among the three?

6.   Consider a cognitive theory of learning. Discuss how the information in the chapter relates to cognitive theory.

7.   As an extension of question six consider Piaget's theory of intellectual development. Discuss how the ideas developed in this chapter relate to the concepts in Piaget's theory.

8.   Discuss the implications of the information in this chapter for curriculum de-

velopment. How might understanding of the contents of this chapter alter how curriculum is typically developed?

REFERENCES

BELTH, M. (1977). *The process of teaching* (New York: David McKay).

BEYER, B. (1984a). Improving thinking skills—defining the problem. *Phi Delta Kappan, 65,* 486–490.

BEYER, B. (1984b). Improving thinking skills—practical approaches. *Phi Delta Kappan, 65,* 556–560.

BRONOWSKI, J. (1974). *The ascent of man* (Boston: Little, Brown).

CARNEGIE FORUM TASK FORCE ON TEACHING AS A PROFESSION. (1986). *The report on teaching as a profession.*

CLINE, S. (1979). Simulation: A teaching strategy for the gifted and talented. *Gifted Child Quarterly, 23,* 269–287.

COSTA, A., ed. (1985). *Developing minds.* (Alexandria Va: Association for Supervision and Curriculum Development).

DAINES, D. (1982). *Teachers' oral questions and subsequent verbal behavior of teachers and students* (Provo, Utah: Brigham Young University). (ERIC 225–979).

DAVIS, O. & HUNKINS, F. (1966). Textbook questions: What thinking processes do they foster? *Peabody Journal of Education, 43,* 285–292.

deBONO, E. (1984). Critical thinking is not enough. *Educational Leadership, 42,* 16–17.

ENNIS, R. (1969). *Logic in teaching.* (Englewood Cliffs, N.J.: Prentice-Hall, Inc.).

FRAYER, D. (1970). *Effect of number of instances and emphasis of relevant attribute values on mastery of geometric concepts by fourth and sixth grade children* (Technical Report 116) Research and Development Center for Cognitive Learning. University of Wisconsin: Madison, WI.

FELDMAN, K. (1980). The effects of number of positive and negative instances and concept definition on the learning of mathematical concepts. *Review of Educational Research, 50,* 33–67.

GALL, M. (1970). The use of questions in teaching. *Review of Educational Research, 40,* 707–721.

GOOD, T. & BROPHY, J. (1984). *Looking in classrooms,* 3rd ed. (New York: Harper & Row).

GOODLAD, J. (1984). *A place called school* (New York: McGraw-Hill).

HINTZMAN, D. & LUDLAM, G. (1980). Differential forgetting of prototype and old instances: Simulation by an example-based classification model. *Memory and Cognition, 8,* 378–382.

HOLMES GROUP (1986). *Tomorrow's teachers* (East Lansing, Michigan: Holmes Group).

KERMAN, S. (1979). Teacher expectations and student achievement. *Phi Delta Kappan,* June, 79–84.

LINK, F., ed. (1985). *Essays on the intellect* (Alexandria Va.: Association for Supervision and Curriculum Development).

LIPMAN, M. (1984). The cultivation of reasoning through philosophy. *Educational Leadership, 42,* 51–56.

MARKLE, S. (1980). Teaching conceptual networks. *Review of Educational Research, 50,* 55–67.

NICKERSON, R. (1984). Kinds of thinking taught in current programs. *Educational Leadership, 42,* 26–36.

PAUL, R. (1984). Critical thinking: Fundamental to education for a free society. *Educational Leadership, 42,* 4–14.

SISK, D. (1975). Simulation: Learning by doing revisited. *Gifted Child Quarterly, 19,* 175–180.

SMITH, F. (1975). *Comprehension and learning* (New York: Holt, Rinehart, and Winston).

STANLEY W. (1985). Recent research on concept learning: Implications for social education. *Theory and Research in Social Education, XII,* 57–74.

STANLEY, W. & MATHEWS, R. (1985). Recent research on concept learning: Implications for social education. *Theory and Research in Social Education, 12,* 57–74.

TENNYSON, R. (1978, December). *Content, structure and instructional control strategies in con-*

cept acquisition. Paper presented at the meeting of the American Psychological Association, Toronto.

TENNYSON, R. & COCCHIARELLA, M. (1986). An empirically based instructional design theory for teaching concepts. *Review of Educational Research, 56,* 40–71.

TENNYSON, R., YOUNGER, J. & SUEBSONTHI. (1980). Acquisition of mathematical concepts by children using prototype and skill development presentation forms. *Journal of Educational Psychology, 75,* 280–291.

TRACHTENBERG, D. (1974). Student tasks in text materials: What cognitive skills do they tap? *Peabody Journal of Education. 52,* 54–57.

WOOLFOLK, A. & McCUNE-NICOLICH, L. (1984). *Educational psychology for teachers,* 2nd ed. (Englewood Cliffs, N.J.: Prentice-Hall, Inc.).

3

THE TEACHING ACT
a general approach to instruction

INTRODUCTION

In the first chapter of this book you were introduced to the concept of information processing. This was followed by a description of information processing outcomes in Chapter 2. Both the content that is learned and the intellectual skills that are developed through information processing activities were described.

The purpose of this chapter is to introduce a three-phase approach to teaching. This approach outlines the steps a teacher takes in developing any learning experience and provides a framework for using the teaching models explained in later chapters. These models are designed to teach the content and thinking skills described in Chapter 2 using the three-phase approach to teaching.

The basic steps in the three phase approach to teaching are:

1. The planning phase
2. The implementation phase
3. The evaluation phase

These phases are sequential and interrelated. In other words, a teacher in developing any learning experience first plans, then implements the plans, and finally evaluates the success of the learning activity. Each of the teaching models described in the following chapters is analyzed by describing how a teacher plans when using the particular model, how the model is implemented, and how the process and content outcomes of the model are evaluated. In this way, the general approach to teaching described in this chapter is combined with the outcomes in the previous chapter to provide a conceptual framework for the information processing models to follow.

Planning

All teaching begins with planning. This simply means that teachers consciously consider not only what they want the students to learn but also the means to accomplish it prior to conducting a lesson. The process may be as simple as classroom veterans merely thinking about what they want their students to achieve on a particular day to as complex as beginning teachers writing detailed lesson plans that include several separate parts. In any case the teacher considers goals and procedures for the class prior to entering it. We will illustrate desirable approaches to this process in detail as this chapter and those that follow are developed.

The value of planning in guiding instruction is well documented in the literature (Peterson, Marx, & Clark, 1978; Clark & Yinger, 1979; McCutcheon, 1980). The McCutcheon study interestingly indicates that careful planning, in addition to being an instructional aid, significantly increases a teacher's confidence and security in the classroom. We are all periodically unsure of ourselves in new or unique teaching situations, and this finding suggests that thorough planning can be a powerful aid in reducing our anxiety and increasing our self-assurance as we approach a lesson.

Identifying goals and objectives is the first step in the planning process. In the next section of the chapter the terms are each defined, and we present different approaches to their preparation. At this introductory point in our discussion merely keep in mind that they mark the beginning of planning.

After goals and objectives are identified, the teacher considers possible techniques that could be used to reach the goal. Teachers with a number of alternatives at their disposal will have a better chance of matching an appropriate procedure to the goal than will those whose repertoire is limited. This is what the models that are described later in the text are all about. In other words, the major focus in this book is on the implementation of plans, and we are introducing the phases of teaching here to provide a logical context for the material that follows.

Implementation

Having determined the goal and the means to achieve it, the teacher is prepared to go into the classroom and actually teach the lesson. This is called implementation. The activity can take many forms such as lecture, discussion, laboratory, simulation, and others. This is the phase that students, parents, legislators, and the general public focus on when education is discussed, and when anyone informally or intuitively thinks of teaching, they are actually thinking about this phase.

Evaluation

The third stage in the teaching act is evaluation. Here the teacher attempts to determine if the students have reached the goals identified in the planning stage and thereby assesses the extent to which the teaching has been successful.

The evaluation process can be formal through the use of tests and quizzes as measurement devices or informal by observing students' comments, questions, and nonverbal reactions. The results of the evaluation process will then help the teacher make decisions about the next set of goals in the ongoing teaching process.

Though described above as three separate phases, the continuity and interrelationship of the phases should be emphasized. The goal that a teacher has for a particular group of students should determine both what is taught (content) and how it is taught (process) and should influence the manner in which learning is evaluated. This relationship is shown in Figure 3.1.

Some of the relationships shown in Figure 3.1 are readily apparent while others may require some discussion. Obviously, goals will affect the implementation and evaluation phases in that a teaching activity is implemented in order to help students reach a goal and evaluation attempts to assess the extent to which the goal is reached. However, implementation and evaluation each impact the other two respective phases. If the evaluation results indicate that the desired learning has not taken place, the teacher must alter upcoming plans to accommodate those results. The goal may have been overly ambitious or

FIGURE 3.1   The Three-Phase Approach To Teaching

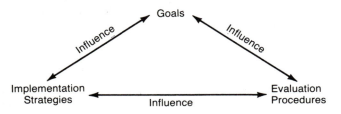

the strategy used to reach the goal may not have been effective. In any case, each phase impacts the other two in a reciprocal process.

We have described teaching as three interrelated phases which proceed from establishing goals to assessment of the goals' attainment. It is conceptualized as a logical operation in which a teacher makes conscious decisions about what to teach, how to teach, and how to determine if the teaching has been successful. In reality teachers do not typically work in such a precise, rational manner (Clark & Peterson, 1986). However, the process is valuable as a way to help you understand teaching and assess the quality of your own work. In this way you have a tool that can aid you in your own professional growth.

Let's turn now to a more detailed discussion of each of the phases.

PLANNING

After studying this section you will be able to meet the following objectives:

1. You will understand the goals approach to writing objectives, so when given examples of goals objectives you will identify each of the four parts.
2. You will understand Mager's behavioral objectives so given a list of Mager objectives you will identify the components of each.
3. You will understand the difference between Mager's, McAshan's, and Gronlund's objectives so when given examples of objectives you will identify the approach used in each.

Preparing Objectives

Introduction.   When behavioral objectives were first introduced as a tool for the improvement of American education, they became a heated issue in circles ranging from state departments of education, through universities, and all the way to the classroom teacher. Many of their early proponents implied that the use of objectives would be a panacea for educational problems, and their enthusiastic zeal further fueled the controversy. Opponents were equally adamant. While some controversy still exists, the issue is much less significant than it was at one time, and the use of objectives is widespread in materials such as county curriculum guides and state-level curriculum frameworks. With the increased emphasis on educational accountability, meaning teachers are being held responsible for student learning, the use of objectives is becoming even more common. Further, the expanding body of literature in teacher effectiveness suggests the importance of carefully considering specific objectives (Rosenshine & Stevens, 1986). Berliner (1985) suggested that the difference between good and effective teachers is that effective teachers, in addition to doing the things good teachers do intuitively, teach directly to precisely stated objectives.

Many textbooks in education and educational psychology use some form of objectives and most public school texts also use them as learning aids. Our view is that objectives are a part of present reality and are here to stay, so we do not argue the issue further. Our purpose is to acquaint you with a variety of approaches to their use so you will be equipped to use them as effectively as possible. Let's look now at some different approaches to preparing objectives.

Mager's behavioral objectives.   An enormously influential approach to the preparation of objectives was introduced by Robert Mager when his book *Preparing Instructional Objectives* was published in 1962. He suggested that an objective ought to describe "what the student will be doing when demonstrating his achievement and how you will know he is doing it" (p. 53).

Mager suggests that a good objective has three parts: (1) an observable behavior, (2) the conditions under which the behavior will occur, and (3) criteria for acceptable performance. The following are examples of objectives written according to Mager's format.

1.   Given ten sentences students will underline the adverbs in each.
2.   Given a slide of the cell showing ten parts, the student will label seven.
3.   Given a series of drawn shapes kindergarten students will circle all the squares.

Mager's system with its emphasis on final behavior requires a great deal of specificity. He contends the effort required to achieve this specificity is worthwhile and even has gone so far as to suggest that students often can teach themselves if they are given well-stated objectives.

McAshan (1974) and Gronlund (1985) among others have been critical of Mager's approach and have offered alternatives to preparing objectives. We will present a detailed discussion of McAshan's approach first because it subsumes Mager's. This will be followed by a description of Gronlund's view of appropriate objectives and how it differs from the previous two.

The goals approach to preparing objectives.   McAshan criticized Mager's objectives because, in his view, they are only evaluation statements, that is, they specify how students will be evaluated but do not identify the educational intent of the teacher. McAshan's approach to preparing objectives can be described as a statement that answers two questions for the teacher:

1.   "What do I want the learner to know, understand, or appreciate?" (or some other educational goal), and
2.   "How will I know if they know, understand, etc.?"

McAshan suggests that the answers to both questions are important and that Mager's objectives only answer the second. His approach is to combine Mager's objective, which he calls the evaluation statement, with a goal. This is how McAshan's objectives subsume Mager's. Keep in mind that from this point on when we refer to an evaluation statement, it is actually a Mager objective or as McAshan sometimes described it, a "Magerism." Let's turn now to a detailed discussion of the goals approach to preparing objectives, or more simply goals objectives.

Goal Statements. All planning begins with teachers' considerations of what they want their students to accomplish during one or more lessons. This desired result is called an *educational goal,* which is a statement of educational intent that is usually couched in general terms. The educational goal answers the question "What do I want the students to know or understand?" The following are examples of educational goals.

1. For first graders to know the vowels.
2. For eighth-grade science students to understand Newton's Second Law.
3. Freshman literature students will understand the difference between a novel and a short story.
4. Fifth graders will understand the difference between similes and metaphors.

Several characteristics are common to each of these goal statements. Each identified the particular student population for which it was designed. Also, the attainment of goals must be inferred rather than observed. We never observe "understanding;" we can only infer it, and it can mean different things to different people. The same is true for "know," "appreciate," and other desired education goals. As with any inference we need something we can observe to help us assess the validity or accuracy of the inference.

Some educators object to the use of goal statements, reacting to their use of mentalistic, nonobservable terms such as "know" or "understand." We're sympathetic to this argument and agree that the use of such terms without behavioral referents can be confusing, if not meaningless. On the other hand they can be useful as a framework to help preserve students of education as they prepare to become teachers, or classroom veterans as they continue in their professional growth. In addition, they are useful in communicating with parents where precise and technical terms might detract from the clarity of an explanation. Because of these reasons we choose to include goal statements in the objectives we write for this text.

Evaluation Statements. An evaluation statement is a specification of educational intent that includes a demonstrated, observable student behavior. Observing this behavior then helps us make a decision about the attainment of the goal and allows the teacher to answer the question "How will I know if the learner knows, understands, etc.?" (the intent identified in the goal).

While the approach to writing objectives varies among educators, most adhere to the need for including an observable behavior in the objective's description. The evaluation statement is a complete objective if Mager's approach is used, while it only specifies how the goal will be evaluated according to McAshan.

The relationship between the goal statement and the evaluation statement requires careful consideration on the part of the teacher. For instance consider again the goal:

"Students will understand the difference between simile and metaphor."

What exactly does this mean? Here are some possibilities.

1. They will state a definition of each.
2. From a list of statements they will identify examples of each.
3. They will write examples of each without help from the teacher.
4. They will write a paragraph that includes examples of each in context.

As you can see "understanding" can be demonstrated in a variety of ways, and no precise definition of understanding exists. Consequently, to clarify their own thinking and to give students a clear picture of what is to be learned, teachers need to specify how the goal statement is to be evaluated. This process has implications not only for planning but for implementation and evaluation as well. For instance, being able to define similes and metaphors is markedly different from being able to embed them in the context of a paragraph and is also significantly different from being able to recognize examples of them in a list of figures of speech. This impacts the form that the evaluation takes.

Specifying the objective also affects the implementation phase. For example, a teacher who wants students to be able to write examples of similes and metaphors in the context of a paragraph would show them sample paragraphs and would also have them practice before the evaluation took place. On the other hand, a teacher who wanted the students to be able to identify examples out of context would present the students with a list of statements which would include similes, metaphors, and other figures of speech and show them how the similes and metaphors are different from the others.

The most appropriate means of evaluating the goal statement depends on a teacher's professional decision using the best information available at the time. There are no rules that can tell the teacher which of the above evaluation statements best measures students' understanding of the concepts. Only the teacher can decide in the overall context of the learning environment. However, Mager and McAshan suggest some guidelines in constructing evaluation statements that can help the teacher in the decision-making process.

Performance. The first step in the process is determining what the learner will be expected to perform to indicate that the goal has been reached. This part of the evaluation statement is called the performance and is probably the most important part of the objective. This is the observable behavior the student demonstrates that allows the teacher to make inferences about the achievement of the goal. For instance, in the illustration with similes and metaphors the students in the first example are asked to state a definition, in the second identify examples, and write examples in the third and fourth. Including an observable behavior in the form of an action verb in the objective is what educators mean when they describe an objective as behavioral.

The following provides some additional examples of behavioral verbs:

select	name	solve	label
construct	derive	compare	classify
list	recite	describe	interpret

Many more could be added to the list, but this gives you a sample of observable performances. They are considered to be behavioral because they describe an overt student act that can be witnessed by the teacher.

EXERCISES

In the following goals objectives determine which part is the goal statement and which part is the observable performance by enclosing the goal statement in parentheses and by underlining the verb which is stated in behavioral terms.

1.   For biology students to know the parts of the cell so that, when given a slide of the cell showing ten parts, the student will label seven.

2.   For art students to understand perspective so that, when given a photograph of a landscape, the student will draw it using three-point perspective.

3.   For physics students to know the second law of thermodynamics so that, without aids, the student will state the law verbatim as stated in class.

4.   Language arts students will know the concept *adverb* so that, when given ten sentences, the student will underline all the adverbs.

FEEDBACK

1.   (For biology students to know the parts of the cell) so that, when given a slide of the cell showing ten parts, the student will *label* seven.

2.   (For art students to understand perspective) so that, when given a photograph of a landscape, the student will *draw* it using three-point perspective.

3.   (For physics students to know the second law of thermodynamics) so that, after a presentation on the subject, the student will *state* the law verbatim as stated in class.

4.   (Language arts students will know the concept *adverb*) so that, when given ten sentences, the students will *underline* all the adverbs.

Condition. In our preceding discussion of goals objectives, no mention was made of the conditions under which the performance would occur. The condition refers to the type of environment in which the individual is placed when the performance occurs and is the second part of the evaluation statement.

The conditions under which a behavior is performed can have important effects on the performance required of the learner. For example, consider the difference between the following two goals objectives:

> For sixth-grade math students to find the area of a circle so that, given the formula ($A = \pi r^2$) and the value for π and r, they can correctly calculate the area.
> For sixth-grade math students to find the area of a circle so that, given a series of word problems, they can correctly solve for the area of a circle.

Note how the conditions alter not only the complexity but also the difficulty of the two tasks. In the first example the learner's task is primarily one of plugging values into an equation and performing the indicated computations. In the second objective, on the other hand, the student is required to do the following:

1.   Read the word problem and recognize that it requires computing the area of a circle.
2.   Remember the equation for finding the area of a circle.
3.   Select the correct values from the word problem and plug these into the equation in Step 2.
4.   Compute the problem.

Obviously, the second problem is more complex and consequently more difficult than the first and, in addition, aims at different types of behaviors or capabilities in the learner. Note how in both objectives the goal statement and performance were the same, but the condition, or testing situation, drastically changed the meaning of the objective. Besides influencing the level of task difficulty and complexity, the condition also influences instructional decisions concerning teaching strategies. A teacher who ultimately wants students to solve word problems involving the area of a circle will provide for experiences that give students practice in this skill. On the other hand, the teacher who only wants students to compute the area of a circle will give students ample practice in computation.

In actuality, the two objectives described above are not mutually exclusive, but rather sequentially related. The objective focusing upon computational skills would probably be used as a stepping stone to the other. Before plunging the student into word problems involving areas, the teacher would probably determine that the student had all the necessary prerequisite skills. Understanding the effect that the condition has on the objective allows the teacher to use such effects in a rational manner to determine the emphasis of different instructional sessions.

Consider once more the illustration with simile and metaphor. In the third example learners are required to write examples of each concept, but in the fourth example they are required to write examples in the overall context of a paragraph. While the actual performance is the same, the conditions are significantly different and probably sequential, as with the example where students are asked to compute the area of a circle.

EXERCISES

In the following objectives, identify the condition by enclosing it in parentheses and putting a C over it. Also, identify the goal statement and performance by enclosing them in parentheses and identifying them with GS and P respectively.

1.   First-grade students will know the vowels so that given the letters of the alphabet they will circle all the vowels.

2.   Freshman English students will understand proper paragraph structure so that given a topic they will write a 100-word minimum paragraph including the components discussed in class.

3.   Third-grade students will know the characteristics of mammals so that from memory they will list at least five characteristics unique to mammals.

4.   Seventh-grade social studies students will know how to read a map so that given a map of Florida and ten coordinates they will find the city closest to each of the coordinates.

5.   Junior high math students will solve linear equations so that given ten equations with one unknown, they will correctly solve for each.

FEEDBACK

1.   (First-grade students will know the vowels) [GS] so that (given the letters [C] of the alphabet) they (will circle) [P] all the vowels.

2.   (Freshman English students will understand proper paragraph structure) [GS] so that (given a topic) [C] they (will write) [P] a 100-word minimum paragraph including the components listed in class.

3.   (Third-grade students will know the characteristics of mammals) [GS] so that (from memory) [C] they (will list) [P] at least five characteristics unique to mammals.

GS
4.   (Seventh-grade social studies students will know how to read a map) so that (given
  C   P
a map of Florida and ten coordinates) they (will find) the city closest to each of the
coordinates.
                                       GS
5.   (Junior high math students will solve linear equations) so that (when given ten
  C   P
equations with one unknown) they (will solve) each.

Criteria. In the preceding paragraphs we have discussed three of the four components of a goals objective. It begins with a goal statement which identifies the learner and broadly describes the educational intent. It is the beginning point in the planning process. The evaluation statement follows the goal statement and specifies how the teacher will determine if the goal has been reached. It includes an observable behavior and the conditions under which that behavior will be demonstrated.

Mager and McAshan also suggest that simply identifying the performance is not enough and a specification of the level or quality of performance is also necessary. This is called the *criteria.*

Criteria for objectives can take many forms. One type of criterion matches the performance of the student against some standard. For example:

> For the student to know the Pledge of Allegiance so that without aids the student will recite the pledge.

Here the criterion states that the student's performance will be errorless. Other standards or levels of performance can be established depending on the age and sophistication of the learner.

Another type of criterion establishes a minimal level of performance. Examples of this type are:

> Junior high social studies students will know the names of the states of the Confederacy so that from memory they will list eleven of the thirteen states.
>
> Sophomore biology students will know characteristics of mammals so that from memory they can list at least five characteristics which are unique to mammals.

Other types of criteria attempt to specify essential components in a performance. For example:

> For senior literature students to know Haiku poetry so that without aids they will write a Haiku poem which is on a proper theme and has the correct number of syllables.
>
> Junior high English students will know how to write a well-organized paragraph so that given a topic they will write a paragraph on the topic which has (a) at least five sentences, (b) an introductory sentence, (c) middle sentences which relate to the introductory sentence, and (d) concluding sentence.

Like the act of writing objectives in general, writing criteria should be viewed as an aid to help clarify thinking about what is to be taught. The attempt to determine criteria prior to instruction forces the teacher to come to grips with the complexity and difficulty of the task to be learned in relation to the children being taught. Once established, there is nothing sacred about the criteria. In view of experiences in the classroom, the teacher may choose to change the criteria (making them higher or lower) or, keeping the criteria the same, the teacher may examine the effectiveness of his or her teaching techniques. Perhaps the greatest benefit of establishing criteria is that it provides the teacher with an opportunity to think about considerations such as these.

Our view of the criteria's value in an objective marks a bit of a departure from Mager and McAshan's original conception. While they suggest criteria should be stated in advance and teachers should literally adhere to the set standard, our view is that the criteria, like the act of writing objectives in general, are more an analytical tool that teachers use to help clarify their thinking as they plan. The criteria serve as a conceptual guide rather than a rigid rule to be followed unflaggingly. In fact most curriculum guides and state-level curriculum frameworks do not include specific criteria in their descriptions of objectives, as you will see in the examples we provide in the next section of this chapter. You will also notice that while we are writing our objectives in this text using McAshan's format we have not explicitly stated criteria in all cases. However, there is conceptual value in considering criteria, so we have included the following exercises as an aid in developing your understanding of criteria and their use.

EXERCISES

In the following goals objectives identify the four components previously discussed in this chapter by enclosing the four components in parentheses and labeling them as follows:

GS–Goal Statement
   C–Condition
   P–Performance
   A–Criterion

1.   Physical education students will volley a volleyball so that, when provided with a volleyball and a wall, the student will volley the ball against the wall 50 consecutive times within 60 seconds.

2.   The elementary science student will know how to read a bar graph so that, given a bar graph, he can list at least five items of information in the graph.

3.   The elementary language arts student will understand antonyms so that, given ten words previously unencountered in this context, the student will write an antonym for each.

4.   Social studies students will know the location of the continents so that, given a blank map of the world, they will label all of the continents correctly.

5.   For the twelfth-grade automotive mechanics student to know how to read a schematic diagram of a transmission so that, given a transmission and schematic, the student will orally match points on the schematic with actual parts.

6.   The distributive education student will be able to identify the three types of advertising displays so that, given six new examples of the three types of displays, the student will identify five of the six correctly.

7.   For elementary science students to know how to graph numerical information so that, given data in table form and graph paper, the student will graph the data. Criteria for graphing are: (a) there should be a title on the graph, (b) the axes should be appropriately placed and labeled, and (c) the points on the graph should be accurately placed.

8.   English grammar students will know how to punctuate the ends of sentences correctly so that, given an unpunctuated paragraph, they will correctly punctutate each of the sentences with either a period, question mark, or exclamation point.

FEEDBACK

GS–Goal Statement
  C–Condition
  P–Performance
  A–Criterion

1.   (Physical education students will volley a volleyball) [GS] (so that when provided with [C] a volleyball and a wall) the student (will volley) [P] the ball against the wall (50 consecutive times within 60 seconds) [A].

2.   (The elementary science student will know how to read a bar graph) [GS] (so that given a bar graph) [C] he (can list) [P] (at least five items of information in the graph) [A].

3.   (The elementary language arts student will understand antonyms) [GS] (so that when given ten words previously unencountered in this context) [C] the student (will write) [P] an antonym (for each) [A].

4.   (Social studies students will know the location of the continents) [GS] (so that when given a blank map of the world) [C] they (will label) [P] (all of the continents correctly) [A].

5.   (For the twelfth-grade automotive mechanics student to know how to read a schematic diagram of a transmission) [GS] (so that when given a transmission and schematic) [C] the student (will orally match) [P] points on the schematic with actual parts. (*Note here that 100% accuracy is assumed when it is not explicitly stated.*)

6. (The distributive education student will be able to identify the three types of advertising displays) (so that when given six new examples of the three types of displays) the student (will identify) (five of the six correctly).
GS
C
P
A

7. (For elementary science students to know how to graph numercial information) (so that when given data in table form and graph paper) the student (will graph) the data. (Criteria for graphing are: (a) there should be a title on the graph, (2) the axes should be appropriately placed and labeled, and (3) the points on the graph should be accurately placed).
GS
C
P
A

8. (English grammar students will know how to punctuate the ends of sentences correctly) (so that when given an unpunctuated paragraph) they (will correctly punctuate) (each of the sentences) with either a period, question mark, or exclamation point.
GS
C
P
A

Gronlund's instructional objectives. Gronlund (1985) believes that objectives should be stated first in general terms such as "understand," "appreciate," "know," "evaluate," or "apply," which are then followed by specific behaviors providing evidence that the learner has met the objective. The following are samples:

> General objective: Knows basic concepts in chemistry.
> Specific behaviors:
> 1. Defines terms in his or her own words.
> 2. Identifies examples of concepts.
> 3. Distinguishes between closely related concepts.
>
> General objective: Understands solutions to problems.
> Specific behaviors:
>
> 1. States law that applies to problem.
> 2. Identifies relevant variables.
> 3. Selects data from given information.
> 4. Computes solution.
> 5. Describes meaning of solution in his or her own words.
> 6. Describes relationship between solution and "real world" example.

Let's look now at the specific characteristics of Gronlund's objectives as illustrated in the examples.

1. The objectives are stated in terms of student outcomes rather than teacher performance. For instance "teach basic concepts in chemistry," is a teacher performance and is not a student outcome. This is a characteristic overwhelmingly agreed upon by objective writers. Virtually all curriculum guides in general use today state objectives in terms of student outcomes. Each of the approaches discussed in this chapter emphasize stating objectives in terms of observable student behavior.

2. Objectives are not stated in terms of the learning process, such as "student learns concepts in chemistry." "Learns" is a student process rather than a student outcome, and Gronlund discourages this type of description.
3. Objectives are limited to a single performance. For example, Gronlund would not state an objective as follows: Students know and understand concepts in mathematics.
4. Objectives avoid specification of subject matter. For instance, he says, "Don't focus on the subject matter topics. (e.g., Student learns the meaning of osmosis, photosynthesis, etc.)" (Gronlund, 1985, p. 11). Instead, objectives should focus on general categories of behaviors.

Gronlund's approach to preparing objectives, or a modification of it, is probably the most popular today among curriculum writers. Compared to Mager it has the advantage of economy in that the objectives are more inclusive than Mager's. One critic (MacDonald-Ross, 1974) suggested that it would take over 10,000 objectives to specify all the outcomes from reading a popular educational psychology text using Mager's objectives while they could be described using 50–100 using Gronlund's approach.

Gronlund's approach is similar to McAshan's in that he suggests that a general objective which identifies the instructional intent should be stated first. For instance, in the previous examples the intent is for students to "know basic concepts" and "understand problem solutions" and the ability to "identify examples" or "select relevant variables" are the evidence that the students have met the instructional intent in each case. Mager only specifies the evidence in his approach, while the intent is missing.

The compromise Gronlund makes is in terms of specificity. First, he does not identify either the conditions under which the performance will be demonstrated nor the criteria for acceptable performance, and second, he discourages the use of specific subject matter topics. This latter feature of Gronlund's objectives is often modified by curriculum writers as they prepare their objectives. For example, consider the following objectives taken from the State of Florida Curriculum Frameworks (1985).

1. Demonstrate the ability to use the properties of the real number system.
    The student will:
    1.01 identify the order properties of real numbers.
    1.02 solve linear inequalities including sets of inequalities.
    1.03 solve equations and inequalities involving absolute value.
    1.04 identify the axioms of the real number system.
    (Algebra II, p. 1)

As you see from the example the objectives essentially follow Gronlund's characteristics except that the topic is identified. Strict adherence to Gronlund's criteria would suggest that the specific topics be left out.

The issue of identifying topics is obviously a matter of the writer's judgment. Often, a compromise between Mager's and Gronlund's approaches may be appropriate. A teacher or curriculum writer may choose to identify topics less specifically than Mager would suggest, while at the same time being more precise than Gronlund would advocate.

EXERCISES

Consider each of the following objectives and identify those that are appropriately stated according to Gronlund's criteria for objectives. If they are inappropriately stated, identify the reason in each case. We are purposely sidestepping the issue of content specificity in these exercises, so do not assess them on that basis.

1. Learns punctuation rules.
   1.1 States rule in own words.
   1.2 Punctuates paragraphs correctly.
2. Teach students parts of speech.
   2.1 Define parts of speech.
   2.2 Provide examples of parts of speech.
   2.3 Have students identify parts of speech in context.
3. Knows basic shapes.
   3.1 Identifies examples of shapes.
   3.2 Draws shapes from memory.
4. Understands geographical terms.
   4.1 States definition in own words and writes definition.
   4.2 Identifies examples in paragraphs.
   4.3 Identifies examples on globes.
5. Applies critical thinking skills to reading material.
   5.1 Distinguishes between observation and inference.
   5.2 Distinguishes between fact and opinion.
   5.3 Identifies irrelevant information.
   5.4 Identifies writer point of view.
   5.5 States implicit assumptions.

FEEDBACK

1. This objective is stated in terms of a learning process instead of a student outcome. By contrast an outcome would be "understands punctuation rules." The subobjectives are stated properly according to Gronlund's criteria.
2. The second objective, both the general objective and the subobjectives, is stated in terms of a teacher performance rather than a student performance.
3. The third objective is properly stated according to Gronlund.
4. With the exception of subobjective 4.1, which identifies two performances in the

same statement, the overall objective is appropriately written. The problem could be solved simply by separating 4.1 into two separate performances.

5.   Objective five is properly written.

SUMMARY

In this section we have focused particularly on the preparation of objectives as part of the overall planning process. Our purpose in including the various approaches to writing objectives and their modification in common practice is to underscore the role objectives play in the improvement of instruction. As we stated earlier, objectives are a means to help teachers clarify their thinking as they plan and are not ends in themselves. Objectives, while not the panacea their enthusiastic proponents initially suggested, can be useful tools in helping guide teachers with their planning decisions. The emergence of the teacher effectiveness research and increasing educational accountability have expanded the already significant role objectives play in guiding teachers and teacher behavior.

The selection of a particular format is a matter of personal preference and teacher judgment, and one approach is no more correct or incorrect than another. We prefer McAshan's goals objectives and have adopted them for use in this text. Your preference may be different.

Regardless of the approach, there is one important characteristic that objectives have in common, however, and we want to re-emphasize that characteristic here. All objectives are written in reference to the *student*. It is a student performance, a student behavior, or a student outcome. By contrast, the following are not student objectives.

1.   To present the causes and effects of the Civil War.
2.   For students to study the development of the Roman civilization.
3.   For students to do a laboratory exercise on the dissection of a frog.

The first example could be described as an objective for the teacher or teacher performance as Gronlund would describe it, and the other two are descriptions of experiences or learning processes that the students would have that would lead to a desired outcome. These are important conceptual as well as practical distinctions. Keep them carefully in mind as you study the material that follows.

A second factor that all objectives have in common is as much economy of expression as possible. An objective should always be stated in as few words as it takes to communicate its meaning. Extra irrelevant wording merely diffuses the meaning and makes the objective unwieldy and cumbersome.

To close this section let's reconsider the example dealing with the Civil

War and see how each of the approaches developed in this section might prepare objectives related to this topic.

MAGER'S APPROACH

From memory students will list the five major causes of the Civil War.

Given three civil and economic results of the Civil War, students will write one implication of each.

McASHAN'S GOALS OBJECTIVES

Students will know the causes of the Civil War so that without aids they will list the five major factors leading to the war.

Students will understand the effects of the Civil War so that given three civil and economic results of the war they will write one implication of each.

GRONLUND'S INSTRUCTIONAL OBJECTIVES

Knows causes and effects of the Civil War.
    Lists causes.
    States effects.
    Writes implications from effects.

IMPLEMENTATION

The planning phase involves the identification of a specific content objective, the implicit thinking skills component, and the selection of a strategy that will be used to help students reach the goal. You are then ready to implement the strategy, or in other words, actually teach the lesson.

While the models in Part II of this text are related to the themes identified in Chapters 1 and 2, they have unique planning and implementation characteristics. Because of these unique features, a general discussion of implementation would not be meaningful here, and instead the planning and implementation for each model will be discussed in detail separately. The remainder of this chapter will be devoted to the evaluation stage of teaching with special emphasis placed on the relationship between planning and evaluation.

EVALUATION

Introduction

As described in the planning section of the chapter, an objective specifies what the student should understand or know and what the teacher will accept as evidence that the knowledge or understanding has been acquired. The type of measurement item should then reflect the intent of the objective. This section of the chapter will be devoted to illustrating the relationship between planning and evaluation by presenting examples of objectives together with corresponding items to measure both content and thinking skills outcomes. Complete coverage of the various ways learning outcomes can be measured is beyond the scope of this text, and readers desiring more information on the topic are referred to any of the leading measurement and evaluation texts in the field.

We will first present sample items designed to measure content outcomes and will then illustrate the measurement of thinking skills objectives. We will use the taxonomy originally presented by Bloom (1956) as a framework for our examples.

Measuring Content Objectives

After reading this section you will be able to meet the following objectives:

1. You will understand the measurement of facts so when given an objective you will write an item congruent with the objective.
2. You will understand the measurement of concepts so when given an objective you will write knowledge and comprehension level objectives to measure the concept.
3. You will understand the measurement of generalizations so when given given an objective you will write items to measure generalizations at the knowledge, comprehension and application levels.

As we saw in Chapter 2, each of the forms of content provides a unique form of information and is learned differently. These differences must be reflected in both the implementation and evaluation phases of teaching. The examples that follow are designed to illustrate how measurement items can be written to accommodate the different characteristics of the content forms.

Facts.   As described in Chapter 2, the acquisition of facts is a type of S-R learning in which the goal for the learner is to link the response (answer) to the stimulus (question). Fact learning is essentially a memory task in which the learner is required to either recall or recognize the fact as it was taught. Table 3.1 provides examples of objectives and items designed to measure recall.

In contrast to recall, recognition items provide the learner with a list of alternatives from which the correct answer can be chosen. Typically, the format for the item will be matching or multiple choice. Examples of objectives and their corresponding measurement items are shown in Table 3.2.

TABLE 3.1   Objectives and Measurement Items for Fact Learning at the Recall Level

OBJECTIVE	MEASUREMENT ITEM
1. For fourth-grade social studies students to know the capital of the state of Washington so that from memory they state the capital in writing.	1. What city is the capital of the state of Washington? _____
2. For chemistry students to know the chemical symbols for the elements in the halogen family so that without aids they will write all correctly.	2. Write the symbols for all of the elements in the halogen family. _____
3. For fifth-grade math students to know the formula for the area of a triangle so that without prompts they will write the formula correctly.	3. What is the formula for the area of a triangle? _____

TABLE 3.2   Objectives and Measurement Items for Facts at the Recognition Level

OBJECTIVE	MEASUREMENT ITEM
1. Literature students will know the author of "The Raven" so that when provided with alternatives they will choose the correct author.	1. "The Raven" was written by A. Longfellow B. William Thoreau C. Herman Melville D. Edgar Allen Poe
2. For eighth-grade history students to know the states of the Confederacy so that given a list they will identify the Confederate states.	2. Which of the following states belonged to the Confederacy? A. Georgia B. New York C. Ohio D. Florida
3. Students will be able to associate words with symbols for the basic geometric shapes so that when provided with squares, circles, triangles and rectangles they will match the correct word with the shape.	3. Draw a line from the shape to the correct word. 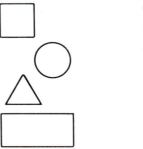

Concepts.   Like facts, objectives for concept learning can be written at a memory level through either recognition or recall, but because of the additional aspects of concept learning more options are available to the teacher. A definition, characteristics, or the relationship to other concepts each reflect a different element of knowledge, all of which are readily measured. Table 3.3 provides sample items designed to measure knowledge of concepts for each of these features. The list of examples is obviously not intended to be exhaustive, and instead is provided as a framework from which teachers can generate their own items.

The teacher should be cautious about measuring concepts only at the knowledge level because the ability to memorize definitions, characteristics, or related concepts does not necessarily mean that the student understands the concept. Concept and fact learning are different in that concept learning involves the formation of a generalizable abstraction while fact learning does not, that is, the learner can generalize from the concept to identify additional examples. Indeed, some people would hold that true concept learning does not occur until an abstraction is formed and the ability to generalize is acquired. Whatever their views on this issue, teachers who have concept learning as one of their teaching goals should be able to write objectives which tap this important dimension.

The most common procedure employed to determine if learners have formed a generalizable abstraction is to ask them to classify additional examples as belonging or not belonging to the concept. This is considered to be comprehension level measurement and objectives for this level, as with knowl-

TABLE 3.3   Knowledge Level Items for Measuring Concept Learning

RECALL	RECOGNITION

DEFINITION

1. What is a parallelogram?	1. Which of the following is the best definition of a parallelogram;
	A. A parallelogram is a four-sided figure with four interior angles.
	B. A parallelogram is a geometric shape with four equal sides and four equal angles.
	C. A parallelogram is a geometric shape with four sides and the opposite sides equal in length and parallel.
	D. A parallelogram is a four-sided geometric shape with two acute interior angles and two obtuse interior angles.

RECALL	RECOGNITION

CHARACTERISTICS

2. What attributes will you find in *all* parallelograms?

2. Which of the following characteristics will be found in *all* parallelograms; (More than one answer may be correct.)
   A. Four sides
   B. All sides equal
   C. Interior angles equal
   D. Opposite sides equal in length
   E. Opposite interior angles equal
   F. Right angles

SUPERORDINATE

3. A parallelogram is a kind of (one-word answer):

3. Of the sets of figures below, identify the one most accurately describing a parallelogram.
   A. Rhombus
   B. Triangle
   C. Square
   D. Quadrilateral

COORDINATE

4. Write the names of all the four-sided figures you can.

4. Which of the following are four-sided figures?
   A. Trapezoid
   B. Pentagon
   C. Circle
   D. Triangle

SUBORDINATE

5. Write the names of all the types of parallelograms you can.

5. Which of the following are parallelograms?
   A. Rhombus
   B. Trapezoid
   C. Square
   D. Rectangle

edge, can be of a recognition or a production format. Recognition objectives require the learner to identify new examples from a number of alternate items. Production objectives require the learner to provide examples which have not been previously mentioned in class. Examples of these two types of objectives and corresponding measurement items are provided in Table 3.4.

TABLE 3.4   **Comprehension Objectives for Concept Learning and Corresponding Measurement Items**

OBJECTIVE	MEASUREMENT ITEM

RECOGNITION

1. For fourth-grade students to understand the concept of *adjective* so that, when provided with examples and nonexamples, they will correctly classify each.

1. Circle *all* the examples below which are adjectives.
   A. go
   B. big
   C. dog
   D. the
   E. happy

2. For third-grade science students to understand the concept of *carnivore* so that, when provided with examples of carnivores and noncarnivores, they will correctly classify each.

2. Circle all the animals that are carnivores.
   A. wolf
   B. cow
   C. rabbit
   D. lion
   E. bear

3. For chemistry students to understand the concept of *diatomic,* so that when provided with examples and nonexamples of diatomic molecules they will identify all the diatomic ones.

3. Which of the following are diatomic molecules?
   A. H_2
   B. NaCl
   C. H_2SO_4
   D. Cl_2

PRODUCTION

1. For first-grade math students to know the concept of *greater than* so that when given a number they will provide three examples of numbers that are greater than the given.

1. Write down three numbers that are greater than ($>$) 10.

2. High school literature students will know the concept of *simile* so that without aids they will construct three original (i.e., not discussed in class) similes.

2. We've been studying similes in class. Now it's your turn to write your own. Write three similes that haven't been discussed in class.

3. For third graders to know the concept of *rhyme* so that without aids they will write five rhyming pairs of words.

3. In the spaces below write five *pairs* of rhyming words.

The key to the illustrations in Table 3.4 is the recognition or production of new or original examples. It is important that teachers avoid using examples for measurement that they have used to initially teach the concept. If the same ones are used for both teaching and measurement, the students will merely recall the examples, and the measurement will be at the knowledge level. This is legitimate if teachers are only attempting to measure learning at this level but it is not if they are trying to determine whether or not the learning will transfer to new situations.

We should emphasize again that the preceding illustrations of measurement formats at the comprehension level by no means exhaust all the possibilities for such measurement items. For example, students could be presented with a new example or nonexample of a concept and be asked to explain why it is or is not an example. This helps develop the skills of critical thinking in that the learners are required to relate the observed characteristics in the example to a set of criteria (the set of characteristics needed for a valid concept). In another instance students could be asked to explain the definition using original examples. The format for the items is probably not critical. More important is that the teacher understands the rationale behind types of measurement items and knows how to use each appropriately.

Generalizations.   Several parallel features exist in the measurement of concepts and generalizations. Like concepts, knowledge and comprehension of generalizations can be assessed, and knowledge is typically determined by having students recall or recognize the generalization. Comprehension is analagous for the two. Concept learning at this level is determined by having the student identify or produce unique examples, and comprehension of a generalization is measured by having the students identify situations in which the generalization applies. At this level the student only determines where the generalization could apply but does not actually produce the predictions or explanations characterizing application. When problems are solved, predictions made, or explanations offered on the basis of the generalization, students are working at the application level. The behaviors expected of the students at the different levels are shown in Table 3.5.

Table 3.6 contains objectives and measurement items for the three levels. We have purposely used the same generalization throughout the illustration to try and clarify differences among the levels. Table 3.7 provides some additional examples.

TABLE 3.5   Different Levels of Learning Generalizations

LEVEL	BEHAVIOR
Knowledge	Student remembers generalizations.
Comprehension	Student understands generalization—can paraphrase it or identify situations in which it applies.
Application	Student can use generalization to solve problems.

TABLE 3.6   Objectives and Measurement Items for Generalizations

KNOWLEDGE

OBJECTIVE	MEASUREMENT ITEM

RECALL

1. For math students to know the Pythagorean theorem so that from memory they will write the theorem in correct form.

1. What is the formula for the Pythagorean theorem?

RECOGNITION

2. For math students to know the Pythagorean theorem so that, when provided with a list of alternatives, they will select the proper one.

2. Which of the following is the Pythagorean theorem?
   A. $A^2/B = C$
   B. $A = \pi D$
   C. $A^2 + B^2 = C^2$
   D. $(C - B)^2 = A^2$

COMPREHENSION

RECOGNITION

1. For math students to understand the Pythagorean theorem so that, when provided with verbal problems, they will identify those in which the theorem applies.

1. Read the following situations and circle the letters of those in which the Pythagorean theorem could be used to solve the problem.
   A. A football player caught the opening kickoff on his own goal line right and ran for a touchdown diagonally across the field. How far did he run? (Assume that he ran in a straight line.)
   B. Mary Jane wanted to make the crust for a pizza pie. The recipe was designed for a 13-inch (diameter) round pie sheet but Mary Jane only had a 9-inch sheet. What should she do to the recipe?
   C. A man had to cross the field illustrated below. Just as he started to enter the field at A he saw a big bull in the field. He decided he'd better go the long way. How much longer did he have to go because of the bull?

A   100 yds.   B

30 yds.

C   D

COMPREHENSION

OBJECTIVE	MEASUREMENT ITEM

PRODUCTION

2. For math students to understand the Pythagorean theorem so that without aids they will describe a situation in which the theorem applies.	2. Describe a situation involving an everyday problem which could be solved using the Pythagorean theorem.

APPLICATION

1. For math students to know how to apply the Pythagorean theorem so that, when provided with verbal problems that require its use, they will successfully solve the problems for the correct values.	1. Solve all the above problems that can be solved using the Pythagorean theorem. Show your work. You need not solve problems that can't be solved by the theorem.

Each of the examples at the application level are production items where the learner is required to solve the problem as is required with the example in Table 3.6 or make a prediction from the information in Table 3.7. An alternative format involving recognition is available, however. Consider the following example.

Suppose the mean temperature of Samoa dropped 20 degrees. Which of the following most accurately describes how the culture would be affected?
a. It would be unaffected because Samoans are not concerned about creature comforts.
b. The Samoans would change their mode of dress and housing to accommodate the change.
c. The Samoans would probably move to another country to avoid the cold weather.
d. Samoa would be less known as an island paradise and would be more closely related to a country such as New Zealand.

From these examples we see that considerable flexibility exists measuring each form of content. Also, an interesting relationship between the complexity and abstraction of the form of content and the level at which it can be measured should be pointed out. We have summarized this relationship in Table 3.8.

Note, however, that higher levels of learning do not automatically follow as a result of teaching concepts and generalizations. Rather, learning at these levels must be planned and taught accordingly. Teachers who have higher cog-

**TABLE 3.7   Objectives and Measurement Items for Generalization Learning
at Comprehension and Application Levels**

COMPREHENSION

OBJECTIVE	MEASUREMENT ITEM

RECOGNITION

1. For fifth-grade social studies students to understand the generalization "Climate affects culture" so that, when provided with a description of a culture, they will identify statements that illustrate the generalization.

1. In the following description underline *all* statements that illustrate the generalization "Climate affects culture."

    The Samoans are a peaceful, fun-loving culture. Life in Samoa in many ways has not changed much in the last hundred years. Many people in Samoa still fish for a living. Because it is warm, many wear the sarong year-round like their ancestors have for centuries.

PRODUCTION

2. For fifth-grade social studies students to understand the generalization "Climate affects culture" so that when given an essay test they will describe at least three different ways in which their own culture is affected by climate. These must be different from the ways discussed in class.

2. Describe three ways that climate affects culture in America. These must be different from the examples discussed in class.

APPLICATION

OBJECTIVE	MEASUREMENT ITEM

1. For fifth-grade social studies students to be able to apply the generalization "Climate affects culture" so that, when provided with a description of a culture and a hypothetical situation, they will make and explain three predictions as a result of the hypothetical situation.

1. What would happen to the culture of Samoa if the mean temperature, which is approximately 70 degrees, were to drop 20 degrees? Make three predictions and explain them.

TABLE 3.8

	CONTENT FORM	POSSIBLE LEVELS OF MEASUREMENT	HIGHEST POSSIBLE LEVEL OF MEASUREMENT
Increasing level of complexity and abstraction	Facts	Knowledge	Knowledge
	Concepts	Knowledge Comprehension	Comprehension
	Generalizations	Knowledge Comprehension Application	Application

nitive abilities as their goal must provide learning activities that help students reach these levels and must construct evaluation items that reflect these learning outcomes. The examples provided are designed to illustrate the different levels for each of the content forms.

Measuring Thinking Skills

At first glance the measurement of thinking skills would seem little different from assessing students' acquisition of the forms of content. Instead of knowledge and understanding of facts, concepts, and generalizations, measuring the learners' ability to find patterns, make and assess inferences and generalize would be the focus.

However, assessing thinking skills has two unique features compared to measuring content outcomes. First, preparing valid and reliable items to measure thinking skills is more difficult and has less historical precedent to use as a framework than has the assessment of knowledge and understanding. As Beyer (1984) has noted, this difficulty is one of the factors that has inhibited the development of thinking skills instruction.

Second, as we said in Chapter 2, the separation of thinking skills and content is impossible, so measuring thinking will always have a concomitant content measurement, and teachers must constantly evaluate their items to be certain that the focus is on thinking with content as a vehicle rather than content being the focus.

We will attempt to accommodate these problems in each of the following illustrations. As they are presented, we discuss factors that need to be considered if the items are to remain valid.

Observation.   As we discussed in Chapter 2, observing is the basis of all thinking and the foundation on which the other skills are based. It is given major emphasis in the elementary schools, while older children, although often incorrectly, are tacitly assumed to be competent observers. However, with older children the problem is usually one of attention or sensitivity rather than the inability to discriminate among objects or events. With younger children many standard measures of perceptual ability exist, and a discussion of them is beyond the scope of this text.

Further, the ability to observe in the mainstream classroom is typically measured informally during the course of learning activities rather than formally with structured observational or paper and pencil items. For these reasons we do not discuss the measurement of observation further here. Instead we want to turn now to a discussion of measuring developmental skills and critical thinking.

Developmental skills and critical thinking.   As with the assessment of content outcomes, measuring thinking skills can be described using production and recognition as a framework. We described developmental skills as the ability to compare, summarize, identify patterns, and make generalizations, explanatory inferences, predictions, and hypotheses. Each of these is either an inductive or a deductive conclusion with the ability to assess these conclusions being one of the two categories of critical thinking. The developmental skills are measured with production items while critical thinking is assessed through recognition.

Let's look now at several examples of objectives and items designed to measure thinking skills.

OBJECTIVE

For students to be able to evaluate summaries, so when given a passage and a series of summary concepts they will identify the most accurate.

ITEM

Read the following passage and answer the question that follows.

Technology is the knowledge and skill that humanity has for using, making and controlling things. In the United States we have a high level of technology. One of its indications is our heavy dependence on time.

Think for a moment about how you use time. When do classes begin at your school? At what time do you go to lunch? How many minutes are there in a quarter of a football game? We have ways of measuring time very accurately. Most of us wear watches on our wrists. This shows how great a value we place on knowing what time it is. We even refer to "split-second timing." For some purposes, we need to measure time in split seconds. What is the record for the 100-yard dash? Can you think of other occasions when "split-second timing" is important?

Anthropologists know about other less technological societies as well. In these societies the time of day is often measured by the height of the sun in the sky. The changes in the shape of the moon may be another way of measuring time.

For some societies the slow change of the seasons is an exact enough measure of time.

We know that hundreds of planes land at and take off from a busy airport each day. The arrival and departure of these planes cannot be controlled by the height of the sun in the sky. By consulting a schedule we learn the plane leaves at 1:50 p.m. We had better be on time.

There are two primary concepts identified in the passage. They are:

a. history and anthropology
b. the United States and technology
c. the United States and time
d. technology and time

There are several factors that should be considered in this example. First, we are assuming that the students had not previously seen or discussed the passage. In order to prepare valid measures of thinking skills it is important that the students are asked to make or assess conclusions not made in the learning activity. As with the assessment of content, if the conclusion has already been discussed, they can merely recall it, and the measurement is actually a knowledge level measurement of content rather than a measure of thinking skills.

Second, the students must be able to read the passage comfortably or the item merely measures vocabulary and reading comprehension. As with any measurement involving reading, an element of reading comprehension exists, but the teacher must be as certain as possible that it is not the only thing being measured.

Third, identifying the key concepts is only one measure of critical assessment of summaries. The teacher may choose instead to write several summary statements and have students identify the most accurate one.

Assessment of summarizing can easily be extended to the critical assessment of generalizations. For example consider the following objective and item based on the previous passage.

OBJECTIVE

Students will be able to critically assess generalizations so given a passage and list, they will identify the most accurate generalization based on the passage.

ITEM

Based on the passage the most accurate generalization of the following is:

a. The higher the level of technology, the more important precise time is.
b. Technology exists to a high degree in the United States.

    c.   While time is measured in many ways, it is valued to a greater extent in this country than in others.

    d.   Anthropology and history are the ways we learn about ourselves and other countries.

The information to assess generalizing inferences can exist in a variety of forms. For example consider the following objectives and items.

OBJECTIVE

Students will be able to think critically so when given information and a series of generalizations they will identify the most accurate generalization based on the information.

ITEM

Look at Table 3.9 titled "Energy and Humankind." Of the following the most accurate generalization based on the chart is:

    a.   As humanity advances the consumption of food increases in proportion.

    b.   As humanity advances, energy tends to require an increasing proportion of the total energy consumption.

    c.   As humanity advances the proportion of its energy consumption taken by transportation decreases.

    d.   As humanity advances technologically, the proportion taken by home and commerce continually increases.

The assessment of explanatory inferences is closely related to the preceding material and can be measured in a similar way. For example consider the following objective and item.

OBJECTIVE

For students to assess explanations so when given information and a series of statements they will identify the most accurate explanation from the list.

ITEM

Consider again the chart entitled "Energy and Humankind." We see that energy consumption due to transportation has increased by four and a half times in the advance from Industrial to Technological. Of the following the best explanation for this increase based on the chart is:

    a.   Primitive energy sources such as humans and animals are no longer used.

    b.   The variety of energy sources has increased.

    c.   The use of fossil fuels has increased.

    d.   The proportion of the energy taken by food has increased.

TABLE 3.9 Data for Inference Measurement Items

	ENERGY AND HUMANKIND*		
	ENERGY SOURCES	ENERGY TYPE	AMOUNT OF ENERGY USED BY EACH PERSON DAILY
Technological Humanity (U.S.)	food fire animal labor rivers wind sun fossil fuels chemical atomic	muscle heat, light animal energy hydropower, wind steam solar power coal, petroleum natural gas electricity nuclear power	10,000 calories — food 66,000 calories — home and commerce 91,000 calories — industry and agriculture 63,000 calories — transportation <u></u> 230,000 TOTAL
Industrial Humanity (Peak 1850–1870)	food fire animal labor rivers wind fossil fuels	muscle heat, light animal energy hydropower, wind steam coal	7,000 calories — food 32,000 calories — home and commerce 24,000 calories — industry and agriculture 14,000 calories — transportation <u></u> 77,000 TOTAL
Advanced Agricultural Humanity (Northwestern Europe in A.D. 1400)	food fire animal labor rivers wind	muscle heat, light animal energy hydropower wind	6,000 calories — food 12,000 calories — home and commerce 7,000 calories — industry and agriculture 1,000 calories — transportation <u></u> 26,000 TOTAL

(cont.)

TABLE 3.9 (Continued)

Primitive Agricultural Humanity (Fertile Crescent in 5,000 B.C.)	food fire animal labor	muscle heat, light animal labor	4,000 calories 4,000 calories 4,000 calories 12,000 TOTAL	food home and commerce industry and agriculture
Hunting Humanity (Europe about 100,000 years ago)	food burned wood	muscle heat, light	3,000 calories 2,000 calories 5,000 TOTAL	food home and commerce
Primitive Humanity (East Africa about 1,000,000 years ago)	food	muscle	2,000 calories	food

*Adapted from "The flow of energy in an industrial society," by Earl Cook, 1972. The authors wish to thank Tom Manning, a science teacher for the Duval County School System in Jacksonville, Florida, for permission to use this chart.

We want to note here that the measurement items do not have to be accompanied by a large chart. However, it is important that the patterns, generalizations, and explanations can be based on information that the students can see or observe, rather than prior knowledge, or the item may be more a measure of recall than a measure of thinking skills.

Pictures, graphs, tables, and maps all provide excellent sources of information from which developmental skills and critical thinking can be measured. Using existing sources can help reduce the time required to prepare the items. The materials can be displayed on the overhead or chart and the teacher then must only write the item. Students' texts can even be efficiently used. Because they are evaluating conclusions based on the chart, table, or graph in the text, having an open book in front of them during the test does not detract from the validity of the item.

This concludes our general discussion of measuring for thinking skills. We provide additional examples when we discuss the evaluation of activities for each of the models in Part II of the text.

EXERCISES

PART I

The following paragraphs describe a teacher involved in a teaching episode. Read the entire episode including the items prepared by the teacher and then respond to the questions which follow.

Mr. Jones, a language arts instructor, was attempting to teach his students the concept of personification. He wanted his students to be able to appreciate the use of personification when encountered in literature. In attempting to figure out exactly how he would teach the concept, he prepared the following objective.

OBJECTIVE

Language arts students will know the concept *personification* so that when shown examples and nonexamples of the concept, they will pick out the examples and explain their choices.

In analyzing his objective, Mr. Jones decided that the most effective way of teaching this concept would be through examples and a definition, so he began his lesson by putting the following definition on the board.

Personification is a literary device in which inanimate objects or nonhuman beings are portrayed as possessing personal attributes.

"Okay, class, who can tell me what the definition means in their own words? Anyone?"

Silence.

"Well, let me give you a couple of examples of what I mean and then I'll ask you to try again. Take a look at these."

The sea raged angry at the wind and rain that upset its solitude.

The car coughed and sputtered and then died, only a quarter of a mile from the summit.

"Now can anyone tell me what the definition means? Sarah?"

"Well, personification means you treat dead things like they're alive," ventured Sarah.

"Anyone else?" asked Mr. Jones. "Bob?"

"It could also mean that you treat things like they have a personality," replied Bob.

"Good, now let me try a few more examples and see if you can tell me if they're examples of personification."

He then put the following examples on the board.

The fog crept in, stealing its way into the bushes and trees in the valley.

The thief was sly as a fox, disguising all the possible clues to the crime.

"Can anyone tell me if these are examples of personification? Jane?"

"I think they both are—because they both treat nonpeople like they're people," replied Jane.

"I don't think so," interjected Larry. "I think only the first one is. The first makes fog look like it's alive, so that means it's an example of personification. However, the second isn't because it's just comparing a thief to a fox."

The lesson continued with Mr. Jones presenting additional examples, and the students categorizing these examples and explaining their answers.

Toward the end of the class meeting, Mr. Jones gave his class the following three exercises.

PERSONIFICATION

1.   Which of the following is the best definition of personification?

A. Personification is a literary device in which something is compared to something else.

B. Personification occurs when a writer exaggerates something to achieve an effect.

C. Personification is a literary device in which two dissimilar objects are described.

D. Personification ocurs when a writer gives inanimate objects living characteristics.

2.   Which of the following are examples of personification?

A. The tea kettle rattled and steamed, seemingly eager to be removed from the fire.

B. The ship limped into port, subdued by the damages it had received.

C. The silver bullet struck the vampire just as it neared the girl.

D. The silver moonlight reminded us of the couple of days and nights that had passed many years ago.

3.   Now it is your turn. Write three more examples of personification. These should be examples that have not been discussed in class before.

TO THE READER:

1. Identify the three phases of the general approach to teaching illustrated in Mr. Jones lesson.

2. Mr. Jones gave his students three items to determine their understanding of the concept. For each item, identify the level and whether is was recognition or production.

3. Consider Mr. Jones's items and their level. Discuss the appropriateness of the items according to their relationship with the objective.

FEEDBACK

PART I

1. Mr. Jones's activity can be described as follows:

Planning: During this phase the teacher determined his objective and decided how he was going to teach the lesson.

Implementation: In the implementation phase the teacher presented a definition together with examples of the concept. This occupied the largest portion of the scenario.

Evaluation: In this phase the teacher gave the class three exercises to complete.

2. The items can be classified as follows:

1.	Knowledge	Recognition
2.	Comprehension	Recognition
3.	Comprehension	Production

3. Probably the most appropriate item was number 2. This item was most congruent with the objective that Mr. Jones formulated. Item 1 provides some information about the students' grasp of the concept but actually measures learning at the knowledge level. This item, alone, would not be an appropriate item to measure attainment of the concept.

Item 3 would also be an excellent way to measure the students' understanding of the concept. In this instance, however, it would be inconsistent with the objective which stated that students will *identify* examples as opposed to stating their own examples.

EXERCISES

PART II

The following exercises are designed to give you practice in constructing your own measurement items. Try to write an item for each exercise before turning to the feedback section.

1.   The concept equal or equal to (=) is one taught to all elementary math students. Write an item to measure understanding of this concept. This should be a comprehension level item which measures students' ability to recognize examples.

2.   The ability to sequence is necessary to understand most stories. A student who is able to do this can tell which part of a story came first, which part came next, and so on. Write a recognition item which will measure this ability. (To do this it may be necessary for you to provide a story for the student.)

3.   In watching the moon come up on successive nights you might have noticed that it rises a little later each night. A generalization summarizing these observations could be "The moon rises an hour later each night." Write an application level item to measure students' ability to apply this generalization in a new situation.

4.   The following are data collected by a chicken farmer. Using these data, construct an item designed to measure students' ability to recognize valid generalizing inferences.

Number of Eggs per 100 Chickens in Artificially-lighted and Non-lighted Henhouses

	SPRING	SUMMER	FALL	WINTER
Lighted	88	85	85	87
Non-Lighted	83	86	80	75

FEEDBACK

PART III

1.   A recognition item that measures students' understanding of the concept *equal to* would be the following.
Which one of the following is true?

A. $\text{卌} = \text{////}$

B.   ••• = ••••

C. $\triangle\triangle = \triangle\triangle\square$

D.   0 0 0 0 = 0 0 0 0

The above item assumes that students can count. If this assumption is not valid, then performance on the item would be influenced by students' ability to count, and consequently, the item would not be a valid measure of student's understanding of the concept. Also, students should have previously learned that the symbol " = " means equal.

2.   As mentioned in the exercise, an item of this type requires that the students have

available materials that they can sequence. Accordingly, an item designed to measure students' ability to recognize a sequence might appear as follows:

After reading the following story, turn your paper over and answer the question which follows.

Mary was walking to school when she saw dog chasing a kitten into a narrow pipe. When she went over to the pipe and looked inside, she saw not one kitten, but four. Just then she heard a man say, "Are those your kittens?" Turning around, she saw an old man with white hair smiling at her. "No," she said, "But I wish they were." "Well, if you want one, I think you can have one because they don't seem to have any owners. But first you'll have to ask your mother." Mary was fidgety all day at school, anxious to return home to ask her mother about the kittens.

Question: Arrange the following events in the order in which they appeared in the story by placing a "1" by the first thing that happened, a "2" by the second, and so on.

_____ Mary saw the old man.

_____ Mary looked in the pipe.

_____ Mary saw the dog chasing the cat.

_____ Mary arrived at school.

Having students turn the page before answering the question also incorporates the element of memory. If this is not desirable, the question could be answered with the story available. Also, the question as it now exists measures reading ability because students must be able to read to answer the question. To eliminate this dimension, the story could be read orally, and students could be asked to sequence pictures of the story.

3.   An application level question could appear as follows:

George, an amateur photographer, wanted to photograph the full moon coming up over the Atlantic. He noticed in the newspaper that there would be a full moon in three days. He also noticed that the moon had risen that evening at 9:45. What time did he have to get down to the beach on the night of the full moon to catch it coming up?

This question places the student in a novel situation and requires the student to utilize the generalization as well as the data in order to solve the problem.

4.   In measuring students' ability to recognize valid inferences, the common procedure is to provide a number of inferences and ask students to select the inference which is most supported by observation. A question such as this could be written as follows:

Look at the data in the chart. Which of the following statements is most supported by observation?

A.   Chickens lay the most eggs when it is warm.
B.   The shorter the day, the more eggs chickens lay.
C.   The amount of light chickens receive influences the number of eggs they lay.
D.   The more sleep chickens get, the more eggs they lay.

Here the students are required to relate the inferential statement to the observations in the data table. Their analysis would require that they reject choice A because the chickens with lighted conditions laid more eggs in winter than summer. Choice B would be rejected for the same reason. Choice C would be accepted because the chickens with unlighted conditions laid more eggs in summer when they received more light. There are no data to either support or reject choice D. Consequently, choice C would be the best answer. A student given practice in this type of analysis would be developing his thinking skills and increasing his ability to process information in his everyday world.

In this item as well as the others, the reader will see alternate ways in which the presented ideas could be measured. These examples are but *one* possible way of measuring the content and processes illustrated here. It is hoped that these, as well as other ideas presented in this book, rather than narrowing the thinking of the reader, will serve as a springboard for new ideas.

REFERENCES

BERLINER, D. (1985, April). *Effective Teaching.* Paper presented at the meeting of the Florida Educational Research and Development Council, Pensacola, Florida.

BEYER, B. (1984). Improving thinking skills—defining the problem. *Phi Delta Kappan, 65,* 486–490.

BLOOM, B., ed. (1956). *Taxonomy of educational objectives. Handbook I: Cognitive domain* (New York: McKay).

CLARK, C. & PETERSON, P. (1986). Teachers' thought processes. In M. Wittrock, ed. *Third handbook of research on teaching,* 3rd ed. (New York: MacMillan), pp. 255–296.

CLARK, C. & YINGER, R. (1979). *Three studies of teacher planning.* East Lansing, Michigan: Michigan State University Institute for Research on Teaching, Research Series No. 55.

Curriculum Frameworks. (1985). Florida Department of Education. Tallahasee, Florida: State Department of Education.

GRONLUND, N. (1985). *Stating objectives for classroom instruction,* 2nd ed. (New York: MacMillan).

MacDONALD-ROSS, M. (1974). Behavioral objectives: a critical review. *Instructional Science, 2,* 1–51.

MAGER, R. (1962). *Preparing instructional objectives* (Palo Alto, Ca.: Fearon).

McASHAN, H. (1974). *The goals approach to performance objectives* (Philadelphia: Saunders).

McCUTCHEON, G. (1980). How do elementary teachers plan their courses? *Elementary School Journal, 81,* 4–23.

PETERSON, P., MARX, R., & CLARK, C. (1978). Teacher planning, teacher behavior, and students' achievement. *American Educational Research Journal, 15,* 417–432.

ROSENSHINE, B. & STEVENS, R. (1986). Teaching functions. In M. Wittrock, ed. *Third Handbook of Research on Teaching,* 3rd ed. (New York: MacMillan), pp. 376–391.

4

THE INDUCTIVE MODEL

INTRODUCTION

The Inductive Model is a straightforward but powerful strategy designed to develop the thinking skills of observation, comparing, finding patterns, and generalizing while at the same time teaching specific concepts or generalizations. In addition, the model has the intrinsic advantages of promoting high levels of interaction and increased student motivation. Its effectiveness depends on the teacher as an active leader as the students process the information. To begin to illustrate these features let's turn to an example of the Inductive Model in action using an actual lesson we have observed. We use fictitious names and we have eliminated some of the dialogue for the sake of clarity and brevity, but otherwise the description is as we observed it.

Mr. Jaurez has his fifth graders involved in a unit on invertebrates and wants them to learn the concept *arthropods.*

He began the lesson by saying, "OK everyone, to start today's lesson I want you all to reach down and grab your upper leg. Squeeze it and poke at it a bit. Now tell me what you felt. Cinda?"

"Squishy," Cinda responded.

"OK," Mr. Jaurez smiled. "What else, Tim?"

"Soft."

"Fine, Tim. Shakakan?"

"A bone is down inside."

"Yes, very good, Shakakan. How do you know that?"

"I can sort of feel it up near my knee."

"Yes, I'm sure you can," Mr. J. replied. "And this bone is part of which of our body systems? Debra?"

" . . . Our skeletal system."

"And what did Shakakan say about the bone's location? George?"

"It was down inside her leg."

"And what does that tell us about our skeletal system? Nancy?"

" . . . "

"Is it on the outside of our bodies or is it on the inside of our bodies?"

"It's on the inside!" Nancy replied quickly.

"Yes, very good, Nancy. Our skeletons are on the inside of our bodies."

"Now what else did you feel? Reginald?"

" . . . "

"Does it feel sort of warm or sort of cold?" Mr. J. queried.

"Warm," Reginald responded immediately.

"Good! And why do you suppose it felt warm? Bill?"

" . . . We're warm-blooded animals," Bill responded after a moment's hesitation.

"Yes! That is one of the important characteristics of people, Bill."

"Now let me have you look at this," Mr. Jaurez said, and with that he reached into a portable cooler and pulled out a live lobster.

The students amid squeals of "Oooh," "Yuk," and "Gross," began to chatter excitedly.

Mr. Jaurez settled them down in a moment and then directed, "Now tell me about this. Sue?"

"It looks slimy."

"And what else? Tammy?"

"It looks like it has a shell on it."

"Excellent! And how might we tell?"

"We could feel it."

"Yes, go ahead."

Tammy then felt the lobster and tapped on it and said, "It feels hard."

"How else does it feel? Leroy?"

"It's cold," Leroy replied after placing his palm on the lobster's back.

"Good! "Now let me show you something else."

Mr. Jaurez then took a large beetle out of a plastic bag and began the same line of questioning as he had used with the lobster. He also displayed a colored transparency of the beetle for the children and told them to look at the image on the screen when they could not see the actual animal.

He then repeated the entire process with a crayfish. We return to the lesson now to see how Mr. Jaurez proceeds.

He continued, "Now look at all three of the animals. What is something they all have in common? Don?"

" . . . Well they all felt hard."

"Yes, excellent, Don, and what does that tell us?"

" . . . "

After a few second's hesitation, Mr. Jaurez continued, "What did Tim say about the way our bodies felt?"

After thinking a moment Don replied, "Soft."

"Yes, exactly! Very good, Don. And what did that tell us about the location of our bones? Kathy?"

"They're on the inside of our bodies."

"That's right, Kathy. Well done."

"So, what do we know about the skeletons on these animals, Don?"

"They're on the outside!" Don excitedly answered.

"Well done, Don. You've identified one of the important features of these animals."

"What else did we find was similar about the animals? Judy?"

"They all felt cold."

"Excellent, Judy. How is that different from the way we feel? David?"

"We feel warm. We're warm-blooded!" David squealed. "These animals are all cold-blooded!"

"Yes, that's outstanding thinking, David," Mr. Jaurez responded with a smile and a wave of his hand.

Mr. Jaurez then continued to direct the students' analysis of the lobster, beetle, crayfish, and their own bodies having them identify the jointed legs in each of the animals, discovering that in this case that we also have jointed legs, and finally having them identify the segmented bodies in each of the animals. Let's return once more to the dialogue and see how Mr. Jaurez completed the lesson.

"Now let's look at the patterns we've found in the animals," Mr. Jaurez directed. "What did we say each of them have in common? Christy?"

" . . . Well, they're all cold-blooded."

"Yes, excellent. That's one common feature of these animals," and with that he wrote 'cold-blooded' on the chalkboard.

"What else? Bob?"

"Skeleton on the outside," Bob replied quickly.

"Good, Bob. That's another important feature," and he again wrote 'outside skeleton' on the board.

"Kirsty?"

"Their legs are jointed."

"Jason?"

"They have segmented bodies."

"Outstanding, everyone! You've identified all the important features of this group of animals. Now does anyone know the name of this animal group?"

After waiting and hearing no response Mr. Jaurez said, "We call these animals arthropods. Everybody say that word now."

The students then responded in unison, "Arthropods!"

Mr. Jaurez then quickly erased the board and then said, "Now give me a definition of arthropods. I'll let someone volunteer."

With some prompting they were able to define arthropods as follows: "Arthropods are animals that have an outside skeleton, jointed legs, segmented bodies, and are cold-blooded." He then extended the lesson by showing the students a clam and asking them to tell him if it was an arthropod or not and upon deciding that it was not, to explain why not. He went on by referring the students to Mrs. Wiggens, the school principal, and having them decide if she was an arthropod. Amid laughter and squeals of delight they concluded that she was not. Mr. Jaurez then went on to ask them why not and probed them to identify a feature that Mrs. Wiggens and arthropods have in common. Finally, he had the students suggest other examples of arthropods and he closed the lesson.

Let's stop now and examine the features of the illustration. As background for the discussion, you may want at this time to refer to Chapter 2 to review concepts and generalizations, the role examples play in learning, and how they may be creatively taught.

Mr. Jaurez helped his students acquire the concept *arthropod* by showing them examples and nonexamples and directed their information processing through his questioning. As the lesson unfolded the students made comparisons between the examples (the lobster, beetle, and crayfish) and the nonexample (themselves) and then identified patterns in the examples. The patterns revealed the essential characteristics of arthropods, and the students then generalized to suggest that these characteristics would be found in all arthropods. This was explicitly stated in a definition. Mr. Jaurez then extended the lesson by having the students analyze other examples (the clam and Mrs. Wiggens) to see if their characteristics fit the patterns. Finally, he asked them for additional examples of arthropods.

Mr. Jaurez's approach was a bit unique in that he began the lesson with a nonexample, while a teacher would typically begin with an example. His reason for doing so was motivational. He wanted to begin with something personal, and something that would promote instant involvement from all the students.

As we discuss the planning, implementation, and evaluation phases of the model we will see how it can be adapted to meet an individual teacher's goals. Keeping this inherent flexibility in mind we can outline the general procedure as follows:

PHASE 1: THE OPEN-ENDED PHASE

1. Show the students an example of the concept or generalization or a nonexample as was illustrated in Mr. Jaurez's lesson.
2. Ask the students to observe and describe the example.
3. Show the students a second example or nonexample.
4. Again have the students observe and describe the second example.
5. Continue the process using as many examples and nonexamples as have been prepared.
6. Ask the students to compare the examples and nonexamples.

PHASE 2: THE CONVERGENT PHASE

7. Prompt the students to identify patterns in the examples.

PHASE 3: CLOSURE

8. Explicitly state the patterns in a definition.

PHASE 4: THE APPLICATION PHASE

9. Apply the definition with additional examples.

While a concept was taught in the illustration, the process is very similar for teaching a generalization. The examples would illustrate the relationship between the concepts in the generalization, and the students would, as with a concept, identify a pattern in the examples.

There are two primary differences between teaching a concept and teaching a generalization. The first is in the use of nonexamples. While they are important in teaching a concept, and particularly important in teaching closely related coordinate concepts, generalizations are often taught without the use of nonexamples.

The second difference exists in their application. Mr. Jaurez had the students apply the concept by giving them additional examples to analyze and then asking them to supply their own. On the other hand, students would apply a generalization by asking for additional examples or using it to explain an observation or set of observations. For instance suppose students have learned, "Intermittent reinforcement leads to persistent behavior and slow extinction." The students could apply it by explaining on the basis of the generalization some behavior such as a gambler at a slot machine or a person who encounters a locked door.

Let's turn now to a discussion of the planning, implementation, and evaluation of Inductive Model lessons.

PLANNING LESSONS WITH THE INDUCTIVE MODEL

After completing this section of the chapter you should be able to meet the following objectives:

1. You will understand planning for Inductive Model lessons so when given curriculum materials in your area of expertise, you will state a specific set of characteristics or a specific relationship according to the critera identified in this section.
2. You will understand the role of examples in teaching abstractions so when given a specific goal, you will identify examples which effectively meet the goal.

The planning process for using the Inductive Model is very straightforward and involves two essential steps. The first of these is the identification of goals.

Identifying Goals

As with any lesson, the teacher must begin with a clear goal in mind. There are two parts to this process, the first of which is the development of observing, comparing, finding patterns, and generalizing skills which is a concomitant goal in any inductive lesson. However, because thinking skills and content cannot be appropriately separated, our experience has shown that focusing on content for the purpose of goal setting is more efficient, and we approach it from a content perspective. Thinking skills are then integrated with the content as the lesson is implemented.

The second part of goal setting is identifying the concept or generalization you want to teach and then deciding *exactly what you want the students to know about it*. This means the goal is explicit to the point that you can identify what you want the students to be able to say or do. As we noted in Chapter 3, the difference between good and effective teachers is related to goal setting and the ability to teach directly to these goals (Berliner, 1985). Further, our experience in working with teachers has indicated that their questioning effectiveness and clarity of language are closely related to how clear they are about their objective. In asking teachers about what they were trying to accomplish after watching a rather vague and uncertain lesson, they usually have difficulty in explaining the goal with precision. Without certainty as to where the lesson is headed, it is impossible to effectively guide the students' thinking.

Mr. Jaurez had a goal that was clear, precise, and exact. He knew that he wanted the students to identify the characteristics *cold-blooded, outside skeleton, jointed legs,* and *segmented bodies* in the examples. Knowing this allowed him to direct the students' information processing smoothly and without observable effort. He was able to time his questions efficiently and provide a student with some additional assistance when necessary. Each of these features are related in part to a clear understanding of exactly what he wanted from the students.

Selecting Examples

The second essential step in the planning process is the selection of examples. Once teachers know exactly what they want the students to be able to say or do, they must then find the examples that will illustrate those characterstics. From the discussion of examples in Chapter 2, we see the process can be as simple as going to a fish market to get a lobster, crayfish, and clam as Mr. Jaurez did, to as demanding as creating a complex simulation and role play which would effectively communicate a concept such as *discrimination*.

In working with teachers we often ask, "What makes an example a good one?" and we typically get responses such as "They're clear," or a similar description. In this instance, *clear* can be described very precisely. An example is clear if the characteristics or relationship identified in the objective are *observable in the examples*. This is why a precise description of what you want the students to be able to say or do is so important. The specificity allows you to determine the effectiveness of the examples.

Mr. Jaurez's examples were excellent. He had identified cold-blooded, outside skeleton, jointed legs, and segmented bodies as the characteristics of the concept. The students could feel the cold bodies of the lobster, beetle, and crayfish, could also feel the hard exterior in each compared to the soft exterior in their own legs, and could see the jointed legs and segmented bodies. The examples fit the criteria for effective illustration of the concept very well.

How many examples are necessary? As we discussed in Chapter 2, Frayer's (1970) work has indicated that three or four well chosen examples will often appropriately illustrate the concept or generalization. Our experience is consistent with this research. However, the basis the teacher will ultimately use to determine the number of examples is the concept or generalization itself. The more abstract the idea and the less prior student exposure to the concept or generalization, the more examples will be needed. Having extra examples prepared is always a good idea. They are available if needed, and they can always be used for evaluation purposes if not.

Once the goal is clear and the examples have been created or identified, the teacher is ready to implement the lesson. Before turning to this phase, complete the exercises that follow.

EXERCISES

1.   Select a concept or generalization from a content area of your choice. State an objective for the students related to the abstraction. Remember, the criterion for an effective objective is: *You know exactly what you want them to be able to say or do.* Mr. Jaurez's lesson illustrates this process well.

2.   Having selected an objective, identify examples that will effectively illustrate the concept or generalization. The criterion in this case is that the characteristics or the relationship identified in the objective should be observable in the examples.

Discuss the objective and examples with your instructor and/or a colleague. They will be able to help you decide if the objective and examples are clear.

IMPLEMENTING INDUCTIVE MODEL LESSONS

After completing this section of the chapter, you should be able to meet the following objectives:

1.   You will understand the phases of the Inductive Model so when given a classroom example you will identify the phases illustrated in the episode.
2.   You will understand the questioning techniques implicit in the Inductive Model so from a classroom scenario you will identify description, comparison, prompting, and repetition questions.

3. You will understand the thinking skills incorporated within the Inductive Model so when given a classroom episode you will identify the thinking skills practiced in the lesson.

The implementation phase of the Inductive Model is relatively simple and can be quite flexible. In the Introduction we outlined the procedure as existing in four distinct phases which was presented primarily as an organizational scheme to help clarify your thinking. We use this scheme as we describe in depth the implementation of the model, but we will also discuss how the model can be adapted to meet students' needs. Let's look at each of the phases now.

Phase 1: The Open-ended Phase

Observation and description.   Phase 1 begins by simply presenting the students with an example (or nonexample) of the concept or generalization which the students are then asked to observe and describe. Because virtually any answer is acceptable, it is labeled *open-ended*. It starts with a question or directive such as:
  "What do you notice here?"
  "What do you see?"
  "Describe this for me," or something similar such as Mr. Jaurez's beginning when he said, "Tell me what you felt." He did the same thing when he showed the students the lobster and said, "Tell me about this." This is a better question than one such as, "How many legs does the lobster have?" or "What kind of animal is this?" The latter two while not wrong or bad have answers that are correct or incorrect and consequently narrow the opportunity to respond.
  As another example consider a teacher who wants students to understand the rule; "Nonessential clauses in a sentence are set off by commas." A sentence would be displayed on the board or overhead such as the following:

The boys in this class, who are among the best looking in the school, did very well on the last test.

The teacher would then continue by saying, "What do you notice about the sentence?" "Tell me something about the sentence." "Describe this sentence for me," or some similar directive. At this point in the activity, these questions are better than others such as: "What is the subject of the sentence?" or another question that has a right or wrong answer.
  As one more example, consider a teacher who wants to teach the concept *representative forms of government*. Information such as the following might be displayed:

The United States is a large, culturally and physically diverse country. Most of its ancestors came from Europe, but it has citizens from every country in the world. The leaders of the country are elected and congregate in Washington, D.C., the nation's capital. Here senators and representatives from the various states work with the president in establishing and administering the law of the land.

As with the other examples, the teacher would begin the processing by asking the students a question such as the following: "What do you notice about this paragraph?" or "Describe this paragraph for me," or some similar directive.

From the illustrations we see that Phase 1, in addition to serving as the springboard for the thinking process, is designed to be an easy, comfortable beginning to the processing for both the teacher and the students. It takes very little time to begin an activity with open-ended questions and the results produced in terms of thinking and motivation more than compensate for any extra time the additional processing might take.

Let's consider more carefully now some of the advantages of open-ended questions.

1. They provide for student success. Because any answer is acceptable, students can respond without fear of failure or reprisal. This opportunity is very motivational. Wlodkowski (1984) identifies emotional safety as a critical variable in motivation; students are 'safe' when they can answer without fear of failure. Our observations are consistent with Wlodkowski's findings. We have personally observed students who moved from hostile or frightened at the beginning of a class to volunteering responses by the end of the period simply because any answer they gave was acceptable. A change such as this in a single class period is really quite remarkable!

2. An open-ended question allows the teacher to call on all the students equally and by name. Even in a large class all the students can be called on several times during the course of a lesson when open-ended questions are used. Several students can be asked to describe the first example, several more the second example, and still more the third until all the students have had a turn. This is again a powerful motivator. Gage and Berliner (1984) suggest that the sound of our own name is the single most powerful emotional orienting stimulus that exists for people. Further, as we noted in Chapter 2, Kerman (1979) reports that teachers who called on all their students equally had improved achievement scores, fewer discipline referrals, and an improved attendance rate compared to teachers who did not concentrate on this practice. This is indeed an impressive result!

The benefits of involving students have also been documented by other researchers (Pratton & Hales, 1986). These investigators found that students taught by teachers who actively involved them in lessons achieved at higher rates than those in traditional, control classes.

The single most effective technique a teacher can use to maintain student attention is to put them in a situation where they know they will be called on. When success and emotional safety are combined with the certainty of being called on, student attention and attitude improve markedly, and with it achievement improves. Perhaps even more valuable is the fact that this process can be put into play with any topic at any grade level under virtually any conditions.

3. The question provides for brisk lesson pacing, a factor that has been found to influence learning (Brophy & Good, 1986; Rosenshine & Stevens, 1986). Pacing refers to how quickly a lesson moves along and should not be confused with the amount of content covered. Teachers can call on many students in a short period of time which results in high levels of student involvement. Again this is a powerful motivator.

4. The question is philosophically consistent with the development of thinking skills. As we saw in Chapter 2, thinking skills development begins with observation and an open-ended question directs the students to start their processing at that point.

As the teacher proceeds through the examples, he or she will use professional judgment to determine the number of descriptions to be requested of the students. This is part of the flexibility inherent in the model. There is no rule that dictates the exact number of descriptions that should be made of each example. With practice teachers quickly become facile with the process and move the students comfortably from example to example. Reading and monitoring the behavior of the students is important here. If they appear eager to continue describing the example, the teacher may continue a bit longer. On the other hand, if the students appear "antsy" or eager to "get on with it," the teacher should move on more quickly.

Comparing.   As the lesson proceeds, the process of observing and describing evolves naturally into making comparisons. The introductory illustration implies that comparisons among the examples are held until all of them are presented, and Mr. Jaurez proceeded this way. However, if you should instead want the students to make comparisons after presenting the first two and continue comparing after each succeeding example, it is perfectly appropriate to do so. The lesson should proceed in a natural and comfortable sequence rather than be tied to a rigid structure.

In the case with the lesson on nonessential clauses, the teacher might have displayed the following for the students:

> The boys in this class, who are among the best looking in school, did very well on the last test.
> Mrs. Adams' salary, which isn't enough to live on, is paid twice a month.

At this point, the teacher would ask the students to describe the second example and might then make comparisons. The students could be directed to begin with a simple question such as: "Now look at both the sentences. What is alike or different about them?"

In the lesson on representative democracy, the teacher might present the students with a second description such as:

> Iran is a Middle Eastern country with a rich cultural heritage dating back to the time of Christ. At the present time, Iran is attempting to preserve this heritage. At the same time, it is struggling to establish itself as a twentieth-century leader in Middle East politics. Endowed with ample supplies of oil, the country is trying to educate its citizenry to take advantage of the physical blessings of the land. Situated between the Persian Gulf and the Caspian Sea, Iran is in a strategically crucial spot in the Middle East. Ruled by a religious leader, the country is experiencing tensions between traditional Moslem values and modern twentieth-century practices.

As with the other examples, the teacher could simply direct the students to make comparisons with a question such as: "Look at both the paragraphs now. How are they similar or different?"

Notice also that in the case with nonessential clauses both sentences were examples, while in the illustration with representative democracy the first was an example and the second was a nonexample. The sequence is a matter of teacher judgment and one arrangement is no more correct than another. Mr. Jaurez actually began his lesson with a nonexample, which is less typical, but again is no less correct.

Making comparisons narrows the range of student responses that will eventually lead to identifying a pattern in the examples. While not as open-ended as observing and describing, a variety of responses will still be acceptable so the teacher can help the students converge on the answer while preserving the advantages that open-ended questioning affords. After similarities in the examples are identified through the comparisons, the lesson evolves naturally into Phase 2.

Phase 2: The Convergent Phase

The open-ended phase is characterized by observations, descriptions, and comparisons where virtually all answers are acceptable. Obviously, however, the lesson cannot continue in this way indefinitely. In that a specific content goal exists, the lesson must progress to an explicit description of the relationship in a generalization or the characteristics of a concept. To reach the goal the teacher narrows the range of student responses and leads them to verbally identify the relationship or characteristics. In that the students' processing results in, or converges on, a specific answer, it is called the "convergent phase." Our introductory lesson nicely illustrates the smooth progression from the open-ended to the convergent phase of the model. Let's examine it now.

In response to Mr. Jaurez's request for a comparison, Don responded,

"They all felt hard," and upon being asked what that told the class, Don had no response. Mr. Jaurez then asked the following questions:

> "What did Tim say about the way our bodies felt?"
> "What did that tell us about the location of our bones?"
> "So, what do we know about the skeletons on these animals?"

In the sequence of questions Mr. Jaurez prompted the students to identify the specific characteristic *outside skeleton* that he had identified in his goal. He continued by smoothly and deftly guiding the student processing until each of the specific characteristics he had identified in his goal had been reached. He came to closure in the lesson by having the students state a definition of the concept. Let's look at these questions a bit more closely now.

Prompting questions. Prompting questions are those designed to elicit an acceptable answer from a student when the student has either not responded or has given an inappropriate response. Mr. Jaurez wanted the students to conclude that the skeleton was on the outside for arthropods. When Don was unable to give this response, he asked another question that he was certain Don would be able to answer when he asked, "What did Tim say about the way our bodies felt?" This was a prompting question. Obviously, a wide range of possibilities exists for prompting, and any question that elicits an acceptable response is a good question.

Prompting is potentially difficult in that teachers must "think on their feet" to generate the most effective question at exactly the time when it is needed. However, it can be very rewarding for both the students and the teacher. It's fun and exciting to get responses from students that they were previously unable to make. In addition it establishes a climate of support between the teacher and students and further amplifies the motivational benefits identified in the open-ended phase. With practice teachers can become very adept with this extremely valuable skill.

The value of prompting is documented in the research literature. Anderson, Evertson, and Brophy (1979) and Stallings, Needels, and Stayrook (1979) both concluded that student achievement was greatest when teachers handle incorrect responses by asking simple questions, providing cues, and otherwise giving assistance rather than leaving the student in favor of someone else or giving the correct response and moving on.

Repetition. Repetition questions are also a valuable aid in helping the students arrive at the conclusions identified in the teacher's goal. They are questions that remind the students of information they have previously identified during the course of the lesson and help reinforce the direction of the processing. Mr. Jaurez used a repetition question to prompt Don when he asked, "What did Tim say about the way our bodies felt?" Other repetition questions in the activity were: "What did Shakakan say about the bone's location?" and "What did we say each of them have in common?"

As teachers we all know that considerable repetition is often required to help establish and reinforce ideas for students. As the lesson converges to closure it is a powerful tool in aiding students' processing.

Phase 3: Closure

Closure is the point at which the students come to the lesson's formal conclusion. When learning a concept, it is marked by the students verbally stating a formal definition, such as Mr. Jaurez's class did when they said, "Arthropods are animals that have an outside skeleton, jointed legs, segmented bodies, and are cold blooded." When learning a generalization, closure is reached when the students verbally state the relationship.

While a formal statement of closure is generally important and is documented in the research (Tennyson, 1978; Feldman, 1972; Brophy & Good, 1986), certain exceptions will occasionally exist. For example suppose the concept *above,* originally introduced in Chapter 2, is being taught to a group of small children. It could be defined as "A position in space where one object is at a higher altitude than is another." Obviously, young students would be unlikely to generate such a statement even with considerable prompting. In this case the teacher would move directly to the application phase in lieu of a formal statement of closure.

Phase 3 is also a good point in the lesson to help the students develop thinking skills related to recognizing irrelevant information. For instance, in the case with the nonessential clauses, they could be prompted to notice that the pronoun at the beginning of the clause is not relevant because the examples began with different pronouns. In the example with representative democracy, the location and size of the countries, among other factors, would be irrelevant. With any topic, it is relatively easy to assess the examples for nonessential information, which in turn sensitizes the students to this important thinking skill.

Phase 4: The Application Phase

The concept or generalization is reinforced by having the students classify examples and generate examples of their own. In many cases application can lead directly to seatwork or homework assignments. For example, in the case of the lesson on nonessential clauses, the teacher might ask the students to verbally provide examples of sentences including essential clauses and others including nonessential clauses. This would be a form of application.

Mr. Jaurez had his students apply the concept when he asked them to determine if the clam and Mrs. Wiggens were arthropods. While not reflected in our introductory illustration, it was interesting to note that several of the children wanted to classify the clam as an arthropod in the actual lesson we observed. They made this classification on the basis of the hard shell and cold-bloodedness and neglected the lack of a segmented body and jointed legs. This interesting tendency underscores the need for practice in thinking skills instruction where the students learn to carefully observe and account for all their observations. Teachers can provide for this practice through questions such as prompting and repetition.

This concludes our discussion of implementing Inductive Model lessons. Turn now to the following exercises designed to reinforce your understanding of the material in this section.

EXERCISES

The following scenario is based on an actual classroom lesson where the Inductive Model was used to teach a generalization. Read the anecdote and answer the questions that follow.

Mr. Reed wanted his students to learn the rule: "When adding *ing* to words the final consonant is doubled if preceded by a short vowel sound but not if preceded by a long vowel sound." He began his lesson by writing the following words on the board.

get   fight
mat   hope

He began by saying, "Look at the words I have written on the chalk-board. Tell me something about them. Sonya?"

" . . . They're all words," Sonya responded.

"Indeed they are," Mr. Reed smiled, "What else? Pat?"

"The ones in the first column have three letters."

"Yes, good! Something else. Jim?"

"The ones in the second column each begin with a different letter."

"Yes they do," Mr. Reed acknowledged. "Bill?"

"They're all one-syllable words."

"Some are verbs and some are nouns," George volunteered.

"Yes, very good observations," Mr. Reed praised. "Now let me show you some more," and with that he wrote the following words on the board.

cut   bite
tip   boat

"Now tell me about these. Gail?"

"They're also verbs and nouns," Gail answered.

"Good! Betty?"

"Some have three letters and some have four."

"Good observation, Betty. . . . Now let me show you some more examples," and he then wrote additional words on the board so his list appeared as follows:

get	getting	fight	fighting
mat	matting	hope	hoping

"Now, what do you notice here? Mike?"

"You added *ing* to all the words," Mike said instantly.

"Yes, and what else? Roger?"

"Each of the words has a vowel in the middle."

"Good, Roger. ... Let's do it once more," and he added *ing* to the words in his second list.

cut	cutting	bite	biting
tip	tipping	boat	boating

"Now let's look at all the words," Mr. Reed requested. "Look at the first two columns in each case and compare them to those in the last two columns, Nikki?"

"The words in the first column all have three letters and those in the third column all have four letters," Nikki replied.

"Good. Anything else? Donna?"

"All the words have a vowel in the middle."

"Yes. Good, Donna. Now compare the sounds of the vowels in the two lists. Roy?'

" . . ."

"Say the words in the first column, Roy."

" . . . get, mat, cut, tip," Roy responded.

"Yes, good. Now say the words in the third column."

"Fight, hope, bite, boat."

"Yes, good, Roy. What did you notice about the sounds?"

"The ones in the first column had a short sound."

"Exactly! And how about the ones in the third column, Jill?"

"They had a long sound."

"That's right, Jill. Good observation. Now look at the words in the second and fourth columns. What do you notice there? Keith?"

"They all have *ing* added to them."

"Yes. Now look at the spelling of the words. What kind of pattern do you notice? Judy?

" . . ."

"Look at the consonants at the ends of the words, Judy. What do you notice?"

" . . . They're doubled in the second column."

"Yes, good thinking, Judy. And how about in the fourth column? Reggie?"

"They're not doubled."

"Outstanding, everyone. Now what did Roy and Jill say about the sounds of the vowels in the words? Kathy?"

" . . . Well," Kathy said hesitantly. "The ones in the first column were short and the ones in the third column were long."

"Yes, excellent, Kathy. And what did we add to each of the words? Sue?"

"*ing,*" Sue replied quickly.

"Now try and relate what we've found here, someone?"

" . . . Go ahead, Don."

" . . . The words in the first column had short vowels . . . and their consonants were doubled."

"Excellent, Don! You've identified the relationship between the vowel sound and the spelling. Now how about the other words? Charlotte?"

"Their vowel sounds were long and the consonant wasn't doubled," she replied.

"Now let's put this together and try and state it in a rule," Mr. Reed requested.

" . . . "

"I'll get you started," Mr. Reed smiled. "When adding *ing* to words . . . Gary?"

" . . . You double the consonant at the end if the vowel sound is short, but you don't if the vowel sound is long."

"Very well done, Gary. You've identified the relationship between vowel sounds and spelling when adding *ing*."

"Now, give me a word, add *ing* to it and explain why the spelling is the way it is. Suzanne?"

Mr. Reed went on to ask the students for several more examples of adding the suffix to words with long and short vowel sounds and he then closed the lesson.

1.   Identify each of the phases in the lesson. Identify the point where the lesson shifts from one phase to another.

2.   Identify a description question in the lesson.

3.   Identify a comparison question in the lesson.

4.   Locate two prompting sequences in the lesson by identifying the first question of the sequence.

5.   Identify a repetition question in the lesson.

6.   Identify the thinking skills in the lesson and give an example of a question that promoted student practice with the skill.

7.   Consider a teacher wanting to teach the principle: "Less dense materials float on more dense materials if they don't mix." The lesson is done by using two vials of the same volume, one containing water and the other containing cooking oil, and placing them on a balance. The mass of the water is measurably greater than that of the cooking oil. The water and oil are then poured together into a third vial and the oil floats.

Answer the following questions based on the information.

a. How many examples did the teacher use?

b. What specific information would the teacher have to prompt the students to identify?

c. What might the teacher do in Phase 4 of this lesson for the application phase?

FEEDBACK

1.   In that the development of the lesson should be smooth and comfortable for both the teacher and the students, the exact beginning and ending point of a phase is

not critical. We have described the phases as distinct for the sake of clarity and presented the exercises for the purpose of reinforcing your understanding of the model. We do not intend the phases to be a rigid structure to be followed precisely. Keep this in mind when reading the feedback.

Phase 1 began when the first words were presented and Mr. Reed asked the first question. It ended when Donna said, "They all have a vowel in the middle." The next question Mr. Reed asked was, "Now compare the sounds of the vowels in the sentences." While this called for a comparison, it was designed to narrow the scope of possible responses and begin to converge on the rule. It marked the beginning of Phase 2.

Phase 2 ended when Sue noted that they added *ing* to each of the words. At that point Mr. Reed began to move the lesson to closure when he asked the class to relate what they had found in the lesson. This marked the beginning of Phase 3. Phase 3 ended when Gary generalized to make the statement relating the spelling and the sound of the vowels. Mr. Reed began Phase 4 when he said, "Now give me a word . . . " and called on Suzanne.

2.   All the questions where Mr. Reed asked the students to tell him about the example or asked them what they noticed, beginning with the first one directed to Sonya, were description questions.

3.   Comparison questions were specified in the question's wording. Mr. Reed called for comparisons when he said, "Look at the first two columns in each case and compare them to those in the last two columns" or "Now compare the sound of the vowels in the two sentences."

4.   When Mr. Reed asked Roy to compare the sounds of the vowels in the two lists, Roy did not respond. He then prompted Roy by asking him to say the words in the first column. This sequence continued until Roy stated that the ones in the first column had a short sound.

The second sequence began when Judy was unable to identify the pattern in the spelling and he responded by saying, "Look at the consonants at the ends of the words. What do you notice?" She was then able to identify the doubled consonant in the second column.

5.   Mr. Reed asked a repetition question when he said," Now what did Roy and Jill say about the sounds of the vowels in the words?"

6.   The students in Mr. Reed's class practiced observing, comparing, finding patterns, and generalizing. The description questions called for observation and a verbal statement of the observation, and comparison questions required that skill explicitly. The students were asked to find a pattern in the spelling, and the question was directed to Judy. The fact that she was unable to answer should not be surprising. Initially, students might have trouble finding and verbally describing the patterns. However, with practice and encouragement, they will begin to look for patterns and relationships in information and will often identify them earlier than expected. This is a clear indicator that they are *thinking,* and this experience is very rewarding for the teacher.

The students generalized when they described the rule in a single statement. As with finding patterns, this is initially difficult for students, but they quickly become adept at the skill and then relish their ability. Their success with this relatively difficult task is then a strong motivator for other experiences.

7.   (a) The teacher used one example to teach the lesson. In any generalization, the examples must show the relationship and neither the vials of liquids alone nor the liquids poured together by themselves illustrated the relationship. However, when the demonstrations were combined, the relationship between density and flotation was demonstrated.

(b) If the students did not specify them in the open-ended phase, the teacher would prompt the class to identify the following:

1. The volumes of the two vials are equal.
2. The mass of the water is greater.
3. The density of the water is greater. (The students would conclude the state ment about density based on their observations of mass and volume.)
4. The oil is floating on the water.

From the information the teacher would then prompt the students to state the relationship: "Less dense substances float on more dense substances if they do not mix."

(c) In Phase 4 the teacher would show the students additional examples, such as cooking oil and syrup, and ask them to predict and explain several factors, such as whether or not the materials would mix; if one floated on the other, which would be the more dense; which the students would predict is more dense, and so on.

INDUCTIVE MODEL OPTIONS

We have emphasized the role of examples as Inductive Model lessons are planned. With experience and practice this process can become very efficient, and veteran teachers may find that they can prepare lessons essentially "on the spot." Consider again the illustration of the concept *metaphor* we used in Chapter 2. (You may note at this point that our presentation in that illustration was essentially inductive.) In this case the concept could be presented with sentences on the board as examples, and an experienced teacher could actually create them while directing the students' processing. Skilled teachers who have goals clearly in mind can often use the Inductive Model virtually "off the top of their heads." This simply means that they generate examples as they go along. As teachers acquire increased confidence in "thinking on their feet," their preparation for Inductive Model lessons can become very efficient.

While this discussion may sound like we are advocating that teachers go into their classes unprepared, nothing could be further from the truth. The key difference lies in having a precise goal in mind and knowing what kind of examples will effectively illustrate the concept or generalization being taught.

Teachers also have considerable latitude in directing the students' proc essing. With older students, classes experienced in thinking skills training, or those at the upper end of the achievement spectrum, they may consider start ing a lesson by displaying two or three examples and immediately directing the students to search for a pattern. The questioning could begin by having the teacher say something such as, "Look at the examples. What do they all have in common?'' This question is obviously narrower than starting with observation, but it is still open-ended and has a time efficiency advantage. It also preserves the essential thinking skills of comparing, finding patterns, and generalizing. It merely de-emphasizes the formal practice in observing.

EVALUATING INDUCTIVE MODEL ACTIVITIES

Measuring Content Outcomes

The content outcomes of a lesson conducted using the Inductive Model can be measured using the procedures we discussed in Chapter 3, and you may want to review the material at this time. To reinforce the ideas presented there, let's take another look at Mr. Jaurez's lesson.

To evaluate the students' understanding of the concept, he could simply show them a variety of other animals, or pictures of other animals and have them categorize the animals as belonging or not belonging to the class *arthropods*. Notice here that pictures are a much better choice than written words. For example consider the following item.
Circle all of the following that are arthropods.

   a.   alligator
   b.   shrimp
   c.   oyster
   d.   dragonfly

In order to respond correctly to the above item, students must know how each of the examples appear. If not, they could understand the concept and still respond incorrectly. This invalidates the item. If pictures are used (assuming the characteristics are displayed in detail), students could respond to the item without knowing the names of the animals, and those with less experience are not disadvantaged compared to the rest of the class.

In the example with nonessential clauses, the teacher could simply present the students with several sentences and have them identify those that are correctly punctuated or ask them to correctly punctuate the sentences.

Measuring Thinking Skills

The primary thinking skill implicit in the inductive model is generalizing, and concomitantly the assessment of generalizations. As with content, you may wish to review the section on the evaluation of thinking skills in Chapter 3 at this time.

As an example of measuring thinking skills, consider the following item involving a teacher who has taught the rule about punctuating nonessential clauses and wants to measure the students' ability to generalize.

The item might appear as follows:

Look at the following information.

1. The American flag is colored red, white, and blue.
2. Clint Eastwood starred in the violent western movie *The Good, The Bad, and The Ugly*.
3. To most conveniently get to New York from Los Angeles you would go through St. Louis and Indianapolis.
4. The United States, Russia, Great Britain, and France all have United Nations veto powers.

Write a generalization about the use of commas based on the sentences.

This form of item would be very useful in the context of a unit on punctuation. Assuming that the students have not been taught a rule about punctuating elements in a series at the time they encounter the item, they would be encouraged to look at the information, find a pattern, and generalize from it. The item could be used as an introduction to a lesson on the rule. If the teacher includes one or more examples on each exercise that the students are required to complete, their thinking and development can be aided tremendously. With practice they become skilled at searching for patterns and the inclination to search will transfer to new situations.

As you see in this example, the thinking skills item is an extension of the process that would be used in the lesson itself. The only difference lies in the individual nature of the item. In the lesson the information is processed in a group effort, while processed individually as the students respond to the item.

DISCUSSION QUESTIONS

1. Consider the motivational features of Mr. Reed's lesson. What did he do that promoted student motivation, and what might he have done to increase it? Compare the lesson to Mr. Alvarez's. What motivational advantages did each have? Consider also the lesson on nonessential clauses. Assuming that the first example referred to the class the students were in and the teacher's name was Mrs. Adams, how did these examples affect motivation?

2. Teachers obviously do not have time to develop an inductive lesson for every concept and generalization existing in curriculum materials. How do they decide what concepts and generalizations to select?

3. Are some concepts and generalizations more conducive than others to being taught using the Inductive Model? If so, what characteristics do they have in common?

4. Are there instances when verbal examples would be sufficient for teaching a concept or generalization? If so, what would these instances be?

5. What are the major advantages of inductive teaching? The major disadvantages?

6. We have briefly discussed options for using the Inductive Model with different age groups. What other factors would have to be considered in using the model with lower elementary students? With advanced high school students?

REFERENCES

ANDERSON, L., EVERTSON, C., & BROPHY, J. (1979). An experimental study of effective teaching in first grade reading groups. *Elementary school journal, 79,* 193–223.

BERLINER, D. (1985, April). *Effective teaching.* Paper presented at the meeting of the Florida Educational Research and Development Council. Pensacola, Florida.

BROPHY, J. & GOOD, T. (1986). Teacher behavior and student achievement. In M. Wittrock, ed., *Third handbook of research on teaching,* 3rd ed. (New York: MacMillan), pp. 328–375.

FELDMAN, K. (1972). The effects of number of positive and negative instances and concept definition on the learning of mathematical concepts. Paper presented at the meeting of the American Educational Research Association, in *Review of Educational Research, 50,* 33–67.

FRAYER, D. (1970). *Effect of number of instances and emphasis of relevant attribute values on mastery of geometric concepts by fourth and sixth grade children.* (Technical Report 116) University of Wisconson: Madison, WI, Research and Development Center for Cognitive Learning.

GAGE, N. & BERLINER, D. (1984). *Educational psychology,* 3rd ed. (Boston: Houghton-Mifflin).

KERMAN, S. (1979). Teacher expectations and student achievement. *Phi Delta Kappan, 60*(10), pp. 79–84.

PRATTON, J. & HALES, L. (1986). The effects of active participation on student learning. *Journal of Educational Research, 79,* 210–215.

ROSENSHINE, B. & STEVENS, R. (1986). Teaching functions. In M. Wittrock, ed. *Third handbook of research on teaching,* 3rd ed. (New York: MacMillan), pp. 376–391.

STALLINGS, J., NEEDELS, M., & STAYROOK, N. (1979). *How to change the process of teaching basic reading skills in secondary schools* (Menlo Park, CA: SRI International).

TENNYSON, R. (1978). *Content structure and instructional control strategies in concept acquisition.* Paper presented at the meeting of the American Psychological Association, Toronto.

WLODKOWSKI, R. (1984). *Motivation and teaching: A practical guide* (Washington, D.C.: The National Education Association).

5

THE CONCEPT
ATTAINMENT MODEL

INTRODUCTION

The Concept Attainment Model is an inductive teaching strategy designed to help students of all ages learn concepts and practice analytical thinking skills. Based upon fundamental concept-learning research (Klausmeier, 1985; Tennyson & Cocchiarella, 1986), the model uses positive and negative examples to illustrate concepts that can be as simple as *square* and *dog* or as sophisticated as *oxymoron* and *socialism*.

The design of this model, first suggested by Joyce and Weil (1972), is based on the research of Jerome Bruner and his associates who investigated how different variables affected the concept-learning process. These researchers originally entitled their work *A Study of Thinking* (Bruner, Goodnow, & Austin, 1956), the title of which, in hindsight, was perhaps a bit ambitious. Though concepts form one of the most important dimensions of learning and cognitive development, subsequent research has shown a multitude of other components to comprise the total realm of thinking (Gagne, 1985; Good & Brophy, 1980).

A Study of Thinking was, however, a major watershed in modern psychology. It refocused researchers' attention from external variables viewed in terms of stimuli and responses to the cognitive processes and strategies that learners use when they attempt to learn a concept. Out of this came impetus for the field of information processing, and a byproduct of this research is the current emphasis on thinking skills.

Before we continue, let's review briefly some of the dimensions of concept learning first introduced in Chapter 2. A concept is an abstract idea that can be described through a definition, examples and nonexamples, characteristics, or its superordinate, subordinate, and coordinate relationships to other concepts. For example, the concept *noun* can be described as a part of speech (superordinate concept) that names a person, place, or thing (characteristics). The definition identifies a superordinate concept and the concept's essential characteristics.

The concept could be illustrated with examples such as *mother, Chicago,* and *ball,* and nonexamples such as *run, large,* or *quickly.* Notice that the nonexamples all illustrate coordinate concepts, that is, run is a verb, large is an adjective, and quickly is an adverb. Verb, adjective, and adverb are concepts coordinate to the concept *noun.*

Concepts play a central role in our lives. They are used to reduce the complexity of the environment, for example, our eyes are physically capable of detecting millions of different shades of color but we group them into a small number of relatively simple categories such as red, green, brown, and so on. They also help reduce the necessity of constant learning. For example, when we know the concept *square,* we eliminate the need to learn each individual instance of a square and instead merely classify them as members of the concept. Concepts also provide direction for instrumental activity. Concepts like *knife, table* and *fork* allow us to enter homes or restaurants anywhere in the world and use these implements to feed ourselves. The utensils will vary in a number of nonessential ways, but our grasp of the concept allows us to use plastic forks at a picnic and fine silverware in a restaurant in a similar way.

Finally, concepts provide us with the building blocks for ordering and relating classes of events. This occurs in two primary ways. One is through superordinate, subordinate and coordinate relationships. Knowing that a salmon is a fish, which is also a vertebrate, allows us to infer a number of properties to each. For example, knowing that vertebrates have spinal chords allows us to infer this property to both salmon and other fish. Similarly, knowing that all fish have two-chambered hearts allows us to infer this same property to salmon. Second, concepts are related through generalizations and cause and effect relationships. At a very simple level they can consist of relationships such as "fires are hot." At a more complex level, arithmetical and physical science relationships are described in precise equations (e.g., $A^2 + B^2 = C^2$).

Concept learning is a natural activity as evidenced by the enormous number of concepts small children bring with them to school. They typically know letters, lower numbers, colors, shapes, parts of the body and a myriad of relational concepts such as *bigger, above* and *behind* before they enter school. They learn the concepts through examples. For instance, a parent wanting to teach the concept *car* to a two-year-old points to cars as positive examples and either deals with negative examples in a somewhat formal way ("That's a bus." "That's a truck.") or does so in a responsive fashion when the child inappropriately labels a negative example as a positive example (e.g., "No, that's not a car. It only has two wheels. That's a bike.").

Unfortunately, the use of this successful, inductive, example-dependent approach is greatly reduced when the child enters school. The one-to-one teaching relationship and its personalized feedback is lost, the teaching approach becomes expository, and examples are often replaced with words. To illustrate the inadequacy of words, consider the following true anecdote.

A father was reading to his six-year-old son and as they read, they encountered the word *dissolve*. "What's *dissolve*, Dad?" his son asked. After several futile attempts at explaining the concept, the father tried a different approach. (Think for a second how you would verbally explain this concept to a six-year-old.) As a solution to his problem the father led his son into the kitchen, took out the salt and pepper and shook some salt into one glass of water and some pepper into another. He stirred both and asked his son what he saw. "It's gone, Dad," the child said, pointing at the glass of salt water. "That's *dissolve*, son," his dad said.

For certain concepts (such as dissolve) and other abstract concepts that are difficult to describe in words, examples may be the only effective teaching alternative.

The Concept Attainment Model is designed to capture these essential features of concept learning while at the same time extending the thinking skills of the students. To illustrate this process, let's look now at a teacher using the model in a typical school setting.

Mr. Haynes, a third grade science teacher, began his class by calling the students' attention to a bag on the desk at the front of the room.

He said, "Class, today we are going to learn another important idea on science. To do this we're going to use a slightly different approach. I'm going to show you some examples of what the idea is and some other examples of what the idea is not. From those examples and the others that are not examples I want you to try and figure out what the idea is. Let's give it a try."

With that he reached into the bag and pulled out an apple and put it on the table in front of a cardboard sign that said, "Examples." He had sliced the apple in half, and he displayed the two halves for the students. He also placed a book next to it in front of a sign that said "Non-examples."

Then he asked, "What might the concept be? Who has an idea? Sharon?"

"It could be things that we eat."

With that, Mr. Haynes put the word "Hypotheses" on the board, underlined it, and asked, "What do we mean by the term hypotheses? Anyone?"

"It's sort of an educated guess," Mike volunteered.

"Very good, Mike. For our purposes that's a good definition," Mr. Haynes responded. "Our hypotheses will be our educated guesses as to what the concept is." He then wrote 'things to eat' under the word 'hypotheses.' "What else might be a possibility?" asked Mr. Haynes. "Jim?"

"It could also be things that are alive—or at least were."

"Fine," replied Mr. Haynes, writing the word 'living things' on the board under the list of hypotheses. "Any others? Meg?"

"Well, this is a little bit like Jim's idea but it's a little different. How about things that grow on plants?"

"Okay. Does everyone see how living things and things that grow on plants are different? Karen, can you explain that to the class?"

"Well, there are some living things that don't grow on plants. Like animals."

"Excellent, Karen. Do we have any other ideas, class?"

After pausing for a few seconds, he continued, "Well then, let's look at a few more examples." With that, he took out a sliced tomato and put it under the positive example sign and placed a carrot that had been sliced in half under the negative example sign. Then he continued, "What does this new information tell us? Let's first look at the hypotheses we have. Are they still all acceptable? Steve?"

"It can't be things to eat," Steve responded.

"Please explain why, Steve."

"Well, carrot is not an example and we eat carrots."

"Very good, Steve," Mr. Haynes smiled. "The added information we have forced us to eliminate that hypothesis."

"What about the rest of the hypotheses? Sherry?"

"We also have to eliminate both plant products and living things because carrot is a plant product, and it's something that was alive."

"Excellent, Sherry. You've not only identified what hypotheses had to be eliminated, but you've also explained why we could no longer accept them. Now, we have no hypotheses left. Do we have any new ones? Ken?"

"How about things that we eat that grow above the ground?"

"And why did you suggest that, Ken?"

"A tomato and an apple grow above the ground, and none of the nonexamples are things that grow above the ground."

"Very good explanation, Ken. Any others? Shawn?"

"How about things that we eat with seeds in them?"

"Okay. Any others, Marsha?"

"This might sound silly, but how about red foods?"

"Let's think about that for a moment, everyone. Are all of our examples red foods?"

"Yes!" the class exclaimed in unison.

"Are any of our nonexamples red foods?"

"No!" they again shouted.

"So is 'red foods' an acceptable hypothesis?"

"Yes!"

"Indeed it is," Mr. Haynes said enthusiastically. "Let's put that up on the board. Any others, class?"

After waiting a few moments, he continued, "If there are no further hypotheses at this time, let's continue."

With that he reached into his bag and brought out an avocado, which he placed in the positive group and a piece of celery that he placed in the negative group.

"Now let's look at the hypothoses again. How about 'red foods'?"

"We have to eliminate it now because an avocado isn't red, and it is an example," Dana stated.

"Excellent, Dana. How about 'things with seeds'?"

"That's still OK, because all of the examples are foods that have seeds in them."

The lesson continued with Mr. Haynes providing additional positive examples: an acorn, peas in a pod, a squash, and an ear of corn. These were contrasted with negative examples: head of lettuce, artichoke and potato. After students had narrowed their hypotheses to things with seeds, Mr. Haynes introduced the term "fruit" and had the students analyze the concept in terms of the characteristics in the examples. He then asked the students for a definition of the concept. Finally, he had the students cut up the examples and passed these around for examination. He then had the class take out a piece of paper and categorize additional examples as either positive or negative examples of the concept *fruit*.

Let's look now at Mr. Haynes' lesson to begin to identify the structure of the Concept Attainment Model. The model exists in two cyclical phases which are followed by closure and application. The phases can be outlined as follows:

Phase 1: Presentation of Examples

Mr. Haynes explained how the activity would proceed and then he displayed for the students an example and a nonexample. This display marked the beginning of Phase 1.

Phase 2: Analysis of Hypotheses

Phase 2 began when the students hypothesized a name for the concept. They suggested labels such as "things to eat," "living things," and "things that grow on plants."

The cyclical nature of Phases 1 and 2 was illustrated when, after the initial ideas were hypothesized, Mr. Haynes provided an additional example and nonexample. This amounts to cycling back through Phase 1. At that point the students then returned again to Phase 2, determining what hypotheses were acceptable and which ones had to be rejected based on the examples. They also suggested additional hypotheses at that point.

The process of presenting examples, analyzing hypotheses, presenting additional examples, and continuing to analyze hypotheses continued until all the hypotheses but one were eliminated.

Phase 3: Closure

When the analysis process has eliminated all but one of the hypotheses, the students are then asked to define it explicitly and identify the characteristics. Mr. Haynes arrived at closure when he asked the students for the definition of *fruit*.

Phase 4: Application

In the final phase the students apply the concept by classifying examples or generating their own. This phase is identical to the application phase in the Inductive Model.

We will discuss each of these phases in more detail, but now we want to turn to a discussion of planning for Concept Attainment activities.

PLANNING CONCEPT ATTAINMENT ACTIVITIES

After reading this section of the chapter you will be able to meet these objectives:

1. You will understand content appropriate for the Concept Attainment Model so when given a list of goals you will identify those most appropriately taught with the Concept Attainment Model.
2. You will understand the selection of examples so when given a content goal you will prepare a list of examples that will effectively illustrate the concept.
3. You will understand the sequencing of examples to promote thinking skills so when considering a topic of your choice you will prepare and sequence a set of examples to maximize students' practice with thinking skills.

The planning process for teaching Concept Attainment lessons is similar to planning for Inductive Model activities. We will discuss the similarities as well as the differences in planning for the two models in the paragraphs that follow. The first consideration is the identification of goals.

Identifying Goals

Content goals. The content goals for a Concept Attainment and an Inductive Model lesson are essentially the same. The only difference would be that the Inductive Model is designed to teach both concepts and generalizations, while the Concept Attainment Model's focus is limited to concept learning. Deciding on exactly what you want the students to know about the concept is no less important with one model than it is with the other. Mr. Haynes was teaching a group of young children so he had identified *seed contained in the edible part of the plant* as the essential characteristic of the concept *fruit.* A biology teacher would attach a more sophisticated set of characteristics to the concept, such as the fruit being an enlarged and ripened ovary, but Mr. Haynes was teaching an essentially valid concept for third graders. The important aspect of Mr. Haynes' planning was that he knew exactly what he wanted from his students, which we have previously identified as an important feature of effective teaching. Having a precise goal in mind allowed Mr. Haynes to select examples that would help the students reach the goal.

Thinking skills goals.   The thinking skills students employ in a Concept Attainment lesson are more demanding than those used with the Inductive Model and consequently they require a more experienced and developed learner. For instance, students initially only observe and describe the examples in an Inductive lesson, while in a Concept Attainment activity they are asked to hypothesize a label for the concept. This is a considerably more demanding process. Also, as the lesson progresses, students in an Inductive activity focus on the processes of observing, comparing, and finally generalizing, while in a Concept Attainment lesson they continue to hypothesize and analyze the hypotheses. At each step the processing for a Concept Attainment lesson is more demanding, and the teacher must keep that in mind as the lesson's goals are considered. We will readdress the thinking skills involved with Concept Attainment activities in the Implementation section of the chapter and will offer further suggestions when we discuss developmental considerations for using the model.

Selecting Examples

The principles involved in selecting examples to teach a concept are the same regardless of the procedure involved. As you have seen with the Inductive Model and as you will see when you study the Deductive Model, the most important factor in selecting examples is *identifying those that best illustrate the characteristics of the concept.* Mr. Haynes chose good examples when he used the apple, tomato, and avocado. In each case the students could see the essential characteristic—the seeds—in the examples.

Mr. Haynes also was clever in his choice of squash, peas, and corn. Using them as examples would then encourage the students to generalize to include them in the concept *fruit,* and without them the learners would continue to classify the foods as vegetables, which is the concept we attach to them based on our eating experiences.

The examples are selected so that *each* contains the *combination* of essential characteristics and *none* of the nonexamples contain the same combination. As another case, consider the concept *homophone* which can be defined as: A word identical with another in pronunciation, but varying in spelling and meaning. Appropriate examples would be:

    fare — fair
    reed — read

However, any one of the words alone, such as *fare* or *reed* would not be an appropriate example because no single word is capable of illustrating the characteristics.

This process can be further illustrated with an example taken from the work of Tieman and Markle (1983). They illustrated this process with the concept *chair.* In their analysis they concluded that the critical characteristics were: (a) some type of back support, (b) designed for a single person, and (c) appropriate height for sitting. The nonessential characteristics were number of legs, material they were made of, and size of the back.

In compiling their positive examples, they included a number of pictures which contained the essential characteristics and in which the nonessential characteristics varied. In addition, they chose negative examples in which the essential characteristics were missing. A stool was chosen as a nonexample to illustrate the importance of a back, and a loveseat was a negative example because it is designed for more than one person.

To further illustrate this process, consider the concept *proper noun,* and identify the essential and nonessential characteristics. Then analyze the following positive examples in terms of your list:

1. Mary
2. New York
3. John
4. Chicago
5. United States
6. George Washington

Something is missing. Your list of essential characteristics should have included the idea that a proper noun names a specific person, place or *thing.* There are no specific things in the list of positive examples. To insure that the concept is complete, we would need to add positive examples such as the following:

    German Shepherd
    Honda
    Old Testament

In selecting negative examples, an attempt should be made to vary the nonessential characteristics and to represent all the things that the concept is not. The following is a list of some possible nonexamples for the concept.

chair, common noun (thing)	boy, common noun (person)
run, verb	town, common noun (place)
above, preposition	heavy, adjective
is, helping verb	slowly, adverb
and, conjunction	

From the list we see that the negative examples serve to differentiate *proper noun* from other parts of speech. When both the positive and negative examples are used, the learner can form a complete concept which is not confused with related concepts.

A helpful planning tool in the selection of negative examples is the process of analyzing the target concept in terms of coordinate concepts. Examples of these coordinate concepts then become the negative examples for the lesson. For example, consider again the concept *metaphor* used as an illustration in Chapter 2. An analysis would suggest the use of simile, personification and hyperbole as valuable negative examples as shown in Figure 5.1. From the analysis of *proper noun* we see that the same procedure was used.

Sequencing Examples

Having selected the examples and nonexamples, the final planning task is to place them in a sequence designed to most effectively promote practice in thinking skills. If the development of thinking skills is an important goal for the teacher, examples should be arranged in such a way that the students' opportunity to use these skills is maximized. The shortest or quickest route to a concept may not give students this opportunity, nor may it be the best way to insure optimal retention of the concept. To illustrate these points, let us consider an example from literature.

Onomatopoeia is defined as: (1) the naming of a thing or action by a vocal imitation of the sound associated with it, or (2) the use of words whose sound suggests the sense. A concept attainment lesson on the concept *onomatopoeia* might begin with the following examples:

Yes   1. The faucet dripped and dropped until it nearly drove the sleep-starved man insane.

FIGURE 5.1   Coordinate Concepts as Negative Examples

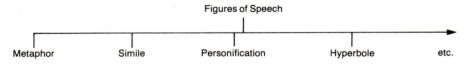

No   2. The tranquility of the night was broken only by the sound of a distant radio.

Yes   3. The outboard engine hiccuped and then roared into action.

No   4. The wind was calm and the night was warm and the sweet smell of jasmine was in the air.

Yes   5. The brakes creaked and screeched as the huge train neared the station.

The examples were selected because they are obvious or salient examples of the concept. The use of such examples would result in the students attaining the concept quickly. As an alternative to this sequence, the following could be presented as the first two examples of the concept.

Yes   1. The rustling leaves gathered around the couple's feet.

Yes   2. The rapid rattle of the machine gun broke the silence of the morning.

Their initial inclusion would result in slower attainment of the concept and more practice in thinking skills for the students. In general, the more obvious or salient the initial examples, the quicker the concept is attained and the less opportunity the students have to practice thinking skills.

Let's look now at a second simpler example. Suppose the concept is *numbers with perfect square roots*. Consider the following two sequences.

SEQUENCE A	SEQUENCE B
4 Yes	1 Yes
5 No	1/2 No
9 Yes	81 Yes
15 No	7 No
16 Yes	64 Yes
2 No	12 No
25 Yes	9 Yes

In sequence A the pattern is quickly and clearly established. Many students would probably correctly hypothesize the concept after two positive examples. On the other hand, the concept is less obvious in sequence B, and it would provide the students with a greater opportunity for hypothesizing and analysis of the hypotheses. In organizing sequence B, the teacher was not trying to hide information from the students nor trying to trick them. Instead, the teacher wanted to maximize the students' opportunity to practice thinking skills.

For any set of examples a number of sequences could be designed. The organization depends on the judgment of the teacher and is a function of the goals of the lesson and the students involved.

We want to emphasize at this point that while alternating the positive and negative examples in the sequence is convenient, it is not a requirement.

In organizing the list, you may want to place two or even three positive examples together, and perhaps do the same with the negative examples. This is totally appropriate. We will illustrate this process further in the feedback for the following exercises.

This completes our discussion of planning for Concept Attainment activities. Turn now to the exercises designed to reinforce your understanding of the material in this section.

EXERCISES

1.   Look at the content goals listed below. Identify which are appropriately taught with the Concept Attainment Model. For those that are inappropriate, explain why.

2.   For each of the content goals identified in question 1 as appropriate for Concept Attainment, prepare and sequence a list of examples that would help the students attain the concept.

3.   Select a topic of your choice and design a sequence of examples that will maximize the students' practice with thinking skills.

GOALS

A. An English teacher wants her students to understand *adverb*.

B. An elementary teacher wants his students to understand *soft*.

C. A science teacher wants her students to know why two coffee cans released at the top of an inclined plane roll down the plane at different speeds.

D. A science teacher wants his students to understand what miscible fluids are.

E. A literature teacher wants her students to know the time period in which Poe did his writing.

F. A history teacher wants his students to know that the life style of the American Indians has changed considerably with the coming of white people.

FEEDBACK

1.   Goals C, E, and F would not be appropriately taught with the Concept Attainment Model. Let's briefly consider each of the goals separately.

(C) A teacher wanting students to know why two coffee cans roll down an incline at different rates has an objective which requires an explanation. Explanations include concepts but are broader than the concepts themselves. As such, they are not amenable to Concept Attainment. The material could be taught using the Inquiry Model, which is described in Chapter 7.

(E) A literature teacher who wants his students to know the time period during which Poe wrote has an objective that calls for factual information, that is, "Poe wrote in the first half of the nineteenth century" is a fact. Facts are not taught as the content goal in a Concept Attainment activity.

(H) "The life style of the American Indian has been changed considerably by the coming of white people" is a generalization. This content objective is not appropriate for a Concept Attainment activity but can instead be taught by the Integrative Model, which is discussed in Chapter 6 or by the Inductive Model described in Chapter 4.

2.   Each of the other goals involves the learning of a concept and are appropriate for Concept Attainment. Let's now consider sequences of examples for each.

(A)   For the concept *adverb* a sequence might be the following:
Yes   The hunter ran quickly after the fleeing deer.
No   Jimmy ran his car off the road.
Yes   Kit Carson stole quietly up to the working beaver.
No   The grizzly bear rummaged in the garbage can.
Yes   The cowboy rapidly fired his pistol until the chamber was empty.
No   The book was about knights in armor.
Yes   Susan lovingly hugged her small child.
Yes   The magnificently powerful tiger slithered through the dense under growth.
Yes   The miner very quickly filled his sacks with the dust.

Obviously, there are many other ways that a sequence of examples could be prepared to allow attainment of the concept *adverb*. The prepared sequence illustrates only one possibility. The important point is that each of the *yes* examples shows an adverb used in the sentence, while none of the *no* examples contains an adverb. The last two examples were selected to provide for a complete and accurate concept. Adverbs, in addition to modifying verbs, also modify adjectives and other adverbs. A sequence which did not include examples of this would teach an incomplete concept. Note the number of examples in the illustration shown above. The sequence shows six *yes* examples and three *no* examples. There is no rule that suggests that the number of examples and nonexamples should be the same nor that they should alternate. The sequence is a function of teacher judgment.

Consider the sequence again. The teacher in this case was trying to maximize the students' thinking skills. The thinking that went into the organization of the examples can be described as follows:

On the basis of the first two examples the students might form hypotheses about hunting, hunters, mountain men, or wildlife. The wildlife hypothesis would have to be rejected, however, as a result of the second nonexample. In turn the third positive example would require the rejection of hunting, hunters, and mountain men, and the process would continue through the remainder of the examples. From the sequence you can see how a clever and attractive sequence designed to promote thinking skills can be organized with very little effort.

(B) A sequence of examples for the concept *soft* might be the following:

1.	Piece of terry cloth	Yes
2.	Piece of sandpaper	No
3.	Chamois skin	Yes
4.	Diaper	Yes
5.	Drinking glass	No

6.	Sponge ball	Yes
7.	Toy car	No
8.	Wadded facial tissue	Yes
9.	Piece of chalk	No

The positive examples could be indicated by smiling faces, plus signs, or the word *yes*. Note again that the *yes* and *no* examples do not always alternate. There is no rule that says every *yes* must be followed by a *no* or vice versa. As with the number of examples, the ordering of the examples depends on the judgment of the teacher.

(E) An appropriate sequence to teach *miscible fluids* might appear as illustrated in the following example. Notice that the actual fluids should be used if the examples are to be most effective. Using the actual fluids (a form of realia) would allow the students to directly observe the characteristics of the concept. If a compromise is required, a combination of actual fluids for some examples and models for the other examples would be the next most effective. The least effective form of example would be the use of words alone.

The following is a possible sequence.

1.	Water and alcohol	Yes
2.	Benzene and gasoline	Yes
3.	Water and oil	No
4.	Benzene and alcohol	No
5.	Water and hydrochloric acid	Yes
6.	Oil and sulfuric acid	No
7.	Water and ethyl ether	No
8.	Benzene and toluene	Yes
9.	Vinegar and water	Yes
10.	Hydrogen and oxygen	Yes

Hydrogen and oxygen is a case where a model could be used very effectively. The model could represent the different sizes of the respective elements and could show the mixing process. While words are most commonly used in an instance such as this, a model would be vastly superior.

3.   The examples and sequences will be highly individual. Check with a colleague or your instructor for feedback. Keep in mind as you design the sequence that all the positive examples *must* illustrate the concept and none of the negative examples *can* illustrate it. Also, use your imagination, and try to design the sequence cleverly to promote thinking skills by the students.

IMPLEMENTING CONCEPT ATTAINMENT LESSONS

After reading this section of the chapter, you will be able to meet the following objective:

You will understand the procedures involved in implementing a Concept Attainment activity so that when provided with a case study illustrating a teacher using this model, you will:

  (a) identify examples and characteristics of the concept, and hypotheses suggested by students;
  (b) explain how the teacher in the case study promoted the development of thinking skills with the sequence of examples.

The implementation phase of the Concept Attainment Model is very flexible and fun for both the teacher and the students because the process can be presented as a type of game which, combined with its inherent sense of the unknown, results in increased student motivation.

Phase 1: Presenting Examples

After the activity has been explained, or once the students have gained some experience with the procedure, the lesson begins with the teacher presenting the students with examples. Typically, it starts with an example and a nonexample presented together and identified as such. However, there is nothing inherently "wrong" with only presenting a positive example. The only disadvantage in not including an initial nonexample is that the scope of possibilities for hypothesizing can be so great that the lesson becomes unwieldy.

Mr. Haynes began his lesson by presenting an apple as an example and a book as a nonexample. Using a nonexample that was so distant from the example was simply designed to keep the possibilities for hypothesizing quite open. A teacher could as appropriately have chosen something much more closely related to the concept, such as milk, or another food. This would have narrowed the possibilities for the students significantly and would have reduced the emphasis on processing.

Now let's look again at the concept *proper noun* discussed in the previous section. A sequence of examples might begin as follows:

  1. New York   Yes
  2. automobile   No

The method of indicating whether the example is positive or negative may vary with the age of the students. The words *yes* or *no,* plus and minus symbols, and the placing of objects in yarn circles on the floor with one being positive and the other negative have all been used with similar success.

Phase 2: Analysis of Hypotheses

Following the presentation of the initial example or examples the teacher asks the students to hypothesize possible categories that would encompass the positive example. Using the previous illustration with proper noun they might include responses such as the following:

a. Cities
b. Cities over a million people
c. States in the United States
d. States composed of two words
e. Places

Herein lies one of the major differences between the Concept Attainment and Inductive Models. With the Inductive Model the conceptual load on the learner is initially less. For instance, suppose *proper noun* were to be taught using the Inductive Model. The teacher might begin by showing the students the words *New York* but would then ask, "What do notice about these words?" In turn the following could be responses:

a. Two words.
b. They begin with capital letters.
c. The first word has three letters.
d. There is one vowel in each word.

We want to emphasize here that the important difference is in the skill the students are asked to demonstrate and *not* the fact that an example and nonexample were presented in the first case, while only an example was presented in the second. With the Concept Attainment Model, the students are asked to hypothesize a label which is an inferential process, while with the Inductive Model they are only asked to observe. They may, and often do, go beyond observation naturally, but the only requirement is that they observe and describe.

The Cyclical Process

Having presented the students with the initial examples and having solicited the first set of hypotheses, the teacher then cycles back through Phases 1 and 2 by alternately presenting examples and analyzing the hypotheses. Returning to the example *proper noun,* the teacher might present the following:

3. New Jersey   Yes

This would be followed by a systematic analysis of the hypotheses, which might follow a procedure such as:
"Now let's look at *cities*. Is it still an acceptable hypothesis?"
The students would then conclude that *cities* would have to be rejected, and they would be asked to explain why it was not acceptable. A response

might be: "New Jersey is not a city and it is an example, so *cities* would have to be rejected." The same procedure would be followed with each of the hypotheses.

After each of the hypotheses has been analyzed, the teacher calls for additional possibilities, and the process again cycles through Phases 1 and 2. For instance, suppose the example

4. home   no

was presented. The teacher would then ask the class to analyze each of the hypotheses in the light of the new data, and again would ask the students to explain *why* the hypothesis was acceptable or had to be rejected. This procedure would then be repeated for the entire sequence of examples.

The purposes in asking the students to explain why they accepted or rejected an hypothesis are twofold. First, it helps the students develop their thinking by having them articulate their own reasoning, and second, the verbal description aids uniformity of understanding. For example, if a student decides that an hypothesis is acceptable or not, and the discussion moves to a second hypothesis, other members of the class may not understand why the first one was accepted or rejected. Asking individuals to explain their reasoning makes the thinking skills visible to all the students rather than to only those who voluntarily participate (Beyer, 1983, 1984) and helps any uncertain students to stay abreast of the activity.

Now let's look again at the thinking skills involved and compare them to the Inductive Model. Analysis with the Concept Attainment Model actually requires some reversals in thinking. For example, New Jersey is *not* a city, but it *is* an example, so the hypothesis is rejected. Similarly, when the nonexample *home* was presented, the hypothesis *places* would have to be rejected because home *is* a place, but it *is not* an example.

Notice that the hypothesis *places* can actually be revised instead of being totally rejected. Instead of *places* the students may want to suggest *special places* as a modification. This process is not only acceptable but should even be encouraged.

By contrast, suppose in an Inductive lesson the teacher has presented the following examples.

1. New York
2. automobile
3. New Jersey
4. home

The students would then be asked to compare the four examples. Some responses might be:

1. Two of the words are not capitalized.
2. Two of the examples have two words in them.
3. The first and third examples have the word *New* in them.
4. The second and fourth examples end in 'e'.

From these illustrations we readily see that while the procedure for the two models is somewhat similar, the skills required of the students are significantly different.

It is important that during the analysis of hypotheses the teacher refrain from passing judgment. It would be inappropriate at this point to say, "You've got it!" or "That's it!" if a student should hypothesize the label the teacher has in mind. Doing so makes the Concept Attainment activity a guessing game in which the teacher has the answer and is keeping it from the students. Instead, the teacher should try to communicate that the solution to the problem of identifying the concept lies not within the teacher but in the data (examples). Doing so places the responsibility for identifying and verifying the concept on the student. Through the process of analyzing data and making inferences, students become not only more proficient at these thinking skills but also more autonomous learners.

In the previous example, if the students initially hypothesized *proper noun* among the other hypotheses, the teacher would simply add it to the list and let the activity continue naturally. As the lesson proceeds, the data will eventually require that all the hypotheses but one be eliminated.

The cyclical process in Phases 1 and 2 can be summarized in a series of steps as follows:

1. Teacher presents positive and negative examples.
2. Students examine examples and generate hypotheses.
3. Teacher presents additional positive and/or negative example(s).
4. Students analyze hypotheses and eliminate those not supported by the data (examples).
5. Students generate new hypotheses.
6. Lesson recycles through steps 3 through 5 until all the hypotheses but one have been rejected.

Phase 3: Closure

Once the students have isolated an hypothesis that is supported by the examples the lesson is ready for closure. At that point the teacher asks the students to identify the critical characteristics of the concept and state a definition. The definition will reinforce the students' understanding of the concept by including within it an identification of a superordinate concept and the concept's characteristics. For example, in the case of *proper noun* the teacher would help the students state a definition such as the following:

A proper noun is a noun (superordinate concept) that names a particular person, particular place, or particular thing (characteristics).

Having stated the definition, the students are prepared for the application phase of the model.

Phase 4: The Application Phase

The application phase for the Concept Attainment Model is identical to that for the Inductive Model. The concept is reinforced by having the students classify additional examples as positive or negative and/or they generate additional unique examples of their own. In Mr. Haynes' lesson the students identified additional examples as being fruits or not, and in the example with *proper noun* they could be asked to identify proper nouns from a list of words or to generate some proper nouns of their own.

This essentially completes our discussion of implementing Concept Attainment lessons, but before moving to the next section we want to briefly discuss three questions that are often asked about the procedure. The first is, "What do I do if I get to the end of my list of examples and the students haven't eliminated all but one of the hypotheses?" If your set of examples and nonexamples is complete, this possibility will only occur when one hypothesis is a synonym for another. In that case you can retain both and when all the others have been eliminated, note that the two are synonymous.

The second is, "What do I do if the students eliminate all the hypotheses but one before all the examples are used?" Here the answer is simple. Simply allow the lesson to come to closure, and use the remainder of the examples as part of the application phase.

Finally, students will often disagree on whether or not an hypothesis should be accepted or rejected. The controversy is usually resolved with some additional examples, so you may at that point tentatively retain the hypothesis knowing that some additional data will require its rejection.

Options for Implementing Concept Attainment Activities

Developmental considerations.   In order to most effectively implement a Concept Attainment activity, the developmental level of the students must be considered. For young or inexperienced learners or those used to teacher-centered expository lessons, the Concept Attainment procedure may initially be confusing. This problem is short-lived, however, if the teacher takes a little extra care in introducing the activity. The second problem involves the thinking skills required when the students analyze the hypotheses. As we noted in our description of the phases of implementation, the students are required to do some reversals in their thinking. The ability to conclude that *cities* must be rejected because New Jersey *is* an example, but *is not* a city takes some practice, and students will not automatically be good at it. This is one of the reasons having the students articulate their thinking is so important.

A procedure teachers have found useful in dealing with this problem has been to practice a Concept Attainment activity with a simple topic and with the teacher actively "walking" students through the procedures. The reason for using a simple topic is to reduce the cognitive load; students do not have to learn the target concept being taught and the procedures for the activity at the same time. In selecting a simple practice concept, teachers have used tangible objects found right in the classroom and have focused on such simple categories as "wooden objects," "girls with red hair," or "containers."

A second adaptation teachers often make when using the procedure with young children is to increase the emphasis on the positive examples, and reduce the number of negative examples. Young children have difficulty dealing with the notion of something that *is not* an example. The practice of inferring categories and doing rudimentary analysis of hypotheses is excellent for young children, however, and with modification they become quite skilled with the procedure.

In introducing the activity the teacher should make clear from the beginning that this is a new type of activity and the way that students will learn it is by having the teacher guide them through it. Mr. Haynes' lesson in the Introduction illustrates a teacher effectively introducing the procedure. In the actual classroom lesson we observed on which the anecdote was based the teacher did considerably more prompting to help the students analyze their hypotheses than was illustrated in the written scenario. We abbreviated the description in the interest of clarity.

As students' facility with the procedure develops, they usually become very attracted to it and often ask if they can "play the game." Teachers have found the model very effective as a form of review and to add variety to classroom activities. Also, experienced learners become adept at generating their own sequences of examples and "playing the game" with each other.

Finally, the model has been found to be an effective procedure for introducing the *scientific method* to students. As everyone who has taught science will likely agree, most texts introduce the scientific method early in the book and it is never heard of again. As a result, students memorize the steps with virtually no understanding of the way it works. Much about the methods of science can be learned from doing Concept Attainment activities. We will save the details of the discussion for Chapter 7, where we discuss the Inquiry Model.

Concept Attainment II.   The Concept Attainment Model can be modified to increase the emphasis the activity places on student thinking. By changing the procedure slightly, the students are placed in a situation where they not only get practice in analyzing hypotheses, but also learn to improve the efficiency of their processing.

We will describe two modifications. We are calling the first of these Concept Attainment II.

Concept Attainment II is an example of a selection strategy. As illustrated in the previous sections on the basic Concept Attainment activity (which will be called Concept Attainment I, or C.A. I), only the first two examples are presented with subsequent ones being presented sequentially and one at a time. Concept Attainment II (C.A. II) is similar to C.A. I in that the first two are presented and labeled positive and negative respectively. However, C.A. II differs from C.A. I in one primary respect. In a C.A. II lesson, all the examples are displayed to the student from the beginning of the activity.

After presenting all the examples and labeling two, the teacher asks the students to hypothesize concept names, which are listed on the chalk board. The students scan the remaining list for those which might substantiate or refute the hypotheses on the board. Students then choose an example from the list and indicate whether they think it is positive or negative. They also state what changes, if any, would be made in the hypotheses if their classification is correct. The teacher then verifies the classification. If the classification was correct, the appropriate changes are made in the hypotheses. If the classification is incorrect, the hypotheses are reanalyzed in light of the new information. The students then select additional examples and repeat the analysis process until one hypothesis is isolated.

A typical Concept Attainment II lesson might begin something like this. The teacher, wanting to teach the concept of *carnivorous animals,* might provide pictures of the following animals. (Carnivorous animals are those characterized by their meat-eating habits.)

EXAMPLES

dog–yes	beaver
car–no	tiger
tree	hamster
cow	mouse
cat	

Students might respond to this information with the following hypotheses which would be listed on the board.

EXAMPLES		**HYPOTHESES**
dog–yes	cat	living things
car–no	beaver	animals
tree	tiger	domestic animals
cow	hamster	mammals
chair	mouse	carnivores

One way to test all of these hypotheses is with *cat.* If cat is a no, then all the hypotheses would need to be rejected. However, cat is a yes, so this example provides no basis to reject any of the hypotheses.

The students might then decide to choose beaver as the next example. If beaver is a yes, all the hypotheses except *carnivores* and *domestic animals* are acceptable, but if beaver is a no, *carnivore* and *domestic animals* would be the only acceptable hypotheses. The teacher would verify beaver as a no because beaver is *not* an example of the concept *carnivore.* Therefore, the hypotheses *living things, animals,* and *mammals* would have to be rejected. Domestic animals and carnivores would be retained as viable hypotheses because beaver was a *negative* example of the concept, and dog and cat have been classified as positive examples. Now look at the list and see if you can determine a way in which students could investigate the hypothesis *domestic animals.*

EXAMPLES		HYPOTHESES
dog–yes	cat–yes	domestic animals
car–no	beaver–no	carnivores
tree	tiger	
cow	hamster	
chair	mouse	

Consider the choices *cow* and *tiger.* The two choices provide slightly different information. The difference is enough to make one a more efficient choice. First, consider tiger. If tiger is a yes, *domestic animal* must be rejected because a tiger is not a domestic animal. If tiger is a no, it merely says that the category cannot be rejected but it actually isn't supported either. The data exist as "neutral" with respect to the hypothesis because tiger may be a no for reasons other than the fact that it's not a domestic animal. Remember that when the student selects examples and examines hypotheses, he does not know what the concept is, and must infer this from the information provided.

Now, consider cow as a test of the hypothesis *domestic animal.* If cow is a no, *domestic animal* is rejected, because cow is a domestic animal, and succinct information about the inference is obtained. However, if cow is yes, not only is the category not rejected, but it is directly supported (again because cow is a domestic animal). The choice of cow as an example provides more information about the hypothesis than does the choice of tiger. Therefore, cow is the more efficient choice. The reverse would be true if we had wanted to test the hypothesis *carnivorous animal.* In that case, tiger would be a more efficient choice. With practice, students become efficient at gathering data, obtaining maximum information with each example. A major benefit to students in a C.A. II activity is the practice they get in the process of analysis. In a limited sense students are designing their own investigation or experiment.

Concept Attainment III. A second modification of the basic procedure is designed to further increase the cognitive load on the learner. As with C.A. II, it requires more sophisticated analysis by the students and helps them improve their efficiency, but it goes one step farther. The processing is basically the same as it is in C.A. II. However, rather than seeing the first two examples identified and the remainder displayed for them, they see the first two identified and they must then *supply their own examples.* For example, consider the following activity which is designed to teach the concept *vegetables with edible roots.*
Suppose the teacher shows the class:

carrot   yes
corn   no

Some possible hypotheses might be:

orange-colored vegetables
vegetables with edible roots
vegetables rich in vitamin A
vegetables that are eaten raw

The responsibility of providing an example to test these hypotheses now rests with the students. The students could test the hypotheses by selecting additional examples of vegetables. An efficient choice might be *radish.* If radish is a yes, *orange-colored vegetables* and *vegetables rich in vitamin A* are eliminated, but if radish is a no, *vegetables with edible roots* and *vegetables that are eaten raw* are eliminated. For this activity, radish is a yes, which leaves *vegetables with edible roots* and *vegetables that are eaten raw* as possible concepts. The task of the students would now be to examine these hypotheses further. A choice now might be *potato.* Potato as a yes would further support *vegetables with edible roots* but would force rejection of *vegetables that are eaten raw.* Because of the concept being taught, potato would be a yes, causing the latter hypothesis to be rejected and lending further support to the hypothesis *vegetables with edible roots.* Students would then continue to test the hypothesis and, in so doing, would be both reinforcing and enlarging their notion of the concept. In planning for a C.A. III activity the teacher should have additional examples available for use if the students' examples do not provide for a complete picture of the concept. If their use is not necessary during the course of the lesson, they could be used at the end of the activity as a means of evaluating the concept learning.

One unique pedagogical advantage of C.A. III is the opportunity it affords the learner actively to gather data. C.A. III is more lifelike or realistic than the other two Concept Attainment formats in that students can more actively pursue a concept which they do not fully understand. Because students are not limited to the examples the teacher provides, they can use more of their own initiative and creativity to investigate hypotheses.

Other advantages can accrue from a C.A. III lesson. In the course of the lesson, the teacher has a number of opportunities to point out similarities between the procedure followed in the lesson and procedures followed by scientists. For example, the idea of the tentativeness of scientific proof can be illustrated by comparing the procedures of scientists with procedures used by students engaged in a C.A. III activity.

Consider the investigation of *vegetables with edible roots* as an example. While the students could cite a number of examples of vegetables with edible roots, all of which would support the hypothesis, they could never really say the hypothesis had been *proven*. In a similar way, scientists as they discover new principles or demonstrate the validity of old ones haven't really "proven" these principles to be true. This is philosophically consistent with the view that knowledge should be regarded as tentative rather than absolute and that hypotheses and theories are either supported or rejected but never proven. There always exists the possibility that data discovered at a later date will cause an hypothesis to be rejected. An advantage of a C.A. III in this respect is that the philosophical view of the scientific search can be illustrated with a concrete example rather than an abstract discussion.

SUMMARY

In the preceding sections of this chapter, the Concept Attainment Model was described as a means of teaching concepts inductively, that is, the learner begins with examples and develops the concept rather than beginning with a concept definition and moving to the examples. It is based on the assumption that one of the best ways to learn a concept is by seeing examples of it. Because examples are central to the Concept Attainment activity, special attention must be paid to their selection and sequencing. As with selecting examples for any concept, their quality depends on the extent to which the characteristics are observable.

The model is implemented by presenting positive and negative examples of the concept in a predetermined order. After each example is presented, students analyze hypotheses, rejecting those which have become inaccurate in light of the data (examples) and forming additional hypotheses based on the new information. The cycle of data-analysis, hypothesis-examination, hypothesis-generation continues until the concept is attained and the teacher brings closure to the lesson by having the students identify the concept's characteristics and stating a definition. The concept is then applied through the classification or generation of additional examples.

In introducing Concept Attainment lessons to students, the teacher should first help the class through an activity using a simple category that puts minimum cognitive load on students. In addition, thinking skills are best developed through overt practice in which students share and explain the thinking processes they went through in arriving at their answers.

The following exercise consists of a short case study in which a Concept Attainment activity is illustrated. Read the case study and answer the questions that follow.

EXERCISES

Read the following anecdote illustrating a Concept Attainment activity and answer the questions using information from the scenario.

Miss Johnson wanted her class both to have a concept of *canine* and to develop their thinking skills.

She cut pictures of various animals and plants from magazines and pasted them on poster paper. She then began the activity by saying, "Today we are going to do a Concept Attainment activity. Who remembers what a Concept Attainment activity is? Jerry?"

"It's where you give us examples and we have to figure out what the concept is."

"Good, Jerry. Today I have a category in mind, and I'm going to show you some examples that fit into the category. I'm also going to show you some examples that don't fit into the category. What you must do is figure out the category from the examples I show you."

Miss Johnson then showed the following pictures (in order) and noted whether they were a "yes" or a "no." She showed a German Shepherd (yes) and an oak tree (no).

1. "I know what you're thinking of, "Mary volunteered. "It's an *animal*."
2. "It could be *pet*," John added.
3. "I think it's *mammal*," Phyllis put in.
4. "Let's take a second and look at those hypotheses. Phyllis, where did you get *mammal*?"
5. "Well, a German Shepherd has hair and live puppies and nurses its young so it's a mammal."
6. "Okay," replied Miss Johnson, "and I think we can all see where Mary and John got *pet* and *animal*. Let's go on and look at some more data." She then showed a collie (yes) and a magnolia tree (no).
7. "I think it's *dogs*," Judy added.
8. "Okay, let's put that on the board. Now let's go a bit further," Miss Johnson said. She then showed a beagle (yes) and a Siamese cat (no).
9. "It can't be *pet*," Kathy quickly said, "because Siamese cat is a *no* and it's a pet."
10. "It can't be *animal* or *mammal* either," Mike noted, "because a cat is both an animal and a mammal."
11. "Let's continue," Miss Johnson requested. She then showed a fox (yes) and a leopard (no).
12. "It can't be just *dog*, Don asserted. "Maybe it's *dog family*."
13. "I'll show you another picture," Miss Johnson said. Then she showed a picture of a wolf (yes).

14. "It must be *dog family,*" Denny stated. "All the yes's support the idea of *dog family.*"
15. Miss Johnson then added, "What do we call *dog family?*" After hearing no response she said, "Animals in the dog family are called *canines.*"
16. Miss Johnson then suggested, "Let's look at these pictures again (the yes's) and see what they have in common."
17. "They all have four legs," Sharon noted.
18. "They make a barklike sound, I think," Ann added.
19. "They have prominent teeth," Jimmy said.
20. "They all have hair," Jane suggested.

The lesson continued as Miss Johnson helped the class form a definition for *canine.* Then she showed them some additional pictures and asked them to classify them as *canine* or not.

Using information from the anecdote, respond to the following questions.
1.   Identify all the positive examples of the concept.
2.   Identify all the characteristics of the concept that were presented in the anecdote.
3.   Identify all the statements in the anecdote that were statements of hypothesizing.
4.   How did Miss Johnson's sequence of examples promote the development of students' thinking skills in the activity?
5.   What could Miss Johnson have done to further enrich the concept the children attained?
6.   What did Miss Johnson do that did not quite follow the procedure of a concept attainment activity?
7.   Where in the anecdote did Miss Johnson make students' thinking processes explicit?

FEEDBACK

1.   The examples of the concept in the anecdote are:

German Shepherd	Fox
Collie	Wolf
Beagle	

The other examples cited in the anecdote, such as Siamese cat, were those that were not canines. The negative examples further clarify the concept by showing what it is not, while the positive examples show what the concept is.
2.   The characteristics cited in the anecdote are:

Four legs	Prominent teeth
Barklike sound	Hair

Note that none of these attributes alone is sufficient to describe the concept. However, *together* they provide an adequate description for the purposes of the lesson.

3.   The hypotheses that students made were:

1.	"It's an animal."	7.	"I think it's dogs."
2.	"It could be pet."	12.	"Maybe it's dog family."
3.	"I think it's mammal."		

4.   Miss Johnson's sequence was presented as follows:

Yes	1. German Shepherd	No	6. Siamese cat
No	2. Oak tree	Yes	7. Fox
Yes	3. Collie	No	8. Leopard
No	4. Magnolia tree	Yes	9. Wolf
Yes	5. Beagle		

Consider now a second partial sequence.

Yes	1. German Shepherd	Yes	3. Wolf
No	2. Siamese cat	No	4. Leopard

The sequence Miss Johnson used allowed students much more opportunity to practice their thinking skills than would the second because the first few examples that she used were more general and allowed for a variety of hypotheses. In the second sequence, "cat" as the first negative example would eliminate "animal" or "pet" as initial hypotheses, and "wolf" as the second positive example would probably cause the students to immediately identify the concept. The first sequence, by contrast, allowed many hypotheses which were successively narrowed until the concept was isolated.

5.   Miss Johnson could have further enriched the concept by including other positive examples, such as "jackal" and "coyote," to broaden the concept for the students.

6.   Miss Johnson presented examples two at a time rather than singly. This is not critical and demonstrates the flexibility in the procedure. The only argument against this practice is that it might increase the cognitive load on young or inexperienced students to the point where they have some difficulty processing the information.

7.   There were several points (e.g., line numbers 9 and 10) in the lesson where students voluntarily made the logic behind their answers explicit. Miss Johnson made a conscious effort to encourage this when she asked Phyllis to explain her hypothesis in line 4.

This completes the implementation section of the chapter. You should now be able to plan and perform Concept Attainment activities. Let's turn now to a discussion of evaluation for Concept Attainment lessons.

EVALUATING CONCEPT ATTAINMENT ACTIVITIES

After reading this section you will be able to meet these objectives:

1. You will understand the evaluation of Concept Attainment activities so that given two items, you will select the one which is most appropriate for measuring students' understanding.
2. You will apply evaluation procedures for Concept Attainment activities so that given a description of a concept, you will prepare a valid item to measure student understanding of the concept.

Students' attainment of a concept can be measured in one or more of four primary ways which are outlined as follows:

1. They identify additional examples of the concept not previously encountered.
2. They identify the concept's characteristics.
3. They relate the concept to other concepts.
4. They define the concept.

The most common, effective, and efficient way of measuring Concept Attainment is by asking students to provide or identify additional examples of the concept. Easy to prepare and unlike a statement of definition or characteristics if the teacher uses unique examples, it is a valid way of measuring whether or not the students have formed a generalized abstraction. For instance, consider the following item again using the example *proper noun*.

From the following list select the choice which is a proper noun:

a. rapidly   c. Alaska
b. sofa   d. went

A variation of this format is to ask students to provide examples of the concept rather than identify examples from the list.

A second form of measurement is to ask students to identify characteristics of the concept. Generally, an item of this type will be at the recall level because the characteristics have already been identified during the activity. However, even recalled characteristics can be a legitimate measurement of concept learning, especially if used in conjunction with asking the students for new examples. An illustration of this type of item could be the following:

Circle all the following which are characteristic of mammals:

a. Naked skin   d. Scaly skin
b. Lays eggs   e. Regulated body temperature
c. Four-chambered heart f. Nurses young

Concepts can also be measured by having students relate them to other concepts. Here the teacher asks the students to identify coordinate, superordinate or subordinate concepts, or a combination of these. The following item is an example of this type of format.

If "figures of speech" is superordinate to the concept *metaphor,* which of the following are coordinate to this concept?

a. Simile   c. Personification
b. Trope   d. Meter

This item tests students' understanding of the relationship between metaphor and concepts which are also figures of speech. Similar items can be designed to measure superordinate and subordinate relationships. Use of items such as these assumes that the teacher has discussed these relationships in class.

A fourth method of measuring for concept learning is to ask students to provide a definition of the concept or to identify the correct definition from a list of alternatives. This type of measurement item is most like items used to measure students' knowledge of characteristics because it typically involves recall of information.

As is probably apparent from this discussion, there is no one best way to measure students' attainment of a concept. Each of the various items described tells the teacher something different about students' understanding, and the best method is a combination of these.

We have provided here a brief description of the measurement and evaluation process in concept learning. A general discussion of the measurement process is described in detail in Chapter 3, and you may wish to review this material now. You should be able to complete the two exercises on evaluation which follow.

EXERCISES

1.   Below are three items designed to measure students' comprehension of the concept *between*. Identify the best measurement item and explain why it is the best. To help evaluate these items you will need to refer to the teacher's objective which is: For kindergarten students to comprehend the concept *between* so that, given examples of the concept, they will identify the one which is an example of the concept.

Item 1. (Teacher reads if necessary.) Place an X where the ball is *between* the bats.

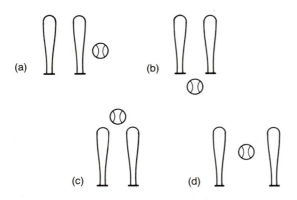

Item 2. Color red the instances where one object is between the others.

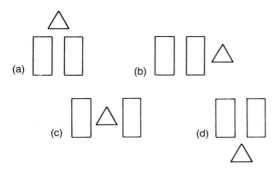

Item 3. Identify the best definition of *between*. (Teacher reads if necessary.)
a. *Between* is a relative position in which an object exists in place with two or more other objects placed on opposite sides of the original object.
b. *Between* is a relative position in space in which an object is placed close to a second and third object.
c. *Between* is a relative position in space in which an object exists with other objects on the side of the original object.
d. *Between* is a relative position in space in which two objects surround a third object on either side.

2.   Prepare a written item which could be used to measure students' comprehension of the concept *commutative property*. (The commutative property refers to the quality of numbers that allows the order of addition and multiplication operations to be reversed, e.g., 2 + 3 = 3 + 2 or 9 × 5 = 5 × 9.)

3.   Prepare a written item to measure children's concepts of *far* and *near*.

FEEDBACK

1.   Item 1 is the best choice for measuring *between*. The students are asked to identify an example of the concept, which is perhaps the best way of measuring concept learning. Also, the directions and choices are clear. Item 2 has two primary problems.

First, the directions are not completely clear, and second, based on the directions, both choices (b) and (c) are technically correct even though the teacher presumably wants the students to check choice (c). Item 3 is unacceptable for two reasons. First, it is inconsistent with the objective which states that the students will identify examples. Second, the choices are overly wordy and abstract, and the student would be most apt to identify the correct choice on the basis of a recalled definition rather than a comprehension of the concept.

There are, of course, other legitimate ways of measuring the concept. For example, a teacher could give students objects and ask them to place one *between* the others, or the teacher could ask students to draw a dog or cat *between* two trees.

2.   The teacher could measure the concept in the following way:

Identify the choices below which illustrate the commutative property.

a. $6/3 - 2; 3/6 = 1/2$

b. $6 - 3 = 3; 3 - 6 = -3$

c. $4 \times 3 = 12; 3 \times 4 = 12$

d. $4 + (3 + 2) = 9; (4 + 3) + 2 = 9$

e. $9 + 5 - 4 = 5 + 9 - 4$

Again, there are other ways of measuring students' understanding of the concept. This example is offered as one appropriate method.

3.   One possibility for preparing a written item for concepts such as *far* and *near* might be the following. As with the other items a variety of possibilities exist. We are presenting this one in the hope that it might stimulate your thinking about additional ways of measuring students' understanding of concepts.

Circle the number of each example that illustrates people or objects *near* each other.

1.

2.

3.

4.

5.

6.

7.

8.

DISCUSSION QUESTIONS

1.   In this chapter differences between early, naturalistic concept learning and initial school learning were contrasted. What are some reasons for these differences? Would there be any advantages to making early concept learning more structured? Any disadvantages?

2.   In implementing Concept Attainment activities in diverse classrooms, we have noticed that students who do not typically participate can become quite actively involved. What might be the reason for this?

3.   What would a Concept Attainment activity be like if only positive examples were used? Only negative? What is the optimal mix of positive and negative examples?

4.   What are the advantages of using coordinate concepts as negative examples in Concept Attainment activities? Disadvantages? What can be done to minimize these disadvantages?

5.   The amount of time that a teacher waits after asking a question has been found to be an important determinant influencing the quality of student answers (Rowe, 1974). How important is wait time in a Concept Attainment activity? When should it occur?

6.   In what areas of the curriculum is it hardest to provide adequate examples for Concept Attainment activities? Easiest?

7.   In what order should C.A. I, C.A. II, and C.A. III activities be introduced to students? What can be done to help students understand similarities and differences between the different strategies?

8.   In terms of C.A. I, II, and III:
   A. Which is easiest to implement in the classroom?
   B. Hardest?
   C. Which require the most prior planning?

9.   How could the thinking skills developed in C.A. II and III be evaluated?

REFERENCES

BEYER, B. (1983). Common sense about teaching thinking skills. *Educational Leadership, 41,* pp. 44–49.

BEYER, B. (1984). Improving thinking skills—practical approaches. *Phi Delta Kappan, 65,* pp. 556–560.

BRUNER, J., GOODNOW, J., & AUSTIN, G. (1956). *A study of thinking* (New York: John Wiley).

GAGNE, E. (1985). *The cognitive psychology of school learning* (Boston: Little, Brown and Company).

GOOD, T. & BROPHY, J. (1980). *Educational psychology: A realistic approach,* 2nd ed. (New York: Holt, Rinehart and Winston).

JOYCE, B. & WEIL, M. (1972). *Models of teaching* (Englewood Cliffs, N.J.: Prentice-Hall, Inc.).

KLAUSMEIER, H. (1985). *Educational psychology,* 5th ed. (New York: Harper and Row).

ROWE, M. (1974). Wait-time and rewards as instructional variables, their influence on language, logic, and fate control: Part one, wait-time. *Journal of Research in Science Teaching, 11,* 81–94.

TENNYSON, R. & COCCHIARELLA, M. (1986). An empirically based instructional design theory for teaching concepts. *Review of Educational Research, 58* (1), 40–71.

TIEMAN, P. & MARKLE, S. (1983). *Analyzing instructional control: A guide to instruction and evaluation* (Champaign, Illinois: Stipe).

6

THE INTEGRATIVE MODEL:
a synthesis of reasoning with content

INTRODUCTION

To begin the discussion of the Integrative Model let's briefly review the material in the two previous chapters. Both followed the theme of combining thinking skills with content goals and were developed with the thinking skills model and the forms of content originally presented in Chapter 2 as a framework. Chapter 4 focused on combining content with the inductive skills of comparing, finding patterns, and generalizing using a teaching procedure that promotes interaction, student motivation, and positive classroom climate. In Chapter 5 the inductive skills were reinforced and the deductive skills were introduced in a spirit of investigation and inquiry.

We are now at a point where the inductive skills, the deductive skills, and content can be combined using a model that synthesizes all three (Eggen & Kauchak, 1985). For this reason we are calling it the Integrative Model. Its flexibility will allow teachers to focus on content, on thinking skills, or on both equally according to their goals. We want at this point to respectfully acknowledge Hilda Taba (1965, 1966, 1967) on whose work the origins of the Integrative Model are based.

To introduce the model, let's examine a teaching episode based on actual classroom practice. (We will abbreviate the dialogue for the sake of simplifying the illustration, but it will capture the essence of the process.)

Mrs. Soo is involved in a science unit on amphibians with her fourth graders. To begin her day's lesson she displayed the following information for the children on a poster and then began to process the information.

After directing the class to study the chart for a moment she began the activity by saying, "Look carefully at the part that tells what toads eat. What do you notice here? Mike?"

"Well, they eat earthworms," Mike responded.

"And what else? Kathy?"

"Spiders," Kathy answered.

"Also grasshoppers," David volunteered.

"Yes, very good, everyone," Mrs. Soo smiled. "Now look at the frogs. What can you tell me about what they eat? Judy?"

"They eat insects," Judy replied.

"Also earthworms," Bill added.

"Now, let's go a bit farther," Mrs. Soo encouraged. "Look at both the frogs and the toads. How would you compare what they eat? How is it the same or different?"

"They both eat insects," Tim noticed.

"John?"

"They both eat earthworms too," John offered.

"The food for each seems to be almost the same," Kristy added tentatively.

"Very good, Kristy," Mrs. Soo smiled. "Why do you suppose that the food seems to be the same?"

After some hesitation Brad volunteered, "The frog and toad live in about the same places."

"What tells you that, Brad?" Mrs. Soo probed.

" . . . It says on the chart that the frog lives on land, in the water and in trees, and it says for the toad that he lives on land and in the water," Brad responded.

"Yes, excellent, Brad," Mrs. Soo praised. "You have supported your conclusion with information that you observed on the chart. Very well done."

"Also, the frog and toad are very much alike," Sonya offered.

"What do you see that tells you that, Sonya?" Mrs. Soo continued.

"From the pictures we see that they look about the same," Sonya replied.

"Also, they both start from eggs and then become tadpoles," Jim added. "On the chart we see pictures of the eggs and the tadpoles."

"Very good everyone!" Mrs. Soo enthused. "You're all thinking very well. Now here's a tough one. Suppose that frogs and toads were quite different rather than being very similar. What might happen to them then? Donna?"

" . . . Maybe the food that they would eat would be different," Donna suggested.

"Can you give me an example of where that would be the case, Donna?" Mrs. Soo queried.

Toads	Characteristics	Food	Habitat
Broad flat back Clumsy No tail	Eggs Tadpoles Dark Colors Shorter back legs Rough warty skin Poison on skin	Earthworms Insects Spiders	Water Land

Frogs	Characteristics	Food	Habitat
Narrow back Moves fast No tail	Eggs Tadpoles Different Colors Long back legs Smooth skin Poison under skin	Insects Spiders Earthworms	Water Land Trees

" . . . A frog and a mouse are different and they eat different foods," Donna replied.

"Yes, excellent example, Donna," Mrs. Soo smiled. "Anything else, anyone?"

Sue noted, "Perhaps they wouldn't live in the same places. Frogs and mice don't live in quite the same places."

"Yes, good suggestion, Sue," Mrs. Soo commented.

"You've all done very well everyone. Now try and summarize what we've discussed about frogs and toads here and talk about animals in general."

After some prompting Joel said, "Animals that are pretty much the same, such as living in the same place and looking about the same, eat the same food."

"Yes, Joel, that's a good summary. Could we go a bit farther?"

Again with prompting the class finally derived the statement, "Animals with similar characteristics will have similar habits, such as living in the same place and eating similar food."

We'll stop the illustration at this point and begin a description of how Mrs. Soo's learning activity synthesized content and thinking skills in the same lesson. Let's look now at the lesson's characteristics.

Mrs. Soo first displayed some data for the students and then began a questioning sequence that guided the students through an information processing experience. She began by simply asking the children to focus their attention on a particular portion of the data, to observe, and to verbally describe their observations. The question she used to initiate the activity was, "Look at what toads eat. What do you notice here?" As we discussed in Chapter 4 this type of question, in addition to focusing on the fundamental thinking skill of observation, has the added advantage of being open-ended, which promotes student success, high levels of interaction and brisk lesson pacing.

Mrs. Soo continued this process with her initial focus on toads and then shifted to frogs using the same line of questioning. After examining the information specific to each animal, she had the students compare the two by identifying their similarities and differences. This question began to narrow the focus of the analysis but still remained open-ended preserving the advantages that open-endedness allows. At this point the children were practicing the basic inductive skill of comparing, and then extended the process to summarizing when they made the more general statement, "Frogs and toads eat the same kinds of foods."

The analysis process then smoothly shifted to the use of deductive skills when Mrs. Soo asked, "Why do you suppose the foods are essentially the same?" At this point the students were asked to provide an explanation for the comparison or suggest a cause for the observations they had made. Brad offered the explanation when he said, "The frog and toad live in the same places," and it was expanded when Sonya suggested, "The frog and toad are very much alike."

At that point Mrs. Soo began the development of critical thinking when she asked each of the students to confirm their explanation. She asked, "What tells you that, Brad?" and "What do you see that tells you that, Sonya?" As we discussed in Chapter 2, one of the characteristics of critical thinking is the ability to document a conclusion with facts or observation. At this point the critical thinking process could be extended if the conclusions were not warranted by the data. For example, suppose a student suggested that the reason frogs and toads eat the same foods was that they look the same. An assessment of the conclusion would lead to its partial refutation by noting that the colors of the two animals are different, toads being similar in color, and frogs varying in color. As the process develops, an alert teacher can capitalize on these opportunities when they occur.

Mrs. Soo took the process a step further in the development of deductive skills when she asked, "Suppose that frogs and toads were quite different rather than being very similar. What might happen to them then?" This is a hypothetical question, which in turn calls for hypothetical reasoning. This develops the students' deductive skills by increasing the abstraction of the question, requiring a more advanced form of thinking. Mrs. Soo also required a form of documentation in this step when she asked Donna for a case where the hypothetical suggestion would hold true.

Finally, the activity was summarized when Mrs. Soo asked the children to generalize from the data they had been processing. They first stated, "Animals that are pretty much the same, . . . eat the same food," which was extended to a broader generalization when the class derived the conclusion, "Animals with similar characteristics will have similar habits, . . . "

At the same time the children were practicing the thinking skills they were acquiring considerable content. They first learned basic information such as:

Frogs and toads are not the same animal.
Frogs and toads live in about the same places.
Tree frogs exist, but tree toads do not.
Frogs and toads eat many forms of insects and worms.
Toads tend to be more bulky and less agile than frogs.

In addition to the basic information the students also learned broad generalizations such as, "Animals with similar characteristics have similar habits." From this we see that teachers who are content oriented in their teaching can as effectively as process-oriented teachers include the Integrative Model in their repertoire of techniques and have the advantages of a model that promotes student involvement, success, and motivation.

In summary, Mrs. Soo taught a lesson where developmental thinking skills, critical thinking, and content were all combined. This is the essence of the Integrative Model, where each of these elements is synthesized into a complete whole.

Let's look now at the basic sequence in the questioning process as was illustrated in Mrs. Soo's activity. We will discuss modifications and the flexibility inherent in the model as the chapter is developed, but for now we will briefly outline the phases of the model for sake of an overview.

Mrs. Soo went through a series of phases which can be described as follows:

Phase 1: Describe

In the first phase the students were encouraged to describe the data in one portion of the chart. The information in the illustration was in the form of a matrix with each portion of the matrix being a cell, so Phase 1 was the description of the information in a particular cell.

Phase 2: Compare

Phase 2 is a natural outgrowth of Phase 1. Once the information in two related cells has been observed and described, comparisons are made between the two. The students at this point identify the similarities and differences between the cells. The comparison may range from a simple description of what is the same and what is different for young children to the summary of a general pattern for older students.

Phase 3: Explain

The natural evolving process continues in Phase 3 when the students are asked, once having identified similarities and/or differences, to explain why they exist. At this point the processing shifts from inductive to deductive and the students' thinking is moved an additional step. In addition, the documentation of the explanation through observable information on the chart is an important part of the phase, and a teacher whose goals are focused on critical thinking would particularly want to emphasize this aspect of Phase 3.

Phase 4: Hypothesize

Phase 4, as with Phase 3, is the natural extension of the previous step. After similarities and differences have been explained to the extent that the data allow and to the satisfaction of the teacher, the students are asked to respond to a hypothetical situation that goes beyond the information displayed for them. They are asked to think more generally and more abstractly than in each of the previous phases, and the reasoning process is extended by one more step.

Phase 5: Generalize

The activity comes to closure when the students are asked to summarize the information and form one or more generalizations that would describe the patterns illustrated in the chart. Teachers may have a lesson relatively narrow in scope and have a single generalization that is the content goal, or they may have a broadly scoped lesson that would allow several generalizations to be formed. We will illustrate each as we detail the description of the model.

Let's turn now to a description of the planning, implementation, and evaluation phases of the Integrative Model.

PLANNING INTEGRATIVE MODEL LESSONS

Identifying Content Goals

After completing this section of the chapter, you should be able to meet the following objective:

> You will understand the planning process for Integrative Model lessons so when considering a topic of your choice you will prepare a lesson including all the characteristics of effective data displays.

As we have seen from the illustration in the Introduction, a goal intrinsic to the use of the Integrative Model is the development of inductive and deductive thinking skills together with critical thinking. The development of these skills is one of the major themes in this text. As we pointed out in Chapter 2, however, content and thinking skills fit hand in glove and one cannot be appropriately separated from the other. For this reason and because the planning process is more easily begun from a content orientation, we begin our discussion of planning with a consideration of content goals.

After the goal has been clearly identified, the teacher considers the teaching procedure that will best promote the students reaching the goal. In Chapter 4 we saw that goals best delivered with the Inductive Model are specific and precisely stated, and they usually involve only one concept or generalization unless closely related coordinate concepts are being taught. By contrast some units and topics are not conducive to explicit and precisely stated single objectives. Let's look now at a series of topics taken from actual classroom experience.

For instance, consider a history teacher who wants to deal with the topic of immigration. Here he would likely discuss representative immigrant groups and analyze dimensions such as their reasons for coming, contributions, characteristics, and rates of assimilation. From a study such as this a number of important conclusions would be made, but dividing the topic into a series of separate lessons with each involving a different goal would be cumbersome and less meaningful for the students.

As another example, consider a primary teacher who is doing a unit on the seasons. In this case she might want the children to see how the food, clothing, and recreational activities in one season compare to those in a different season. Again the teacher's goal would be oriented toward a series of conclusions rather than specifically emphasizing the acquisition of a single, explicitly stated goal.

Finally, consider an algebra teacher who wants her students to be able to write equations and solve percent mixture problems. Here the goal is very clear. However, as opposed to teaching a concept with specific characteristics such as *regular polygon,* it is difficult to isolate the different aspects of the problem-solving process while retaining a perspective of the overall problem. The algebra teacher's goal may seem a bit removed from the others, but it can also be effectively met with the Integrative Model, as we illustrate when we discuss the implementation phase.

Let's look now at each of the three goals and identify their common features. First, by contrast with goals effectively reached with the Inductive or Concept Attainment Models, goals appropriately met using the Integrative Model are broader in scope and involve the acquisition of a series of generalizations, inferences, or problem-solving skills rather than a single, precisely stated goal that is relatively narrow in scope.

Second, the topics involve coordinate ideas that can be compared. For instance, the lesson that provided our introductory illustration was a comparison of frogs and toads, which are coordinate topics. Two or more of the four seasons are coordinate ideas as are Italian, Chinese, and Puerto Rican immigrants (or any other set of immigrant groups). A series of percent mixture problems are also coordinate topics.

Since the number of topics involving coordinate ideas is vast, the Integrative Model is a very general procedure that can be adapted to virtually all grade levels and a wide variety of curriculum areas. For instance, consider the following brief list of goals:

A literature teacher wants to study different authors, the characteristics of the society at the time they wrote, and the patterns in their writing.

A life science teacher is doing a unit on different biomes and the life forms and attributes of each.

A primary class is studying the food groups and is comparing good and bad eating habits.

An art teacher wants to compare the art forms of several different historical periods.

A music teacher is studying the characteristics of different popular music forms, such as country, jazz, rock, and pop.

An elementary teacher is doing a unit on the classic topic of community helpers.

A seventh grade geography teacher wants to do a unit on Eastern Europe. Part of the goal would be to consider the climate, geography, culture, and economics of the area and compare them to their counterparts in Western Europe.

A sixth grade teacher wants to do a unit on the colonies, comparing the geography, climate and economics of the Northern and Southern Colonies.

If you generalize from the examples, you see that the list of topics that can be appropriately taught with the Integrative Model is virtually endless. Let's turn now to the next step in the planning process which is a means for capturing data.

The Data Retrieval Process

Once having identified a topic and series of goals related to the topic, the teacher is prepared to move to the second step which is the capturing of information in a way that will allow the students to process it. As illustrated in the introduction to the chapter, the data often are displayed on a chart organized in the form of a matrix. We discuss this means of data retrieval initially and later show how other forms of displaying information can be efficiently employed for use with the Integrative Model.

We said as we discussed goals that the topics involve coordinate ideas that can be compared to each other. This was illustrated with the example involving frogs and toads. Look now at the following matrices related to the first three goals we discussed in the last section.

PERCENT MIXTURE PROBLEMS   **SOLUTION EQUATION**

1) How many kilograms of water must be added to 69 kilograms of an 80% acid solution to produce a 70% acid solution?

$$(0)n + (.80)69 = (.70)(69 + n)$$

2) How many kilograms of water must be added to 20 kilograms of a 10% salt solution to produce a 5% solution?

$$(0)n + (.10)20 = (.05)(20 + n)$$

3) A druggist has 20 grams of a 10% alcohol solution. How many grams of a 6% alcohol solution must be added to form an 8% alcohol solution?

$$(.06)n + (.10)20 = (.08)(20 + n)$$

4) How many kilograms of water must be evaporated from 60 kilograms of a 5% salt solution to produce a 25% salt solution?

$$(.05)60 = (.25)(60 - n)$$

Data retrieval options.   The data retrieval process is very flexible and the teacher has a variety of options in preparing the data displays. In responding to these options the teacher has the opportunity to make several decisions in gathering and organizing the information.

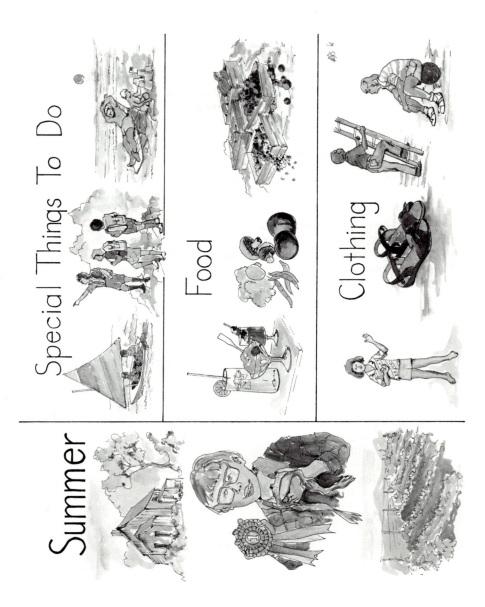

Summer

Special Things To Do

Food

Clothing

Winter

Special Things To Do

Food

Clothing

TABLE 6.1

REASONS FOR COMING	CONTRIBUTIONS	CHARACTERISTICS	ASSIMILATION
ITALIANS			
Small farms divided up between sons no longer could support families Large estates controlled large parts of land Population increase Poor land, wooden plows, lack of fertilizers and irrigation led to poor crop yields Very few factories or plants to work in Heavy taxes from government—few services Bad weather for several years encouraged many to leave Stories of wealth in America	Vegetable farms Construction industry Music Art Active in local politics Importers Food industry Tradesmen Sports	Poor Catholic Large families Tight family structure Farmers in old country Most could not read or write, slightly poorer rate of literacy than rest of U.S. population Worked as laborers English language added quickly by second generation	First generation: very religiously oriented, parochial schools Second generation: more intermarriages, people moved away from birthplace Third generation: public and parochial schools; those who lived in home town maintained close ties; those who moved away from home "Americanized"
CHINESE			
Overpopulation Lack of upward mobility—status fixed Inefficient war-lords—high taxes Active recruitment—promise of high wages Crop failures caused widespread famine	Railroad construction Mine workers Owned businesses within "China Towns" (banks, newspapers, stores)	Most came over as coolie laborers Taoism or Shintoism Tight family structure Most illiterate—those who could, read Chinese, slightly poorer rate of literacy than rest of U.S. population	Men as job hunters Mostly western U.S. Lived together Major influx from 1868–1890 Established "China Towns" Little social association with others Eager to preserve Chinese customs

PUERTO RICANS

Low standard of living compared to U.S.
Large increases in population brought about by medical advances
Puerto Rico very densely populated
Few factories or plants to work in
Land poor for agriculture
Open assess to U.S.—short distance to travel
Relatives wrote back to publicize "good life" in America

Garment industry
Service trades (maids, butlers, chauffeurs)
Agricultural workers

Worked as laborers or opened merchant shops
Retained many of former customs
Slow rate of adaptation of bilingualism

Catholics
High rate of illiteracy
Large families
Thrifty
Skilled or semi-skilled
Social
Small, dark complected

1946–present
Mostly Northeast particularly New York City
Conflict over housing
Public schooling
Church still important in older people's lives
Juvenile delinquency

As you see from each of the examples, the data are typically displayed in a matrix which exists in the form of parallel ideas compared along several dimensions. For instance in the immigrants example in Table 6.1 the parallel ideas are the Italian, Chinese, and Puerto Rican immigrant groups and the dimensions are *reasons for coming, contributions, characteristics,* and *assimilation.* In the case of the frog and toad the dimensions were their *appearance, characteristics, what they eat,* and *where they live.* You can see the dimensions for the seasons, and for the algebra example they are the problems and their respective solution equations.

Let's consider now the factors that lead to the choice of topics and the dimensions on which they are compared. The teacher must make three decisions which are as follows:

1. The number of ideas or concepts to be compared depends on the teacher's goal for the lesson and the scope of the topic. Lessons are most effective with a minimum number of two, such as the frog and the toad, but may range to as many as is desired. In the second example the teacher chose three immigrant groups but could have chosen four, five, or more. Obviously, increasing the number of parallel topics will increase the scope of the lesson, which means the data analysis might not be completed in a single class period. This is perfectly appropriate. In fact, teachers often find the matrix an excellent mechanism for the organization of an entire unit of instruction. In this case a portion of the chart is covered each class period until the unit is complete.

The choice of topics is also a function of teacher judgment. In the case of the immigrants lesson, the teacher wanted to consider representative immigrant groups from around the world and arbitrarily chose Italians, Chinese, and Puerto Ricans on that basis. If in the judgment of the teacher, a different choice is more relevant or better fits the goal for the topic, the decision would be made on that basis.

In the case of the seasons the decision is virtually a natural. It is intuitively sensible that two or more of the four seasons would be selected. In our example the teacher chose summer and winter. Using all four of the seasons will merely broaden the scope of the lesson.

2. The selection of the dimensions for comparison is another decision the teacher makes, and again it is a function of the goal for the lesson or unit. The selection of *reasons for coming* and the other dimensions of the immigrants topic depends on what the teacher wants the students to derive from the lesson. As with many classroom decisions, the teacher may involve the students to the desired extent. There may be one or more topics that they are interested in and the teacher may allow them to incorporate the ideas.

3. The decision as to what information exists on the display and who gathers it is also left up to the teacher who may choose to gather all the information, have the students gather it all, or combine the two, so both the

teacher and the students provide some of the data. The issue is less a function of who collects the information and more the form in which it exists, as we discuss in the next section. In fact some teachers combine the overriding thinking skills goal, a content goal, and the goal of developing student research skills all in the same lesson or unit. Some even put the students completely in charge by taping large pieces of poster paper on the walls and having the students actually write information or paste pictures on the charts.

Let's turn now to a brief discussion of desirable ways of presenting the data.

Effective data displays.   While any means of capturing information will "work," certain displays of data are more conducive to student processing than others. However, the means for presenting information is very flexible and can be easily adapted to a variety of situations. There are two essential characteristics in an effective display.

The first is that the chart contains "processable" information. We are coining the term "processable" to mean that the information is in such a form that the students can summarize it and generalize from those summaries. The most conducive type of information for processing is factual or as nearly factual as possible. Next best is a series of relatively narrow generalizations or a mixture of the narrow generalizations and facts. Least desirable is a series of relatively broad generalizations. For example, consider the immigrants chart shown previously with the data arranged as in the display on page 178.

As you see from the display of information, the data are much less conducive to analysis in this form than they were previously. Note that the previous chart development, while essentially a series of generalizations, is still very conducive to analysis.

The second desirable chart characteristic involves the inclusion of information that will provide for the process of documenting conclusions. Look again at the questioning sequence in the chapter's introductory lesson. In Phase 3 Mrs. Soo asked the students to explain why the frog and the toad would eat the same food. Brad then noted that the animals live in essentially the same places. Upon being asked to support his response, he was able to point to the section of the chart which identified the environment for each. If that section of the chart had not existed, Brad would not have been able to provide the documentation. For this reason including enough information in the chart so the students are able to verify their responses through observation is very important. We illustrate this process in greater detail as we discuss implementing Integrative Model lessons.

Your planning process is now complete and you are prepared to direct the students and guide them as they process the information. Let's turn now to the implementation phase.

REASONS FOR COMING	CONTRIBUTIONS	CHARACTERISTICS	ASSIMILATION
ITALIANS			
Economic problems Political problems Overpopulation	Varied	Religious Lower class	Rapid assimulation after first generation
CHINESE			
Overpopulation Economic opportunity Political problems	Railroad construction Mine workers Business	Religious Lower class	Slow assimulation
PUERTO RICANS			
Overpopulation Economic opportunity	Service trades Agriculture	Religious Lower class	Relatively rapid assimulation

EXERCISE

Consider a topic in your area of study. Prepare a matrix that could be used with an Integrative Model lesson. Carefully develop the material so that the matrix has the following characteristics.

1.   Two or more parallel topics which can be compared to each other.
2.   A series of dimensions on which the topics will be compared.
3.   Data in a form specific enough so that it is "processable."
4.   Data inclusive enough to allow students to document conclusions about the information in the chart.

Present the information to your instructor or a colleague and have them assess it for the previous four characteristics. You will then be prepared to implement the lesson.

IMPLEMENTING INTEGRATIVE MODEL ACTIVITIES

As we saw in the Introduction, the activity is implemented in five distinct though strongly interrelated steps, which we have identified as phases. While the illustration implied a sequence beginning with Phase 1 and continuing through Phase 5, the process is actually very flexible. We first discuss each of the phases in a straightforward and rather prescriptive way. The purpose in this discussion is to make the procedure as clear as possible.

After completing this section of the chapter, you should be able to meet the following objectives:

1.   You will understand the phases in the implementation of the Integrative Model so when given a classroom episode where the model is used, you will identify:
    (a)   each of the phases in the procedure.
    (b)   where the students were documenting a response.
2.   You will apply the questioning skills involved in the Integrative Model procedure so when given data in a matrix, you will write an appropriate sequence of questions based on the data.

After the initial information is presented we identify modifications, such as sequencing options, different forms of data retrieval and accommodation of varying age groups, that will assist teachers in adapting the Integrative Model to their own teaching situations. If questions arise as you read the initial description of the phases, keep them in mind. They should be answered for you as you study the possible modifications in the procedure.

Phase 1: Describe

Phase 1 marks the beginning of the analysis process and the point at which the students are introduced to the activity. As the lesson begins, the teacher simply directs the students' attention to a particular cell in the matrix and asks them to observe and describe the information. With the immigrants chart the teacher could begin by saying, "Look at the Italians' 'reasons for coming.' What can you tell us about it?''

With the chart on the seasons the teacher might direct the children, "Look at the types of clothes people wear in the winter. What do you see there?''

The algebra teacher might suggest, "Describe the first problem for us.''

This type of beginning has the same advantages that exist in the beginning of an Inductive Model lesson. First, it breaks the ice for the students. They are introduced to the activity and they can respond with no danger of failure. As a result, a high level of interaction quickly develops and the pace of the lesson is brisk, both of which are inducements to student attention. In addition, the question allows the teacher to accept all student responses, a factor found to be positively correlated with student achievement (Gall, 1984).

Second, the question allows the teacher to check the students' perception of the information. In describing what they see the teacher can determine if the students are perceiving the information as intended.

Third, the process is consistent with the development of thinking skills. Observation is the beginning point for any thinking skills activity, and the lesson begins with observation.

Finally, it takes pressure off the teacher until the flow of the lesson is established. Merely directing the students to describe what they see is a nice, easy, comfortable way to begin a lesson, and establishes the 'win-win' climate we discussed in Chapter 4.

As the teacher directs the students' processing in Phase 1, there are two decisions to be made which will be determined in part by the responses from the students. The first involves the beginning point on the chart. Typically, the students would be directed to the upper left corner to begin making descriptions, mostly because we are trained to begin reading in the upper left and it is a habit. However, there is no rule that says you must begin there, and if you have a reason to begin at another point in the matrix, that would be perfectly appropriate.

The second decision involves the length of time the description process is continued within a single cell. Certainly a teacher would not merely ask for one observation and then move on. On the other hand, students—and particularly young children—can make an enormous number of observations, and under these conditions the teacher must decide at what point the activity should be directed away from the particular cell. In referring back to Mrs. Soo's lesson, we see that three different descriptions of the information in the first cell were made. We purposely limited the number of descriptions in the example for sake of brevity, but it illustrates the process.

After completing the description in the first cell, the teacher moves on to a second, just as Mrs. Soo did when she moved from the description of what toads eat to a description of what frogs eat. The analysis is conducted just as it was with the first cell and is essentially the same for each one.

Phase 2: Compare

After completing Phase 1 the teacher is ready to move the students forward. Finding similarities and differences through the process of comparing two or more cells is the natural extension of observing and describing the information in a single cell. In addition, as the students make their comparisons, they are beginning to structure the information to make it more meaningful to them. This is consistent with Wittrock's (1974, 1983) theory of generative learning.

Mrs. Soo began Phase 2 by asking, "Look at both the frogs and the toads. How would you compare what they eat? How is it the same or different?" While this question narrows the scope of acceptable responses somewhat compared to Phase 1, the question is still open-ended and retains most of the advantages that open-ended questioning affords.

With the immigrants chart the teacher could simply ask, "How would you compare the Italians' 'reasons for coming' to the Chinese's 'reasons for coming'?" or "Look at all three immigrant groups. How would you compare the 'reasons for coming' for all three?" The same type of question could then be asked for each of the other dimensions on which the immigrant groups are being compared.

With the seasons of the year the teacher might simply ask, "How would you compare the clothing in the winter to the clothing in the summer?" With very young children who are only beginning to develop their skills in making comparisons, the teacher might have to be more specific in the initial question such as, "Look at the clothing in the winter and in the summer. What do you see in the winter clothes pictures that you don't see in the summer clothes pictures? What do you see in both sets of pictures that is the same?"

A teacher using the series of algebra problems might simply ask, "Look at the first two problems. What are some characteristics that they have in common?" Responses could then be followed by, "Now look at all four problems. How are they similar and how are they different?"

With each of the examples you can see that the processing is smooth and designed to promote a high level of success and interaction. In working with teachers as they first encounter the Integrative Model, we often suggest as they lead students through Phases 1 and 2, "Make it easy on yourself." They appear to sometimes feel that the question asked must somehow be more difficult than the phases would suggest, or they should have to work harder at it. This is not the case. The questioning process should be easy and comfortable for both the teacher and the students.

Phase 3: Explain

If a model can have a phase more exciting than any of the others, with the Integrative Model it is Phase 3. At this point the processing becomes deductive, while with Phases 1 and 2 it was primarily inductive. The phases become interdependent and the students are introduced to critical thinking within the scope of the lesson. While the questioning process in Phase 3 is more demanding than it was in the two earlier phases, teachers quickly become very skilled with practice until it essentially is automatic.

We noted that comparing in Phase 2 is the natural outgrowth of observation and description in Phase 1. Phases 2 and 3 have a similar—although not quite as automatic—relationship. To begin to illustrate this process let's refer again to Mrs. Soo's questioning sequence. In Phase 2 she asked, "Look at both the frog and the toad. How would you compare what they eat? How is it the same or different?"

The students then gave a series of responses ending with, "The food for each seems to be almost the same."

Mrs. Soo then followed the response with the question, "*Why* do you suppose that the food seems to be the same?" Asking the students at this point to explain *why* a certain similarity (or difference) exists marks the shift from Phase 2 to Phase 3. As with the move from Phase 1 to Phase 2, the shift is virtually automatic, and the questioning sequence remains smooth. However, the thinking on the part of the students is significantly advanced. In Phase 2, students are merely asked to identify a similarity or difference, while in Phase 3 they are asked to explain *why* it exists. The students are providing an explanatory inference requiring the identification of a deductive relationship. Identifying this type of relationship marks an advance in the development of their thinking skills. Let's look now at some other possible questioning sequences where Phase 3 emerges naturally from Phase 2.

With the immigrants topic the teacher might ask in Phase 2, "How would you compare the assimilation of the Italians to that of the Chinese?"

An appropriate response might be, "The Italians became 'Americanized' by the third generation but the Chinese did not."

The teacher could then simply ask, "Why do you suppose this happened?"

In the case of the lesson with seasons of the year the teacher could ask, "How would you compare the clothing in the winter to the clothing in the summer?" to which a student might respond, "People wear warmer clothes in the winter," and the teacher could then ask, "Why do they wear warmer clothes in the winter?"

The algebra teacher might request, "How would you compare the equations for the first and third problems?"

The students could respond by saying, "The unknown on the left side of the first equation has a coefficient of zero, while in the third equation the coefficient is .06."

The teacher could then merely ask, "Why?"

We have presented the previous illustrations for the sake of clarity and brevity. Obviously, a large variety of possibilities exists in each case. With practice these possibilities will be easily recognized. However, not every comparison is automatically "explainable." Let's look at this issue now.

Documenting responses. As we just stated, not every comparison automatically lends itself to explanation. In this section we identify the characteristics that make the transition from Phases 2 to 3 effective and in the next section we look at some contrasting examples.

Let's look again at the examples of Phase 3 questions from the last section and see what they have in common:

"Why did the Italians become 'Americanized' by the third generation but the Chinese did not?"

"Why do people wear warmer clothes in the winter?"

"Why is the coefficient zero in the first equation and .06 in the third equation?"

In each of the cases and also when Mrs. Soo asked the children, "Why do you suppose that the food seems to be the same?" the students were responding to a question with *an answer which could be found somewhere on the chart.* This allows the students to document their answers with observable information and introduces them to the concept of critical thinking. For example, in the case with the immigrants the students might respond, "The Italians learned the language more quickly than did the Chinese, which would lead to 'Americanization'." They can document the answer by referring to the 'characteristics' column for the two immigrant groups. In this column it says for the Italians 'English language learned quickly by the second generation,' and for the Chinese 'Slow to learn English language.'

In the primary example the students could answer simply, "It's colder in the winter," and could document their answer by referring to the pictures of the snow in the chart.

The algebra students could note that in the first equation water is being added to the solution, but in the third equation a second solution is being added to the original. They can provide evidence for their answer by simply referring to the respective problems.

Mrs. Soo's students were documenting their answers in Phase 3 when they said, "It says on the chart that the frog lives on land, in the water, and in trees, and it says for the toad that it lives on land and in the water."

The ability of the students to find evidence to support their inference is the critical feature of appropriate Phase 3 questioning growing out of Phase 2 responses. Ideally the evidence exists in the chart, and the students can refer directly to it there. However, it is obviously impossible to anticipate all the possibilities a topic might provide, so being able to provide evidence from somewhere in their background even though it is not on the chart would be a reasonable compromise.

Let's look now at some cases where Phase 3 does not automatically develop from Phase 2.

Explainable comparisons. While Phases 2 and 3 are closely related and the move from one to the other should be smooth and comfortable, teacher judgment is required to effectively manage the processing at this point in the lesson. For example, consider again the topic dealing with frogs and toads. Suppose the teacher asks, "Look at the frog and toad in the left column. How would you compare them?"

The students might then respond, "The toad has rough skin with bumps on it while the frog's skin is smooth." This type of comparison is essentially nonexplainable and asking the students to explain why the difference in their skin exists would not be appropriate. The difference is characteristic of their physiology, and no data exist on the chart, nor in all probability anywhere in the students' backgrounds, that could be used to help form the explanation.

Another example might be, "We see an acid solution in the first equation and an alcohol solution in the third equation." There is no sensible reason why they are different based on any evidence in the chart, and again asking the students why the difference exists would be inappropriate.

We are describing these cases as *unexplainable* comparisons. The teacher's task in guiding the students' processing of the information is to recognize comparisons that can be appropriately explained and ask the students to provide the explanation, and in the same activity leave those unexplainable ones as simple comparisons.

The process need not be a problem for the teacher. For example, suppose the teacher asks for a comparison among the algebra problems and a student says, "The first uses acid and the second involves salt." The teacher can simply say, "Yes, very good. What other similarities or differences do you see?" As the analysis continues a student might say, "The first three equations have plus signs on the right side of the equation, but the fourth equation has a minus sign." At this point the teacher recognizes that there is a reason for the difference and asks the students to provide the reason. This is the essence of recognizing explainable similarities and differences. Exercise 2 is designed to reinforce your understanding of questions that effectively move the students from Phase 2 to Phase 3.

Phase 4: Hypothesize

Phase 4 marks an additional step in the development of the students' ability to process the information. As with the pattern of the model, Phase 4 often can evolve directly from Phase 3. For instance, in the case of the immigrants the teacher might ask, "Suppose the Chinese had learned English quickly. What might have happened to them then?" or with the algebra problems, "What would happen to the first equation if instead of water a 50 percent acid solution were added to the original mixture?" These are questions that require hypothetical reasoning on the part of the students. In spite of some theories' assertions that young children are incapable of hypothetical reasoning, our experience indicates that they are quite capable when the hypothetical question is directly related to the information they have been processing.

The teacher in the lessons on seasons might ask, "Suppose you live in southern California. How might the clothing you wear in winter there be affected?" or "What might the summer clothing be like in Alaska?" In each of these cases the students are required to reason hypothetically, which extends the development of their thinking.

The students can also provide a form of documentation for their hypotheses by providing examples where their suggestion holds true. In Mrs. Soo's class, Donna did this when she used the comparison between a mouse and a frog. In the immigrants example students could consider the rapid 'Americanization' of other immigrant groups with similar language such as the Irish. While this documentation is not as precise as the evidence required in Phase 3, its characteristics are similar.

Phase 5: Generalize

The lesson is summarized and comes to closure when the students derive one or more generalizations that serve to summarize the content. Joel provided the closure in Mrs. Soo's lesson when he stated, "Animals that are pretty much the same, such as living in the same place and looking the same, eat the same food." With some additional prompting they made the more abstract generalization relating characteristics and habits.

The primary students would be prompted to make general statements relating climate and lifestyle. While their development may prohibit them from articulating actual generalizations, they would be able to make statements such as, "You do different things and wear differrent clothes when it's warm than you do when it's cold." As their experience and development advance, they would be able to make conclusions such as, "Lifestyle depends on the climate where you live."

A series of generalizations could be derived from the lesson on immigrants, such as:

"People immigrate primarily for economic reasons."

"The contributions of immigrants from different countries are varied."

"Immigrants tend to come from a lower socioeconomic class of people."

"Immigrants tend to initially settle at the point of original disembarkation."

"Cultures that are closely related will assimilate more quickly than those less closely related."

As you can see from the examples, some lessons are rich with possibilities for generalizing, which in turn can lead to animated discussions as students disagree with some of the statements. When this type of discussion exists, they are truly immersed in the thinking process.

The form of closure in the case of the algebra problems looks quite different, but the underlying process is essentially the same. Commonly, students would be presented with additional problems for which equations would be written. When students can successfully describe symbolically the information in the written problems, they have generalized the process, which would be the teacher's goal.

We want to turn to a more detailed discussion of student development and teacher options, but before doing so please respond to the following exercises designed to reinforce your understanding of the content in this section.

EXERCISES

1.   Read the following classroom episode that illustrates an Integrative Model lesson. Classify each question and statement as a (1) for Phase 1, (2) for Phase 2, (3) for Phase 3, (4) for Phase 4, (5) for Phase 5, or (D) if the question and statement calls for and receives documentation for a response in one of the phases.

Mr. Miller had his social studies class involved in a discussion of family groups and wanted to investigate factors affecting the attitudes of people.

He prepared a chart comparing the characteristics of different groups of people. He brought the chart to class and began by saying, "Everyone look at the chart and let's try to interpret the information."

_____   1.   He went on, "Take a look at the 'Type of Work' column. How would you compare the Iules' work to the Torres' work? Sharon?"

_____   2.   Sharon began, "I would say that the Iules are more craftsmen while the Torres are laborers."

_____   3.   "OK," Mr. Miller smiled. "What would you say in general about the Iules' work? Sherry?"

_____   4.   "Well, they're all self-employed," Sherry noted.

_____   5.   "They are people who work outdoors," Maxine added.

_____   6.   "Why might Maxine have said that?" Mr. Miller queried. "Jill?"

_____   7.   "Sheepmen and cattlemen, which are outdoor occupations, are shown in the Iules' work," Jill offered.

_____   8.   "Look at the 'Attitude' of the Wongs and Torres," Mr. Miller requested. "How are they different?"

_____   9.   "Well," Gary said hesitantly, "The Wongs seem to be concerned with beauty and helping others and the Torres are more concerned with work and food."

	10.	"Very good, Gary. Why do you suppose that is the case? Pat?"
_____	11.	"The Torres are poor while the Wongs are well off," Pat answered.
_____	12.	"And what suggests that to you?" Mr. Miller probed.
_____	13.	"See where it says 'Lower Class' for Torres and 'Upper Middle Class' for Wongs," Carol volunteered.
_____	14.	"Also, the Torres are grape and orange pickers," Vonnie put in.
_____	15.	"What might happen if the Torres were to find secure jobs in one place?" Mr. Miller queried. "Jeff?"
_____	16.	"I think they wouldn't remain lower class," Jeff said.
_____	17.	"What might have made Jeff say that?" Mr. Miller went on. "Iris?"
_____	18.	"They wouldn't have to go to thirty schools so they would get a better education," Iris suggested.
_____	19.	"Also, I think their attitude would change a bit," Susan added. "It's much easier to be interested in middle class values like beauty when you're not hungry."
_____	20.	"They would have a close family life because they wouldn't all be out in the fields," Peggy offered.
_____	21.	"What could we say about all the information we have here?" Mr. Miller asked.
_____	22.	"Well . . . the economic state a person is in affects their values, attitudes, and the way they live to a certain extent," Judy answered.

"Very good everyone," Mr. Miller smiled. "You've done an excellent job."

2.   The interdependent questioning sequence in Phases 2 and 3 is sometimes difficult for teachers. In order to reinforce your skills in this area, complete the following exercise.

Look again at the immigrants chart used as one of the illustrations earlier in this chapter. Based on the chart write a Phase 2 question. Then write the Phase 2 response that is an explainable comparison. Write the Phase 3 question and answer based on the Phase 2 answer. Provide documentation for the Phase 3 answer with data found in the chart.

Chart A

	TYPES OF WORK	VALUES	ATTITUDE		RECREATION	ECONOMY STATE
Iule Family	Weaver 1. Jewelry maker Cattlemen Sheepmen	Data 2.	Data 3.	Data 4.	Hunt 5. Games Stories Stories	Lower-6 middle class
Wong Family	Architect 7. Banker Teacher Student	Confucist 8. Reverence for elders Respect nature fellowman Honor	Concern for 9. others Better to give than receive Very fortunate Beauty in the world is important	Data 10.	Parental 11. decisions Reading Talking Zoo Sisters Brothers Four schools	Upper-12 middle class
Torres Family	Grape picker 13. Orange picker Harvester	Mexican-14. American Religious Brotherhood Nonviolence	People should 15. have equal chance Everyone should have a right to a job All people should have enough to eat	Data 16.	Picking grapes 17. Picking oranges Thirty schools Little parental authority	Generally 18. lower class

188

FEEDBACK

Mr. Miller had his social studies class involved in a discussion of family groups and wanted to investigate factors affecting the attitudes of people.

He prepared a chart comparing the characteristics of different groups of people. He brought the chart to class and began by saying, "Everyone look at the chart and let's try to interpret the information."

__2__	1.	He went on, "Take a look at the 'Types of Work' column. How would you compare the Iules' work to the Torres' work? Sharon?"
__2__	2.	Sharon began, "I would say that the Iules are more craftsmen while the Torres are laborers."
__1__	3.	"OK," Mr. Miller smiled. "What would you say in general about the Iules' work? Sherry?"
__1__	4.	"Well, they're all self-employed," Sherry noted.
__1__	5.	"They are people who work outdoors," Maxine added. (This question and answer is Phase 1 as opposed to Phase 5 because the general statement essentially summarizes the information about the Iules. No attempt was made to generalize beyond the immediate information in reference to that particular group.)
__D__	6.	"Why might Maxine have said that?" Mr. Miller queried. "Jill?"
__D__	7.	"Sheepmen and cattlemen, which are outdoor occupations, are shown in the Iules' work," Jill offered. (In this case, Jill was asked to document the answer that Maxine gave in Phase 1. Notice that she was not asked to explain *why* they worked outdoors, but rather *why she said* they worked outdoors. If she had attempted to explain why they worked outdoors, the activity would have been in Phase 3.)
__2__	8.	"Look at the 'Attitude' of the Wongs and Torres," Mr. Miller requested. "How are they different?"
__2__	9.	"Well," Gary said hesitantly, "The Wongs seem to be concerned with beauty and helping others and the Torres are more concerned with work and food."
__3__	10.	"Very good, Gary. Why do you suppose that is the case? Pat?"

____3____   11.   "The Torres are poor while the Wongs are well off," Pat answered.
(By contrast with question 6, in this case Mr. Miller is asking the class to explain why the attitude of the Wongs and Torres is different.)

____D____   12.   "And what suggests that to you?" Mr. Miller probed.

____D____   13.   "See where it says 'Lower Class' for Torres and 'Upper Middle Class' for Wongs," Carol volunteered.

____D____   14.   "Also, the Torres are grape and orange pickers," Vonnie put in.
(As with question 6, the students are being asked to account for their explanation. Note also that Carol's documentation is actually slightly better than Vonnie's because it is more relevant. The ability to assess the relevance of data is an important critical thinking skill.)

____4____   15.   "What might happen if the Torres were to find secure jobs in one place?" Mr. Miller queried. "Jeff?"

____4____   16.   "I think they wouldn't remain lower class," Jeff said.

____D____   17.   "What might have made Jeff say that?" Mr. Miller went on. "Iris?"

____D____   18.   "They wouldn't have to go to thirty schools so they would get a better education," Iris suggested.

____4____   19.   "Also, I think their attitude would change a bit," Susan added. "It's much easier to be interested in middle class values like beauty when you're not hungry."

____4____   20.   "They would have a closer family life because they wouldn't all be out in the fields," Peggy offered.
(Notice in this sequence that Iris was documenting Jeff's hypothesis, but Susan and Peggy were merely hypothesizing again. No documentation for their hypotheses was called for or received.)

____5____   21.   "What could we say about all the information we have here?" Mr. Miller asked.

____5____   22.   "Well . . . the economic state a person is in affects their values, attitudes, and the way they live to a certain extent," Judy answered.

"Very good everyone," Mr. Miller smiled. "You've done an excellent job."

2.   There are a number of sequences that could be presented. We will present a sample in an effort to reinforce the ideas and stimulate your thinking. We will provide a question and answer for each of the parts as an illustration.

PHASE 2:

Q: How would you compare the characteristics of the Chinese and the Italians?
A: Both worked as laborers when they came to the United States.

PHASE 3:

Q: Why do you suppose they worked as laborers?
A: Perhaps their educational level wasn't high enough.

DOCUMENTATION

Q: What makes you say that?
A: For the Italians it says "Most could not read or write" and for the Chinese it says "Most illiterate . . . "

A second sequence might be as follows:

PHASE 2

Q: How would you compare the contributions of the Italians and the Chinese?
A: The Italians seemed to contribute in more different ways than did the Chinese.

PHASE 3

Q: Why do you suppose the Italians' contributions were more varied?
A: Perhaps because they assimilated more rapidly, giving them more opportunity.

DOCUMENTATION

Q: Why do you say that?
A: It says for Italians "English language added quickly . . . " and "Second generation moved from birthplace," while for the Chinese it says "Slow rate of adaptation of bilingualism," and "Eager to preserve Chinese customs."

MODIFICATIONS OF THE INTEGRATIVE MODEL

Developmental Considerations

We have described the phases in the implementation process in detail, and in doing so we have made an effort to provide examples for a variety of age groups. They ranged from a lower elementary illustration with the seasons to a relatively sophisticated junior high or secondary example with the percent mixture problems. However, several other developmental considerations exist even within these respective groups, and we want to address those now.

The first relates to the medium in which the data are displayed and has implications for planning. In Mrs. Soo's lesson designed for lower to middle elementary students, we saw that a combination of words and pictures were used. The lesson on seasons designed for primary children focused exclusively on pictures. By contrast, the lessons designed for older children used words and symbols.

Any medium appropriate for the developmental level of the students can be effectively exploited for the lessons. For example, consider again the example with the different types of popular music. The teacher in this lesson would not focus on pictures or on words but would instead play excerpts from each of the musical forms. Just as the type of example must be appropriate when teaching a specific concept or generalization, the medium for presenting the data must be congruent with the goals when doing a lesson with the Integrative Model.

The second developmental factor relates to the students' ability to process the information and articulate their conclusions. With young children, the primary activity in Phase 1 will probably be observation and description. However, as the children become more advanced developmentally and more skilled in processing information, they will be able to move beyond simple description to summarizing the data within the cell and generalizing from it. For example, in the case of the immigrants lesson the teacher might direct the students with a question such as, "Look now at all the information in the Italians' 'reasons for coming' cell. Could you summarize the information for us?" This directive might then result in the students suggesting that the reasons were political or perhaps economic, and they might generalize and conclude, "People immigrate for economic reasons." This statement would then allow the teacher to caution the students about overgeneralizing in that the only immigrant group providing the basis for the generalization was the Italians. Recognizing overgeneralization when it occurs is a form of assessing conclusions, which is a fundamental critical thinking skill.

Summarizing and generalizing result in statements that are more general than the data in the chart, which means that the students have gone beyond mere description and have raised the level of their skills. The alert teacher will always be open to the opportunity to encourage the students to practice this advanced processing. With practice, even young children can become quite adept, and as they mature their skills become highly developed. With older students or students thoroughly familiar with the process, the teacher may choose to skip description entirely and move directly to summarizing. Experienced students will realize that they must carefully observe in order to accurately summarize, so observation/description is subsumed in the process.

Young children may initially have considerable difficulty putting their conclusions into words, and they may find stating generalizations particularly hard. Teachers should not worry about this. Part of the overriding goal of the model is to help the children develop their articulation ability. Summarizing and generalizing are skills, and like all skills they improve with practice.

As with the first phase, significant developmental differences exist in the others. Phase 2 will initially be primarily limited to identification of similarities and differences with young children, while older students can be encouraged to subsume simple comparisons by searching for patterns in the information. For example, economic factors exist in the reasons for each immigrant group's arrival, and identifying this similarity represents a pattern. At this point, the teacher could also reinforce the idea of overgeneralizing and note that generalizing from the Italians alone would require caution, but generalizing from three groups is much more sound.

Similarly, the inferences and hypotheses young students offer will be closely related to the information that they see, and they may have a difficult time articulating their ideas. Teachers may have to prompt them for statements until they develop their skills. Even if teachers must virtually "put words in their students' mouths," the students will thereby acquire the experience which will increase their skills development.

Processing Options

Sequencing the phases.   As we have described the phases, a sequence beginning with Phase 1 and moving to Phase 5 is implied. In reality, this sequence can and should be flexible and the teacher should allow it to proceed naturally. To illustrate this flexibility, refer again to Mrs. Soo's lesson. She began Phase 1 by asking the children to describe what toads eat. She stayed in this phase by doing the same thing with frogs. Then she chose to move to Phase 2 and have the children compare what frogs and toads eat. This is a perfectly appropriate option. In fact when asked to describe the information in the second cell, students will often make comparisons instead. Rather than stop them and restrict their responses, the teacher should allow the processing to move to Phase 2. This is what we mean when we say "allow it to proceed naturally." Mrs. Soo then moved to Phase 3 and Phase 4, essentially focusing on only one portion of the chart.

Instead of following this sequence, however, she could have chosen to continue with Phase 1 in another cell, such as 'Characteristics.' She would then have merely stated something such as, "Look now at the characteristics of toads. Describe them for us." This process could then continue for all the cells until the information in the chart had been exhausted. She could then move to Phase 2 and make comparisons among each of the coordinate cells and continue with the process in Phases 3 and 4, finally summarizing the information in Phase 5.

From this discussion, we see the teacher has two distinct options which can be represented symbolically as follows:

$$P_1 \text{ -}P_1 \text{ -}P_1 \ldots P_2 \text{ -}P_2 \text{ -}P_2 \ldots P_3 \text{ -}P_3 \text{ -}P_3 \ldots \quad \ldots$$
$$P_1 \text{ -}P_2 \text{ -}P_3 \ldots P_1 \text{ -}P_2 \text{ -}P_3 \ldots P_1 \text{ -}P_2 \text{ -}P_3 \ldots \quad \ldots$$

Of course the teacher has all the options in between as well. She may analyze four cells with Phase 1, move to Phase 2 with two of the cells, make one inference, and then move back to Phase 1 with another cell. She may even jump from a summary statement in Phase 1 to an explanation for the statement, which would mean that Phase 2 was momentarily skipped.

We have emphasized the relationship between Phases 2 and 3 and have discussed making explanatory inferences as the natural outgrowth of identifying similarities and differences. However, the teacher also has the option of requesting explanations not emerging directly from a comparison. For example, the teacher in the immigrants lesson might direct the students, "Look at the 'Assimilation' column again. We see that the Chinese were mostly in the western U.S., but the Puerto Ricans were in the northeast. Why do you suppose that was the case?" This question may have come after a series of comparisons was made throughout the chart, and the students may or may not have identified the places where the groups initially settled. In this case the sequence the teacher chose would likely have been the first of the options we identified previously. The point here is simply that the teacher need not feel that every explanation required of the students must grow directly out of a comparison.

As in all cases, the teacher's goals for the lesson will properly dictate the sequence. Further, the flexibility provides excellent opportunities for incidental learning, and the lack of restriction allows the students to become creative in their analysis of the information. With practice, possibilities of enormous intellectual growth exist.

Options for documentation.   Our discussion to this point has suggested that student documentation of responses is an important aspect of Phase 3, but it has not been emphasized for the others. However, it can be an important component of each of the phases. For example, refer again to the immigrants lesson and the summary statement, "The Italians immigrated for economic reasons." This response was made in Phase 1, and since more than observation and description are involved, the teacher has the opportunity to ask the students to provide evidence for their conclusion. They could then point to information in the chart, such as:

"very few factories or plants to work in"
"heavy taxes from government"
"poor land"

all of which are economic factors.

The same options exist in Phase 2. For example, students studying the chart on the seasons might suggest, "You can have fun in the summer or in the winter," to which the teacher might respond, "What do you see on the chart that tells you that?" The students could then refer to the smiling faces in the 'Special Things to Do' portion of the chart.

From this discussion, you can see that the process is rich with opportunities to help students develop their thinking skills at the same time as they learn content. Our goal in presenting these options is to increase your awareness of the possibilities, so that you may take increased advantage of them when they arise in your classrooms. Obviously, not every lesson will allow the development of each of the skills or options presented. However, your added sensitivity will allow you to seize the opportunities when they exist. Let's turn now to an additional set of options that can reduce planning time and increase the teacher's efficient use of the model.

USING PREEXISTING MATERIALS: OPTIONS FOR INCREASED EFFICIENCY

To this point our discussion has implied a process where data are gathered and displayed in some form conducive to analysis, usually a matrix. As teachers studying this material, you might perceive a prohibitive planning process that adds to your already busy schedule. This need not be the case, however. In this section we want to discuss how you might conduct activities using the Integrative Model where virtually no time is spent preparing materials, and your planning time is devoted solely to a consideration of goals and the questioning sequence that will best reach the goals.

The process is actually quite simple. You must merely recognize existing materials with the characteristics conducive to the implementation of the model. In the planning section of this chapter, we stated that topics appropriate for use with the Integrative Model have components that are coordinate to each other, and in fact an enormous number of topics are organized in this way. The first option suggests the use of existing charts, graphs, and maps. A second involves existing printed materials. Let's examine these now.

Virtually any chart, graph, or map that contains raw data can be used for analysis with the Integrative Model. For example, consider the following chart taken from a typical chemistry book.

FIGURE 6.1   Example of Chart Found in Text

IONIC RADII*

IA	IIA	IIIA	VIA	VIIA
Li+	Be²⁺		O²⁻	F−
0.60	0.31		1.40	1.36
NA+	Mg²⁺	Al³⁺	S²⁻	Cl−
0.95	0.65	0.50	1.84	1.81
K+	Ca²⁺	Ga³⁺	Se²⁻	Br−
1.33	0.99	0.62	1.98	1.95
Rb+	Sr²⁺	In³⁺	Te²⁻	I−
1.48	1.13	0.81	2.21	2.16
Cs+	Ba²⁺	Tl³⁺		
1.69	1.35	0.95		

*Radii given in angstrom units.

A chart such as this would be found in the text, and the teacher would need do nothing more than direct the students to the page on which it is found. At that point, the analysis process could begin.

As an illustration, consider the following sample questions that would be appropriate for each of the phases.

Phase 1: What do you notice about the group IA ions? Group IIA ions? . . .

Phase 2: How do the radii for the group IA ions compare to the radii for the group IIA ions?

Phase 3: Why do the group IIA ions tend to have smaller radii as a pattern than do group IA ions?

Phase 4: What would happen to the radius of a group IIA ion if it lost only one electron instead of two?

After a series of questions such as the ones above, summary generalizations could be made about the relationship between atomic radii and atomic number, groups of elements, oxidation numbers and other factors.

As with the other examples presented, the teacher obviously has a number of options in analyzing the information. We have presented a single questioning sequence for sake of clarity and brevity.

Consider now the following graph.

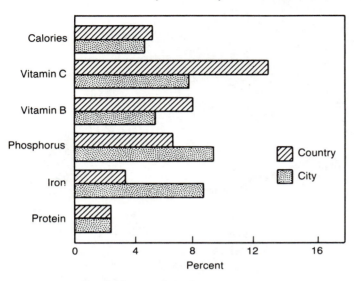

Portion of Households with Calorie and Nutrient Levels
Below Survey Standard by Place or Residence

FIGURE 6.2   Graph Used as Data Source

Let's examine now a possible sequence of phases.

Phase 1:   What do you notice about the nutrient consumption for rural families? For city families?

Phase 2:   How would you compare the nutrient consumption for each group?

Phase 3:   Why do you think the rural families have fewer problems with phosphorous and iron deficiency than do city families?

Phase 4:   If federal money were spent to alleviate problems in the area of dietary deficiency, what type of program would arrest the problem most effectively?

Summary generalizations would be made to bring closure to the information on the graph.

Keep in mind also as you consider these options that this type of analysis does not have to be the focus of an entire lesson. For example, the illustration with the chemistry chart could be embedded within an overall topic of atomic structure, and the entire sequence may take only a few minutes. The same could be the case with the graph relating rural and urban dietary deficiency.

Maps also can be very useful as a form of data retrieval conducive to analysis. Consider the maps on the following pages.

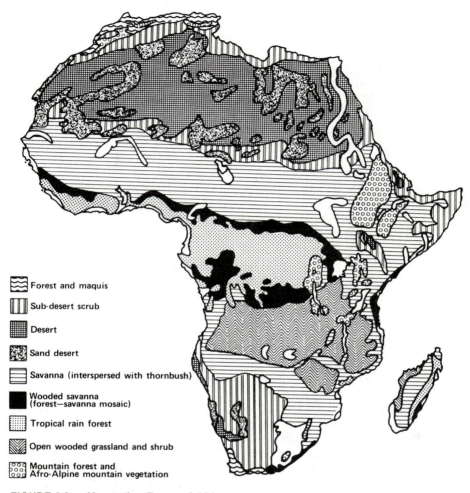

Forest and maquis

Sub-desert scrub

Desert

Sand desert

Savanna (interspersed with thornbush)

Wooded savanna
(forest—savanna mosaic)

Tropical rain forest

Open wooded grassland and shrub

Mountain forest and
Afro-Alpine mountain vegetation

FIGURE 6.3a   Vegetation Zones of Africa

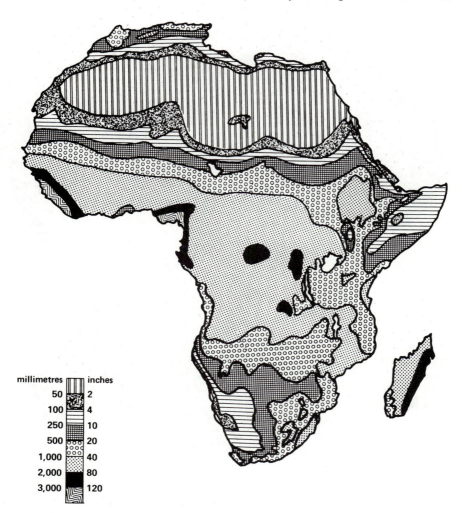

millimetres		inches
50		2
100		4
250		10
500		20
1,000		40
2,000		80
3,000		120

FIGURE 6.3b   Average Annual Precipitation for Africa

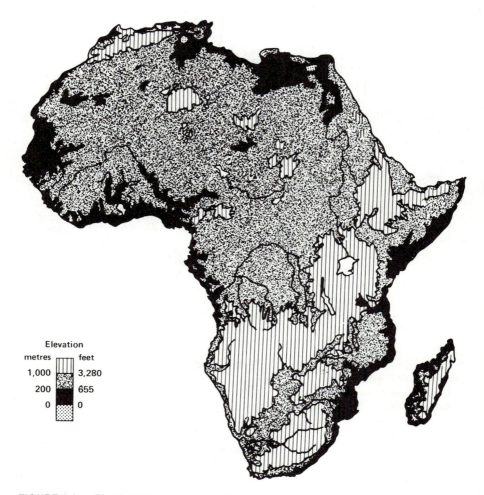

Elevation

metres	feet
1,000	3,280
200	655
0	0

FIGURE 6.3c   Physiographic Regions of Africa

Consider now a possible sequence of analysis.

Phase 1: What do you notice about the locations and amounts of rainfall?

Phase 2: How do the amounts of rainfall compare to the physiographic regions?

Phase 3: Why do the low amounts of rainfall occur where they do? The high amounts of rainfall?

Phase 4: What would happen to the vegetation zones if the amounts of rainfall suddenly changed?

As you see charts, graphs, and maps are very conducive to use with Integrative Model activities. However, options extend even beyond these possibilities. For example, suppose a literature teacher is involved in a unit on American authors which includes biographical sketches and samples of their work. In this case the text itself becomes the source of data and the analysis proceeds from there.

In a situation such as this the teacher has an additional option. During the course of the analysis, the teacher might write some of the students' statements on the chalkboard. After the lesson has progressed to a certain point, the teacher has actually created a brief matrix based on the students' responses. This matrix could then serve as a focus for additional analysis of the information—almost a metaanalysis—which would serve to further reinforce the students' understanding of the content as well as develop their thinking skills. Literature is very appropriate for this type of analysis because the conclusions are much less cut and dried than conclusions in some of the more quantitative areas of study. As a result students could learn tolerance for ambiguity, the ability to reserve judgment, and respect for opposing opinion, among other extended thinking skills.

Many other content areas are equally well suited for analysis using the phases of the Integrative Model. For instance, a geography teacher studying different cultural regions around the world could, on the basis of the text material, describe various features of a region, compare these features in two or more regions and explain the similarities and differences. This processing would be particularly beneficial for the students as a form of review and reinforcement.

As an additional form of review, consider the rules for multiplying, dividing, adding and subtracting fractions. For example, consider the following questions:

> Describe the rules for adding fractions with uncommon denominators.
>
> How are adding fractions with uncommon denominators different from multiplying fractions with uncommon denominators?
>
> Why do you not have to find the least common denominator when you multiply fractions?
>
> What would happen if you found the LCD when you were multiplying fractions?

From this list of questions you can see that the Integrative Model analysis has very wide application with many grade levels and content areas. We hope that this discussion has increased your awareness of the possibilities. We will now turn to a study of evaluating Integrative Model activities.

EVALUATING INTEGRATIVE MODEL ACTIVITIES

Of the models discussed so far, the content and thinking skills outcomes for the Integrative Model are the most complex. As a result, a variety of options exists in preparing items to measure student achievement and growth. We discussed procedures for measuring content and thinking skills in Chapter 3, and you may want to review that material at this time. At this point we want to reinforce the ideas discussed in Chapter 3 with some additional examples. Keep in mind as you read this section that the information is designed to be illustrative and not exhaustive. Our goal in presenting the examples is to stimulate your own thinking about evaluation and perhaps help you generate ideas for some clever test items or other creative systems for measurement.

Measuring Content Outcomes

In the Planning section of the chapter we stated that the Integrative Model, rather than teaching a single, precise concept or generalization is designed to teach systems of generalizations. The evaluation phase of the model would then be similar to measuring students' understanding of generalizations under any normal conditions except the scope of the measurement would be greater. Rather than measuring a single content outcome, several items would be involved to assess the series of generalizations.

To reinforce the information let's look at some additional sample items. For example consider how Mrs. Soo might measure her students' understanding of the generalizations they derived in her lesson. Look at the following item.

Think about the conclusion made about the frog and the toad and their habits. Based on that conclusion, which of the following pairs of animals would likely have the most similar habits?

    a.   a deer and a bear
    b.   a deer and an elk
    c.   a deer and a rabbit
    d.   a rabbit and a bear

This item is designed to measure the students' ability to apply the generalization "Animals with similar characteristics have similar habits," to animals other than toads and frogs. The item has the potential weakness, however, of measuring the students' knowledge of the animals rather than their understanding of the generalization. For example, if the students do not know what an elk is or how it appears, the item would be invalid. To eliminate this possibility the teacher might prepare an item such as the following:

Look at each of the following descriptions of animals. Then based on the descriptions, decide which two will have the most similar habits.

Tony is a swift-running, four-legged animal. He stands about four feet high and weighs over 200 pounds. He has long legs, hooves, and big horns on his head. Tony has fairly sharp teeth in the front of his mouth and large flat ones in the back.

Sam is a muscular, four-legged animal. He has a bulky, strong body covered with thick fur. His teeth are sharp and two of them are a bit longer than the others. Sam is about three feet high and weighs about 350 pounds.

Rocky is a beautiful animal. He stands tall and gracefully on his four slim legs. His small hooves allow him to move swiftly if necessary. He is about five feet tall at the shoulder and weighs over 300 pounds. He is covered with short, light brown hair all over his body.

Blitz is a short animal with a long tail. He has four short legs that are attached to the sides of his body. Blitz can move swiftly for a short distance. He can see in almost all directions with his eyes on the top of his head. His teeth are sharp and stick out a little bit even when his mouth is closed.

In this item the characteristics of the animals are described and the students would make their interpretation on the basis of the description. They would need no prior knowledge of any particular animal. Notice also that any reference to food or where they live is avoided in the description. If they were included, the validity of the measurement would be reduced in that the item is designed to determine the students' understanding of the relationship between *characteristics* and *habits,* such as where they live and what they eat.

An additional value in using the second item would be the potential it has for further discussion. The students based on the descriptions could infer the habitat of each animal, the type of food they would eat, and other habits such as how they would protect themselves. In this way a content measure has the potential for further developing thinking skills.

Measuring Thinking Skills

Thinking skills can be measured at several levels. In the first, the students can be referred to the chart used in the lesson and be asked to form conclusions not developed in class. For instance, referring again to Mrs. Soo's lesson consider the following item.

Look again at the chart involving frogs and toads. Based on the chart, which of the following would be the best conclusion?

    a.   You would be more likely to be harmed by a frog than by a toad because a frog is poisonous and a toad is not.

    b.   A frog would be more likely to survive in a strange place because his habitat is more varied than that of a toad.

    c.   A toad would win a race with a frog because he can run faster.

    d.   Toads get bigger than frogs because the food they eat is different.

In this item each of the choices but (b) is directly contradicted by information in the chart. An item such as this would be a good beginning point in helping students develop their abilities to critically assess information. However, the process can be advanced considerably by changing the level of sophistication. For example, consider the following item.

Look again at the information in the chart. Based on this information which is the best conclusion.

a. A frog is more adaptable than is a toad.
b. A toad's diet is more varied than that of a frog.
c. A toad would probably win a race with a frog.
d. You would be in more danger holding a frog than you would be holding a toad.

In this item, the data in the chart support choice (a) more than any of the other choices, but more interpretation is required by the students in this case than with the previous item.

As we saw from the illustrations, the first level of measuring thinking skills involves asking the students to extend their thinking using familiar data, as was the case with the frogs and the toads. At the second and succeeding levels, the teacher could prepare items similar to the illustrations presented in this section, but the students would have less prior experience with the material. In these cases, the students would be presented with a chart not covered in a lesson and they would then be asked to form or identify conclusions based on the information. These are the types of items we presented in Chapter 3.

Look again at the immigrants chart used previously as an illustration. The following are sample items designed to measure specific thinking skills. For example, consider the following item designed to measure students' ability to form explanatory inferences.

Look again at the chart. Of the following, the conclusion most supported by the data in the chart is:

a. The Chinese came primarily because of adventure while the Puerto Ricans came because of undesirable conditions at home.
b. While the Chinese and Italians came because of agricultural problems at home, the Puerto Ricans came primarily because of population pressures.
c. All three groups came partially because America seemed to offer more opportunities than their homelands.
d. All three groups came because of industrial problems in their homelands.

Consider now the following item designed to measure students' ability to assess hypotheses.

Let's think about some potential immigrant groups. Based on the information in the chart, which of the following immigrant groups would probably have the most difficult time with assimilation?

a. Pakistanis
b. Brazilians
c. Kenyans
d. Greeks

As a final example consider an item designed to measure students' ability to identify irrelevant information.

> Look at the chart. Based on the information in it, which of the following is least relevant to the issue of assimilation?
>
> a. The Italians were Catholics while the Chinese were Taoist and Shintoist.
> b. The Italians learned English more quickly than did the Chinese.
> c. The Chinese were found mostly in the western United States.
> d. The second generation of Italians tended to intermarry with other Americans.

Measuring thinking skills requires careful planning and judgment by the teacher. For instance, if items are based on a chart used in the lesson and the information related to the item has been discussed, it then measures content and not thinking skills. This may be perfectly appropriate if the teacher's goal is to measure content. Our primary concern is that the teacher is clear about what he or she is trying to accomplish and consciously moves toward that goal.

A solution to the inseparability of content and thinking skills is to develop items based on content not covered in the lesson. This also requires caution to be sure that all the information needed to form the conclusions is included in the chart and that the students understand the chart's content. Otherwise, the item measures the students' knowledge of the content or their reading comprehension.

We do not want to suggest, however, that measuring thinking is impossible. With care and practice, you will develop the ability to write items that will not only measure student understanding and thinking but will also serve as a means to promote further student thinking.

DISCUSSION QUESTIONS

1. We briefly discussed an application of the Integrative Model with basic skills when we provided the illustration with number operations. Devise other applications of the model to basic skills activities.

2. Prepare a matrix of the inductive and deductive thinking skills. On what dimensions would they be compared? Prepare another matrix on the Inductive Model, the Concept Attainment Model, and the Integrative Model. Use the matrix as a basis of discussion to help form a schema for the models as discussed in Chapter 2.

3. Phase 5 is analogous to closure for the Inductive and Concept Attainment Models. How is Phase 5 similar and different from its counterparts in the other two models?

4. We discussed prompting and repetition as questioning skills used with the Inductive Model. How might they be employed with the Integrative Model?

5. We said that the Integrative Model belongs in the inductive class of models, and

we also said that forming explanations and hypotheses is a deductive process. Is there an inconsistency in the presentation? If not, why not?

6.   Consider using the Integrative Model in content areas such as art, music, physical education, and technological areas. Discuss how lessons could be designed to promote thinking skills in those areas.

7.   Discuss how data might be gathered and displayed in ways other than using matrices, charts, maps or other written materials.

REFERENCES

EGGEN, P. & KAUCHAK, D. (1985) Thinking skills in the classroom: Where do they fit? How can they be integrated? *Impact on Instructional Improvement, 19*(4), 11–18.

GALL, M. (1984). Synthesis of research on teachers' questioning. *Educational Leadership, 42*(3), 40–47.

TABA, H. (1965). Techniques of inservice training. *Social Education, 29,* 44–60.

TABA, H. (1966). *Teaching strategies and cognitive functioning in elementary school children* (Project No. 2404). Washington, D. C.: U.S.O.E.

TABA, H. (1967). *Teachers' handbook to elementary social studies.* Reading, Mass: Addison-Wesley.

WITTROCK, M. (1974). Learning as a generative process. *Educational Psychologist, 11,* 87–95.

WITTROCK, M. (1983). Writing and the teaching of reading. *Language Arts, 60,* 600–606.

7

DEVELOPING THINKING SKILLS THROUGH INQUIRY

INTRODUCTION

As we have written the material in this text, we have tried to develop the themes of content and thinking skills until they have evolved into an integrated whole. Chapter 4 introduced the basic inductive thinking skills which are combined with the teaching of concepts and generalizations, and this theme was further developed in Chapter 5. In Chapter 6 the deductive skills were added and combined with teaching systems of generalizations. As the chapters have been presented, the content and thinking skills have been expanded in scope and sophistication.

We are now at the point of introducing the concept of inquiry and discussing the goals it is designed to reach and the skills inherent within it. As thinking skills evolve, they culminate in the ability to systematically perform inquiry tasks. The models presented in this chapter are process-oriented teaching strategies designed to teach students a systematic way to approach questions or problems encountered in various content areas. Though originating in science, the process of inquiry can be applied to a wide variety of situations (Driver, 1983; McCollum, 1978).

We can think about inquiry on three levels. In the broadest sense, it can be viewed as a systematic way to investigate a question or problem. Scientists use the process of inquiry to generate and validate knowledge (Brown, Fauvel, & Finnegan, 1981). While this process may seem remote at casual glance, in reality it has a profound impact on our lives. For example, the investigation of disease and other health related matters are all essentially inquiry problems. The tentative conclusions suggesting that smoking, high cholesterol foods, excessive weight and lack of exercise are detrimental to health are the result of inquiry. They originate in studies that ask questions such as: "Why does one sample of people have a higher incidence of heart disease than does another?"

In other cases, such as governmental fact-finding missions, congressional investigations, or probes into alleged inappropriate practice are all questions of inquiry. The airline industry installs the "black box" in aircraft partially to aid in the investigation of accidents. The investigation tries to answer the obvious question, "Why did the accident happen?" They search for the answers in the facts they find related to the accident, and the black box is a valuable source of facts. This is an inquiry problem. The research studies cited as we have developed the content for this text are all based on inquiry problems, such as "Why did the students in one set of classrooms achieve more than those in another set of classrooms?"

Inquiry also occurs on a more personal level. An owner checking his auto's gas mileage under two different sets of driving conditions, such as running the air conditioner or not, has conducted a form of inquiry investigation. Even though the results may be biased by expectations, people who announce they now have more energy because they eat a different diet have partially been involved in the inquiry process.

Inquiry at the most fundamental level can be viewed as a *process for answering questions and solving problems based on facts and observations.* One of our goals in including a discussion of inquiry in this text is to increase our readers' awareness of the powerful role this process plays in our lives.

At the classroom level, inquiry is a teaching strategy designed to teach students how to attack questions and problems encountered in various content areas. As a teaching strategy, the Inquiry Model is operationally defined as a five-step method that proceeds as follows:

1. Question or problem identification
2. Hypothesis generation
3. Data gathering
4. Assessment of hypotheses through data analysis
5. Generalizing

When teachers use the Inquiry Model, they help guide students through these five steps as they wrestle with some problem that is meaningful to them.

On the third level, inquiry is a model designed specifically for the development of thinking skills. Students develop their skills first at the general problem-solving level, and they also practice the specific micro-thinking skills contained within the model, such as generating hypotheses and analyzing data (Beyer, 1984).

We discuss two inquiry models in this chapter. The first is a strategy that teaches students to investigate real questions and problems through data gathering in the form of observations. The second, based on original work by Richard Suchman (1966a), teaches inquiry skills by simulating data gathering through student questioning strategies. Both models have the development of inquiry skills as the major goal but differ in terms of implementation procedures.

To illustrate the implementation of the first type of inquiry in an actual classroom, let's take a look at a home economics teacher using the model.

> Mrs. Hill was beginning a unit on baking breads and other types of baked goods. As she was going over general baking procedures at the beginning of a lesson on bread making, one of the students raised his hand and asked, "Why do you have to knead it so long?"
>
> "That's a good question. Class, any ideas?"
>
> "It's probably to mix the ingredients together well," offered Jill.
>
> "Maybe it has something to do with the yeast," Jim added. "If you don't knead the dough enough, it won't rise."
>
> As she wrote these on the board, she labeled them *hypotheses*. "Let's call these hypotheses or tentative ideas. Does anybody have an idea of how we could find if either of these is correct? Think about it for awhile. Kris, do you have an idea?"
>
> "Why don't we experiment and try these ideas out? We can take the same batch of dough and separate it into several parts. Then we can knead them for different amounts of time. The book recommends about ten minutes. We can do one for ten minutes, one for five and one for fifteen minutes. Then we can bake them like we would normally."
>
> "Good idea, Kris. Class, if we did what Kris suggested, are there any other things that we would need to do to make it a valid comparison? Steve?"
>
> "Well, we'd not only have to use the same dough, but we'd also have to make sure that the kind of kneading is the same. We've found out in here that different people knead differently, and so if we wanted to have a fair comparison, we'd have to make the quality of the kneading the same."
>
> "Good, Steve, anything else, Mandy?"
>
> "Just one other little thing. We know that the ovens in our lab work differently. We'll have to make sure that the baking temperatures are as close as possible."
>
> "Fine, Mandy. Class, temperature of the oven and quality of the kneading are called controlled variables. We try to keep controlled variables the same so that we'll know if the main variable we're investigating—the amount of kneading—makes a difference."
>
> In the lab section, the class proceeded to follow Kris' suggestion, kneading the bread for different amounts of time, baking the different loaves, and tasting and analyzing the results.

Let's return now to our previous discussion of inquiry and see how this lesson relates to the three levels of inquiry discussed earlier. First, students were exposed to a structured way of attacking a question that arose in class and were given specific practice in the subskills contained in the model. From an instructional perspective, the teacher directed the class in the inquiry process through a series of questions that encouraged students to move from a question to hypotheses to data gathering and the subsequent analysis of these data.

In using the Inquiry Model the teacher changed her role as well as students' roles in several important ways. First, she became a facilitator of the process rather than merely disseminating information. As an alternative to pursuing an inquiry activity in the classroom, she could have answered the students' questions directly. In doing so the content of the lesson would have been taught more efficiently in terms of time, but the opportunity for students to experience and learn about the inquiry process would have been lost. Doyle (1983) in a review of articles investigating the type of tasks students are asked to perform in school makes a persuasive argument that students *learn* what they *do*. If they spend their time passively learning facts, they not only develop misconceptions about how and where knowledge originates but also fail to develop the skills necessary to generate their own knowledge (Goodlad, 1984).

This point underscores another important change in both the teacher's and students' roles. As students progress through an inquiry activity, they implicitly learn the structure of the activity itself and also learn the thinking skills which are subcomponents of the model. The teacher helps in this process in two ways by first structuring the activity so students have maximum responsibility for engaging in the processes. Secondly, the teacher can make explicit efforts to directly teach the concepts and skills embedded in the activity. We discuss this in greater detail later in the chapter.

Let's turn now to some considerations a teacher must make in planning for inquiry activities in the classroom.

PLANNING FOR INQUIRY ACTIVITIES

After reading this section of the chapter, you will be able to meet the following objectives:

1.   You will understand the inquiry process so when considering a topic of your choice, you will design an inquiry lesson including all its characteristics.
2.   You will understand the difference between planned and spontaneous inquiry so when provided with a classroom episode, you will determine whether it is planned or spontaneous.
3.   You will understand data sources so when given a description of data gathering, you will determine if the sources are primary or secondary.

Identifying Goals

As with all the models described in this text, the planning process begins with the careful consideration of goals. We have also suggested that goals in general consist of the inextricable relationship between content and thinking skills. With some models the focus may shift slightly, but in all cases both sets of goals exist. The inquiry models follow this pattern.

Content goals.   The Inquiry Model is designed to teach two types of content goals. The first is the identification of cause and effect relationships. In the previous teaching episode the students tried to identify the effect different amounts of kneading would have on the consistency and flavor of baked bread.

Every subject area in the curriculum has topics that contain cause and effect relationships that can be taught with the Inquiry Model. For example, English students can investigate the relationship between an author's life and the content of his writing. An elementary science class can try to identify the causes of improved plant growth. A social studies class can look for the causes of wars and other historical events.

The Inquiry Model can also be used to investigate relationships between concepts that are not necessarily casually linked. These relationships are called *correlational.* For example, a language arts unit on persuasive techniques might investigate the relationship between types of advertising appeals and the product being sold. Or, a social studies unit on jobs and careers could look at the relationship between amount and types of training and subsequent job opportunities and pay. In these examples, there are not clear cause and effect relationships involved. They are more open ended and, consequently, the generalizations that result are not as tightly controlled by the teacher.

Thinking skills.   As we stated in the Introduction to this chapter, some models may have a stronger content than thinking skills focus and vice versa for other models. The latter is the case with inquiry. While cause and effect or correlational relationships can be taught with inquiry models, a teacher with the content as a primary goal would be unlikely to choose inquiry as the procedure. With respect to class time, inquiry is a less efficient means of reaching the goal than another model would be.

A teacher choosing inquiry would have as an important goal the development of the students' ability to recognize problems, suggest tentative answers, identify and gather relevant facts, and critically assess the tentative solution. These are the skills of inquiry, and the development of these skills are the explicit goals of the Inquiry Model.

While the students are the primary investigators in an inquiry lesson, the teacher must carefully plan in order to most effectively facilitate the process. The two primary planning tasks are discussed in the following sections.

Identifying the Problem. Once the teacher has identified a cause and effect or correlational relationship that is to be investigated, the next task is to prepare a question or problem that relates to the relationship. For example, a problem in the noted English example could be "What factors in Poe's life impacted the style of his writing?" And in the science class a problem might be: "What factors affect plant growth?" Ideally, these problems would grow spontaneously out of other class discussions, but they usually have to be carefully planned by the teacher in advance.

This need not be extremely difficult, however. As a class discusses various American authors, the teacher could introduce interesting facts about Poe's life and personality. The inquiry problem could then grow naturally out of the discussion.

The teacher in the elementary science class could develop the investigation of plant growth from the basic concept of plants, the type of plants, and plant parts.

Planning for Data Gathering. In order for the investigation to successfully proceed, the teacher must anticipate a procedure for gathering data which is designed to answer the question or solve the problem. While the procedure for gathering the data should come from the students to the extent possible, the teacher's role in the process is to guide and facilitate the process. This requires planning.

The number of data-gathering options are as broad and diverse as the subject areas themselves. Table 7.1 presents examples of problems and potential data-gathering procedures.

Time. From the preceding paragraphs we can see that an Inquiry lesson is not a single-period, self-contained activity that quickly comes to closure. One of the planning considerations a teacher must make is the scheduling of time to allow the investigation to be integrated with other activities. For example, the English teacher might assign the problem relating authors' lives and their work as a research paper. The students would be asked to select an author, one of which would be Poe in this case, and search for the relationships. As the project unfolds, the teacher can continue with the basic information in the unit or even move on to another unit.

In Chapter 6 we discussed the process of documenting generalizations and explanations with facts. This process can be effectively extended in an inquiry investigation where students would be asked to document their investigations with the facts they find in their library research.

An enormously powerful aid in this case would be a paper that would serve as a model for the students. The teacher could discuss the quality of writing in the paper as well as point out how the author documented the assertions that were made. Our experience indicates that this process rarely occurs in classrooms, but when it does the quality of student work increases dramatically.

TABLE 7.1 Alternative Data Gathering Procedures

QUESTION OR PROBLEM	POSSIBLE DATA SOURCES
1. Relationship of literature content to author's life. (English class)	1. Literature sources plus reference books.
2. Traffic patterns in a city. (Social Studies class)	2. Actual observations of traffic flows at given times and in certain places.
3. Durability of different types of shingles. (Vo Tech class)	3. Shingles placed on floor in high traffic areas.
4. Voter preferences on key issues. (Political Science class)	4. Questionnaires and interviews.
5. Effect of pendulum length and weight on pendulum period. (Science class)	5. Pendulums constructed with different lengths and weights.
6. Historical growth patterns in cities. (History class)	6. Census data and history books.

In the elementary science example, the teacher could guide the students through a process where plants would be grown under different sets of conditions, and their growth would be monitored over a period of weeks. The teacher would simply integrate both the time and the content with the ongoing classroom activities.

Data sources can be classified into two general categories; primary and secondary. Primary data sources come from students' gathering of original data such as observing plant growth and interviewing people. Secondary sources include texts, encyclopedias, and other references in which the information has already been analyzed and interpreted by others. Because secondary sources have been screened through the perceptions and potential bias of others, primary sources are preferred when possible. They also provide students with more opportunities to organize and analyze data. However, if time, cost, or access to the orginal source make gathering primary information impossible, using secondary sources is an acceptable compromise. For example, many questions in history relate to events that are remote in both time and location. In this case careful library research involving good references is appropriate.

The planning for inquiry activities is primarily a matter of organization. Once the goals, sequencing, and scheduling of events are clearly determined, the process proceeds very smoothly.

This concludes our discussion of planning concerns for the Inquiry Model. In the next section we will discuss issues involved in the implementation of the model, but before continuing complete the following exercise.

EXERCISE

Identify a topic and develop an inquiry problem around it. Be certain in the design of the problem that you have considered the following factors:

a. How the problem will be stated and presented to the students.
b. How the data will be gathered.
c. How you will model the process for the students to get them started in the activity.
d. How class time will be spent when the inquiry activity is in progress. Discuss the problem with a colleague to assess its clarity.

IMPLEMENTING INQUIRY MODEL LESSONS

After reading this section of the chapter, you will be able to meet the following objective:

> You will understand the phases of the Inquiry Model so that when given a lesson in which it is used, you will identify each phase.

Having prepared an inquiry problem, anticipated the data-gathering process, and considered the scope and length of the investigation, the teacher is prepared to implement the lesson.

As described in the introductory section of this chapter, the Inquiry Model has five steps:

1. Question or problem definition
2. Hypothesis generation
3. Data gathering
4. Assessment of hypothesis through data analysis
5. Generalizing

We now want to discuss each of these individual steps.

Presenting the Question or Problem

The inquiry investigation begins with the presentation of the question or problem. This process simply amounts to the teacher displaying the written statement on the board or overhead, and being certain that the students understand the language and concepts embedded within it. For instance, the teacher might simply state, "How do you suppose the writers we've been studying have been impacted by the conditions of the society at the time?" or "What kinds of things do you think would help plants grow better?"

There are obviously a variety of ways that the questions can be asked, and the exact form is a matter of teacher judgment. The important thing is to clearly communicate the problem to the students.

Hypothesizing

Once the question or problem has been clarified, the class is ready to try to answer or solve it. In providing a tentative answer, the students are involved in the process of hypothesizing. An hypothesis is an unverified generalization, but for young children it can be presented as a "hunch" or "educated guess." One productive approach to hypotheses generation is brainstorming, in which a number of ideas are produced and subsequently analyzed and prioritized. When using brainstorming in this phase of the model, it is important that students understand that in the initial phases of brainstorming all ideas are accepted.

After the students have developed a list of hypotheses, they are prioritized for the purposes of investigation. Whether or not the inquiry is *open* or *closed* is a factor in this prioritization. In an open inquiry lesson, the teacher does not have a specific generalization in mind but instead wants to have students learn about a general area of the curriculum. Content per se is much less important than providing students with an arena in which to practice their inquiry skills. In a closed inquiry lesson, the content goal is more important and the teacher has a definite generalization as the content outcome of the lesson.

This difference between open and closed inquiry lessons has direct implications for the selection of hypotheses. When the teacher has a specific content goal in mind, he or she will take a much more active role in steering the hypotheses in the direction needed to address the content goal. In a more open inquiry-oriented lesson the teacher can let the hypothesis selection process be more responsive to student interests and needs.

For example, a teacher presenting the problem, "What determines the frequency of a simply pendulum?" would want the students to form hypotheses such as:

"The shorter the pendulum the greater the frequency," and
"The heavier the weight the greater the frequency."

In this investigation the students' data will support the first hypothesis but will require the rejection of the second. In this case the inquiry is closed, and the teacher has both specific content and thinking skills goals in mind. On the other hand, the English teachers' goals would be much more open because the reasons would vary for each author. After all the research papers have been completed, the class could look for patterns in the conclusions that might allow appropriate generalizing.

Data Gathering

However generated, hypotheses are then used to guide data-gathering procedures. The complexity of the process depends on the problem. For example in the case of the investigation involving plant growth, the students could plant some garden vegetable, such as beans, vary the growing conditions, and systematically measure the growth. In the pendulum problem, students would change the lengths, keeping all other conditions constant, and repeat the process varying the weight. These are simple and straightforward data-gathering procedures.

On the other hand, the process of gathering information in reference to American authors would be more demanding and time consuming which would require older and more advanced learners.

While not the case in the examples with the plants or the pendulum, primary data sources are often the most costly in terms of time, resources and effort; secondary sources such as texts and reference books offer the convenience of having other people do the original data gathering. For example, in the introductory anecdote, the teacher could just as easily have referred the class to reference books on the process of baking. However, the students would have less opportunity to directly practice their thinking skills, such as the process of experimenting and the need to control variables, under those conditions. Here Doyle's (1983) suggestion that students learn what they engage in is again appropriate. Original research involving primary data sources is more time consuming and costly, but students learn something different from "mucking about" than from turning to references. On the other hand, the curriculum may not permit large amounts of time spent on original data collection. The important point is that teachers understand these compromises and make conscious decisions with those ideas in mind.

Another decision the teacher must make is whether to conduct the data gathering as a whole class, in small groups, or individually. The most appropriate arrangement often follows naturally from the problem. For example, in the investigation of American authors, the students would most likely work as individuals, while the activity with plant growth would be conducted as a large group, and individuals would measure, water, and care for the plants as the activity progressed. The pendulum investigation would probably be most effectively conducted in pairs.

Data Analysis

In this phase of the model students are responsible for assessing the hypotheses on the basis of the data. In some instances where the data appear in fairly simple form, the analysis process does not require a great deal of effort. In others the process will be much more complex. In certain quantitative investigations, data tables and graphing may be needed in order to use the data efficiently.

At this point in the lesson, it is important that students learn to view the hypotheses as tentative investigative guides. There is sometimes a tendency for students to become attached to hypotheses and to let these hypotheses distort the interpretation of the data. One way to deal with the problem is to sequentially analyze and interpret before turning back to the hypotheses.

A second factor in the assessment of hypotheses is the notion of "right" and "wrong." If the data do not support an hypothesis, the tendency is to describe the hypothesis as *wrong* with the implication being that whoever proposed it made a mistake. This is not the case at all. At the time the hypothesis was proposed, it was the most appropriate answer based on the available information. Added data may require that the hypothesis be subsequently rejected, but the matter of right and wrong should never be an issue.

Generalizing

Closure occurs in an inquiry lesson in several ways. The first is through the acceptance, rejection, or modification of the hypotheses. The second is by tentatively generalizing on the basis of the conclusions. The generalizing process may then lead to new questions, and the inquiry process moves forward. This is the process that goes on continually in the real world. In learning to generalize tentatively, students learn an important lesson about living. They begin to realize that the tidy, structured answers and routines we all strive for often do not exist. In time they develop tolerance for ambiguity, which is a powerful aid in helping them cope with life.

Spontaneous Inquiry

We have discussed the process of inquiry approached systematically. However, one of the greatest benefits in the study of inquiry is a heightened awareness of the possibilities of conducting inquiry investigations that occur spontaneously. Our introductory illustration was based on an actual lesson in which the investigation developed "on the spot." A question arose from the class, and Mrs. Hill was alert and sensitive enough to capitalize on the opportunity when it occurred. A full-scale inquiry lesson was the result.

Other opportunities abound if teachers are aware of the possibilities. In some ways it is like the experience of learning a new word. Suddenly it begins to appear in everything we read. Our goal for you as readers is an increased awareness that will allow you to seize on the opportunities for investigation when they present themselves.

Opportunities often occur when students ask hypothetical questions, as discussed in Chapter 6. For instance, consider the following simple science demonstration where students see an inverted cup of water covered by a card, and the card stays on the cup, preventing the water from spilling.

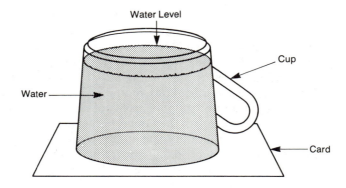

Learners often become very involved with demonstrations such as this and begin to ask a series of questions, such as:

"What if the cup wasn't completely full?"
"What if the cup only had a small amount of water in it?"
"What if the cup were turned 90 degrees?"
"What if we used a liquid other than water?"

These are hypothetical questions. Students could be asked to conjecture answers to the questions and explain why they felt that way. Then each could be readily investigated. For example, the teacher or students could try the demonstration with varying amounts of water. When they found that the card stayed on in each case, they would then eliminate the *amount* of water as a causal variable in the investigation.

Lessons such as this have several advantages. First, motivation often becomes very high. Students see that the investigation results directly from a question they ask. Often students can suggest clever ways to investigate a problem, and a classroom climate of teamwork and cooperative investigation is enhanced. Second, the spirit of inquiry is captured, yet very little time and effort are required from the teacher except to squelch the urge to instantly respond, "It wouldn't make any difference," when a student asks, "What if the cup were only half full?" A much better response would be, "Well what do you think would happen?" and then "Now let's check."

The advantage of inquiry lessons that spontaneously arise from other activities is that students see how the process functionally relates to the subjects they study. The distinction between teacher and student-generated questions is a subtle but potentially powerful one. When students only pursue questions generated by others, they learn that knowledge is external and impersonal rather than functional and integrated. Our view, which is corroborated by others (Goodlad, 1984), is that content is too often presented as preestablished truths. Students are seldom asked to investigate or generate their own. The use of spontaneously generated student investigations can do much to help them understand how knowledge is produced and the relationship of that knowledge to themselves.

Inquiry and Concept Attainment

In our discussion of the Concept Attainment Model we suggested that it could be used to help students understand the scientific method. This is merely the process of inquiry, and Concept Attainment can be effectively used to help students acquire insight into this process. Let's outline the processes.

INQUIRY	CONCEPT ATTAINMENT
1. Problem	1. Problem: What is this concept?
2. Hypothesizing	2. Hypothesizing: I think the name of the concept is . . .
3. Data gathering	3. Data gathering: Students are presented with examples and nonexamples.
4. Analysis of hypotheses	4. Analysis of hypotheses: The rejection of those hypotheses not supported by the examples.
5. Generalizing	5. Generalizing: Forming a definition of the concept.

Concept Attainment can be a very effective tool for the introduction to the processes of inquiry. It takes relatively little teacher time and effort in planning, it can be conducted in a very short lesson, and it can be used to introduce young children to the process before they are developed enough to conduct "full-blown" inquiry investigations.

This concludes our discussion of the General Inquiry Model. In the next section of the chapter, Suchman Inquiry is described. Before turning to that section, complete the exercises that follow.

EXERCISES

Read the following teaching episode which describes a teacher using the Inquiry Model and answer the questions.

Ms. Stanley was beginning a unit on the newspaper in her high school journalism class. She wanted students to understand factors that shaped the form that newspapers took and the role that newspapers played in the total context of journalism. She began her lesson by saying: "Class, today we are going to begin our unit on the newspaper. As an introductory activity, I'd like us to take a look at some newspapers that I've saved from the past week and see what we can discover."

With that she placed newspapers from each day of the previous week on a table in front of the class and put a little sign on each indicating the day of the week.

"Class, what do you notice about these newspapers? Jill?"

"The ones toward the end of the week are fatter than the ones toward the beginning."

"Okay, Anything else, Tod?"

"Sunday looks to be the fattest and seems to have the most color photographs."

"Does everyone agree? Any other observations, Mary?"

"There seem to be more inserts in Wednesday and Thursday's papers."

"Those are all good observations, class. Now I'd like us to go one step farther with one of those, which is the size of the newspaper. I'd like us to investigate factors that influence the size and composition of our daily newspaper."

Saying that, she then proceeded to write the following on the board:

"What factors influence the size and composition of the daily newspaper?"

She continued, "Any ideas, class? How about you, Rob, do you have an hypothesis?"

"It might be feature articles, like things to do on the weekend or travel stuff. Maybe that's what makes some days fatter than others."

"Okay, let's put that on the board under hypotheses. Any other ideas, Sally?"

"It could also be advertising. People have more time to shop for things on the weekend."

"All right, let's put advertising up there, too. Any others, Dave?"

"Another factor could also be sports. There are more sports events on weekends, so that might be one reason why Sunday is so fat."

"That's a good idea, too. Let's stop there in terms of working on hypotheses, and let's spend a moment trying to figure out how we could gather some data related to our hypotheses. Any ideas, Susan?"

"I'm not sure if this will work, but we could count the number of pages that have these different topics on them."

"Interesting idea. Jim, did you have a comment?"

"What about pages that have more than one thing on it? What would we do there?"

The class continued to discuss the procedures they would use to analyze the newspapers and finally arrived at the following table.

TOPIC	NO. OF PAGES	% OF TOTAL
National and International News		
Local News		
Features		
Sports		
Advertising		
Total		

Ms. Stanley then assigned students to seven groups with each group responsible for analyzing a newspaper from a given day of the week. As each group completed its task, it put its information in the form of a table on the board to share with others. When all the groups were finished, Ms. Stanley continued.

"Well, class, what do we have here? That sure is an awful lot of data. To make our job a little bit easier I think we ought to analyze the data systematically. Let's take our hypotheses one by one and see what we find out. Can we look at the "features" hypothesis first? What patterns do you see? Jackie?"

"It looks like in terms of pages there are the most feature articles on Sunday."

"Does everyone agree? Why do you think we see that pattern, Sam?"

"I think it's because people have more leisure time on Sunday to read feature stuff."

"Everyone agree? Joe, did you have a comment?"

"But, look at the percentage column for features on Sunday. It's no higher than any of the others. I can't figure that out."

"Any ideas, class? I see that the bell is going to ring in a few minutes. Let's save the information on the board and continue our discussion tomorrow, beginning with Joe's question."

Answer the following questions based on the information in the scenario.

1. Was Ms. Stanley's inquiry lesson spontaneous or preplanned?
2. Were the data sources that the students used to investigate their problem primary or secondary? Explain.
3. Identify in the teaching lesson where each of these phases occurred.
   a. Question or problem definition
   b. Hypothesis generation
   c. Data gathering
   d. Investigation of hypotheses through data analysis
   e. Generalizing

FEEDBACK

1. Ms. Stanley's actions in the lesson suggested that the lesson was preplanned rather than spontaneous. She had a content goal in mind (for students to understand factors that shaped the form that newspapers took) and came to class with the materials necessary for the activity.

2. Students used primary data sources in pursuing their problem. An alternative secondary source would be to have students look up the information in a textbook.

3. a. Problem identification began when students compared the various newspapers. This phase of the model concluded when the teacher wrote "What factors influence the size and composition of the daily newspaper?" on the board.
   b. Hypothesis generation took place when students offered their ideas (e.g.,

sports, advertising) about factors affecting newspapers and when Ms. Stanley wrote these on the board.

c. Data gathering occurred in small groups as each group analyzed their individual newspapers.

d. The data analyses were just beginning as time ran out. This is not an atypical problem for inquiry lessons, and teachers need to simply adjust to it.

After having examined the hypotheses, the students would cautiously generalize to include other instances.

SUCHMAN INQUIRY: THE ROLE OF QUESTIONING IN INQUIRY

The previous sections of this chapter described the general process of inquiry and how it could be applied in the classroom. In our discussion of the Inquiry Model the problems of time and resource constraints surfaced as major obstacles facing teachers. Often certain problems or topics require greater amounts of time, equipment and effort than can be squeezed out of the curriculum.

In response to these logistical problems, Richard Suchman (1966a, 1966b) developed a modification of inquiry that utilized student questions as alternatives to expensive and unwieldy data-gathering procedures.

Suchman Inquiry has two primary advantages over General Inquiry. First, an investigation can be conducted in the course of a regular class period. This allows the students to experience the complete inquiry cycle in a relatively short period of time, and with practice they become very adept at it. Second, Suchman Inquiry can be used in virtually all curriculum areas with similar effectiveness. As you have seen, the General Inquiry Model can be very time consuming in areas such as social studies and literature. This is appropriate for older students, but younger children often are not capable of managing the scope of the process.

The difference between Suchman and General Inquiry is in the data-gathering process. Suchman cleverly developed a means for gathering data by having the students seek information through questioning. We illustrate this process in the following classroom scenario.

Research conducted on Suchman's form of inquiry was promising; students learned content as well as a control group and improved in their inquiry skills. In a controlled experiment with 196 fifth and sixth graders, Suchman (1966a) found that students exposed to inquiry classes performed as well as a control group that was taught through traditional lecture. More importantly, the inquiry group was able to produce 50 percent more inquiry questions on a posttest task and researchers judged the quality of these questions to be of higher quality and inquiry students to be better motivated.

Let's look now at a lesson illustrating the Suchman Inquiry Model.

Mr. Smith, a biology teacher, was doing a unit on prey-predator relation-ships in the balance of nature. He began his activity by presenting the following situation to his class on an overhead.

In the mountains of the Southwest a number of years ago deer were quite numerous, although the population would fluctuate slightly. There were also wolves in the mountains. Some people from a small town witnessed a wolf pack pull down two of the smaller deer in the herd and were horrified. As a result, the people launched a campaign to eliminate the wolves. To the dismay of the people, the years following the elimination of the wolves showed a marked decrease in the population of the deer. Why, when the wolf is the deer's natural predator, should this occur?

He then went on, "You all remember how Suchman Inquiry works. You are doing the investigating by asking me questions. There are two rules that are important with the activity. What is one of those, Don?"

"The questions must be answerable, 'yes' or 'no'," Don responded.

"Good. And what is the second one? Kathy?"

"The answer to the question must be observable."

"Excellent, Kathy. Now let's begin. Can we get some information to answer this question?"

Steven began, "Have other animals been seen killing deer?"

Mr. Smith responded, "Yes, they have, Steve." With that, he wrote Steve's question on the board with his response.

"Different animals?" Steve continued.

"Yes," Mr. Smith acknowledged, again noting the question and re-sponse under the first one.

"I have an idea!" Pam exclaimed.

"Fine, Pam," Mr. Smith smiled, "but please wait until Steve is fin-ished."

Steve went on, "Does prey-predator balance have anything to do with the problem?"

"That's an excellent thought, Steve, We want to try and answer that. Now, if you were out in the woods looking for evidence, what would you look for to try and answer the questions?" Mr. Smith responded sup-portively.

"I have an idea, I think," Steve said tentatively.

He went on, "After the wolves were eliminated, other predators such as bobcats, coyotes, and large birds, such as eagles, were able to prey more successfully on the deer so their population went down."

Steve then appeared to be finished for a moment, so Mr. Smith re-turned to Pam.

"Jim and I have another idea," Pam suggested.

"Excellent," Mr. Smith praised. "Go ahead."

"After the deer's predator was eliminated, the population expanded so their habitat couldn't support them, and they became susceptible to starvation, and the population went down," Pam said.

"OK," Mr. Smith said. "Can we gather some information to support your idea?"

"Were more bobcats seen in the deer's habitat after the wolves were eliminated?" Ronnie queried.

"No," Mr. Smith said.

"How about coyotes?" Ronnie continued.

"No again," replied Mr. Smith.

"Were numerous barkless dead trees found in the region after the wolves were eliminated?" Sally continued.

"Yes," Mr. Smith said.

"Were deer carcasses found in the region after the wolves were eliminated?" Steve asked.

"Yes," Mr. Smith said.

"Before the wolves were eliminated?" Steve went on.

"Yes," Mr. Smith answered.

"More after?" Steve added.

"Yes," Mr. Smith said.

"Were the carcasses skinny?" Steve continued.

"Yes," Mr. Smith answered.

"Were the deer carcasses diseased?" Steve wondered.

"Some were," Mr. Smith responded.

"Were the deer in the region mule deer?" Jim asked.

"Yes," Mr. Smith said.

"Is hunting eagles against the law?" Bill wondered.

"Yes, it was declared illegal in 1905," Mr. Smith stated.

"Do eagles kill mature deer for food?" Billy continued.

"No, not really," replied Mr. Smith.

"Are the winters in the region quite cold?" Susan asked.

"Yes," Mr. Smith responded.

He then suggested, "Let's look at the hypotheses you've suggested and see how they fit the data."

Joany volunteered, "I think the first hypothesis should be eliminated."

"Why, Joany?" Mr. Smith queried.

"Well," Joany began, "the hypothesis suggested that other predators were the cause of the decline in population, but we've found that there was no increase in the population of bobcats, and the increase in the eagle's population could be because hunting them became illegal."

"Very good, Joany," Mr. Smith smiled.

Bill raised his hand excitedly, "I think we need to change the second hypothesis a bit."

"Go ahead, Bill," Mr. Smith encouraged.

Bill began, "We found that some of the deer must have starved because emaciated carcasses were found and the trees were stripped of their bark, but we also found that some of the carcasses were diseased, which suggests that disease may have caused some deaths."

He continued, "I think the hypothesis should say that after the deer's predator was eliminated, their population expanded so their habitat couldn't support them and they became susceptible to starvation and disease. The wolves take the weakest members, and the herd as a whole is kept healthy."

"Fine, Bill," Mr. Smith smiled.

"We don't know that the wolves do that," Ben noted skeptically.

"I know," Jackie jumped in. "Did the deer carcasses found before the wolves were eliminated tend to be young or old as opposed to the whole range of maturity?"

"Yes," Mr. Smith said.

"That does it then," Jackie asserted. "That supports Bill's idea about wolves taking the weaker members of the population."

The class was satisfied that their hypothesis was supported by the data, and Mr. Smith continued the lesson by discussing the hypotheses that had been formed and linking them to generalizations about prey-predator relationships.

The preceding incident was an illustration of a teacher using the Such-man Model to teach a lesson on ecology. Let's turn now to a description of the model and see how it relates to inquiry in general.

Mr. Smith's activity began with a problem: Why should a population of animals decline rather than expand when their primary predator was elimi-nated? The students then began gathering data when Steve asked if other an-imals had been seen killing deer.

The analysis process then proceeded with the presentation of an hy-pothesis suggesting that the cause of the population decline was an increase in the activity of other predators. A second hypothesis suggesting starvation was presented, which led to the gathering of additional data. The results of the data gathering showed:

1. No increase in number of bobcats (e.g., Were more bobcats seen in the deer's habitat after the wolves were eliminated? No.)
2. A number of barkless dead trees in the area.
3. A number of emaciated and diseased deer carcasses in the area.

This led to the elimination of the first hypothesis and the revision of the second hypothesis to include disease in addition to starvation as a cause for the decline in population. This procedure fit the final steps of General Inquiry in that a cycle of hypothesizing followed by data gathering followed by anal-ysis leading to a revised hypothesis took place. The process of hypothesis for-mation, data gathering, and acceptance or rejection continued until one hy-pothesis was able to account for all the data.

Let's consider the data-gathering process in a bit more detail. First, ac-cording to the steps outlined earlier for the General Inquiry process, hypoth-esizing a solution to the problem precedes the gathering of data. Logically, this is a correct sequence, as the data-gathering process is more efficient when it is based on and directed toward a particular hypothesis. However, students involved in Suchman Inquiry will often begin to gather data before an hy-pothesis has been formed or explicitly stated. This is not a serious problem and usually means that the students are initially somewhat inefficient. As they gain experience with inquiry, their efficiency improves and they will begin to hypothesize explanations before they begin gathering data. At any rate, stu-dent involvement is important, so they should be allowed to initially gather data if they choose. After some data are gathered, the teacher can then en-courage the students to develop a tentative explanation (hypothesis).

The anecdote also illustrates the way in which data are gathered. Stu-dents gather data by asking the teacher questions to which the teacher can respond only yes or no, and the anwers must be factual. These rules allow the responsibility for data gathering and thinking to remain with the students and the teacher can remain a facilitator. Otherwise, the activity can disintegrate into a guessing game. For example, if the first rule did not exist, students could simply ask the teacher to explain the reason, and the inquiry process ceases to exist.

The second is a bit more subtle. A question can be worded so that it is answerable yes or no, but the burden for the thinking remains with the teacher. For example, the question "Does prey-predator balance have anything to do with the problem?" is a question that the students need to answer. They must decide if prey-predator balance is relevant, and if so, is it causal? If the teacher answers the question the way it is worded, the students no longer have to make either decision and they get much less practice with thinking skills. The essence of the model is the practice students get in trying to answer those questions on the basis of factual information. While the means for gathering data are obviously different, the process of analyzing possible reasons is identical to that in the real world. We will discuss the process in greater detail in the section describing implementation.

The activity can be summarized in the following steps:

1. The lesson begins with the teacher's presentation of a problem, which typically asks students to explain why a certain phenomenon has taken place.
2. Students hypothesize a solution to the problem (or just gather data).
3. Data are gathered by the students in the form of questions to the teacher which can be answered yes or no and contain factual information.
4. Hypotheses are revised and more data are gathered, followed by more hypothesizing and more data gathering until a solution accounting for all the data is developed.

These steps will be discussed in detail in the following sections. The next section will be devoted to a discussion of planning for Suchman activities.

PLANNING SUCHMAN INQUIRY LESSONS

After completing this section of the chapter you should be able to meet the following objectives:

1. You will understand topics conducive to inquiry so when given a list of goals, you will identify those appropriate for Suchman Inquiry lessons.
2. You will understand the development of problems:
    a. so when given a series of problems you will select the one that best illustrates the characteristics of an appropriate event, and
    b. so when given a topic you will construct a problem containing the characteristics of an effective Suchman Inquiry problem.

Identifying Goals

Content goals. As with the General Inquiry Model, planning for Suchman Inquiry first involves the identification of appropriate goals. The lesson begins with the presentation of a problem that needs an explanation. This means that the content outcomes of Suchman activities are explanations students generate to explain the problem and ultimately to generalizations based on the explanation. In Mr. Smith's activity the reason for the decline in a population when the population's natural predator was removed was explained and later linked to generalizations about prey-predator relationships. In another example, an English class might be asked to explain why a particular writer's style changed abruptly in the middle of his career, or a social studies class might be asked to explain why a political candidate was elected when all the polls indicated that his opponent would win. Each of the three examples requires an explanation from the students rather than another form of content.

Thinking skills. Again, as with General Inquiry, thinking skills are a primary focus for Suchman Inquiry, and the content and thinking skills are reciprocal and integrated. For example, in recognizing that an alternate reason for an increase in the population of eagles could have been a ban on hunting rather than the availability of deer, Mr. Smith's students were improving their ability to form and critically examine explanatory inferences. This is a skill which is improved with practice and epitomizes the goals of the Suchman Model. Stated another way, a primary goal of Suchman activities is to help students improve their ability to critically assess by using facts the explanations (explanatory inferences) they have formed.

Consider Mr. Smith's activity again. One explanation suggested that other predators reduced the population when the wolves were eliminated. This explanation was rejected when it was found that the bobcat population had not increased. The relating of this datum to the explanation showed well-developed thinking skills. This process was further illustrated when the students related the stripped trees and the emaciated and diseased deer carcasses to starvation and disease as the basis for the decline in population.

The description above shows the strong relationship between content and thinking skills goals in the Suchman Model and illustrates again how content and thinking skills are inextricably related.

Preparing the Problem

After identifying the goals for Suchman Inquiry activities, the teacher's task is to develop a problem which will be the focal point of the activity. When first introduced to the inquiry mode of instruction, teachers often wonder how it can be blended into existing course structures. This becomes particularly difficult because teachers feel responsible for delivering units of content to students in accordance with externally imposed guidelines or prescribed objectives. The solution to the problem lies in the teacher's ability to develop from given units of content, problems which are suitable for inquiry activities. For instance, consider the following topics taken from various content areas that can be structured to fit an inquiry mode of presentation.

1. A social studies teacher wants to teach a unit on major transportation centers in the United States. The unit would include factors which contribute to the growth of the cities.
2. A teacher of American literature wants the class to read a novel such as *The Oxbow Incident* and to understand the human dynamics involved in the story. The study would include such issues as mob behavior and violence and how these psychological themes are blended into the plot of a novel.
3. A teacher of physical science wants students to understand density, buoyancy and Archimedes' Principle as one or more units in the year's study.
4. Psychology students are involved in an investigation of motivation, self-concept, sibling rivalry and other related concepts.

Examples such as these could be cited for nearly every discipline, but instead of examining additional illustrations, let's look now at the examples in more detail.

Consider first the social studies example. In an expository approach the teacher might list and describe factors that are associated with the growth of cities. This description could be followed by selecting several large cities as examples and determining to what extent the factors exist in each. This is a reasonable and legitimate way to deal with the unit.

However, as an alternative, the teacher could introduce the unit in the following way. An outline map showing the location of two fictitious cities might be presented, and the teacher might say,

> "Look carefully at the map. These two cities are both at the mouths of rivers and are both on the coast of this country. Yet one of these two cities has grown into a thriving metropolis while the other has remained insignificant as a population center. Why?"

This is an example of a problem which could be used to start a Suchman Inquiry activity. Continuing with the activity, students would then be called upon to gather data about the problem and to form an explanation which would account for the differences in the two cities.

Let's consider *The Oxbow Incident* example. The teacher could introduce the unit by stating,

> "Three innocent men ride into a Western town, are taken captive, are tried and hanged for a crime they didn't commit. Why did this happen?"

Again, the students as inquirers can, through their investigation, determine what might cause such an event to happen.

The psychology teacher might present a situation in which students are asked to explain why one brother in a family becomes a scholar and honor student while the other becomes a delinquent.

In designing problems (events) for use in the classroom the teacher has two primary considerations to keep in mind. The first is the background of the learner. Mr. Smith's activity could not have succeeded if his students had not known that deer are browsers and that bobcats and eagles sometimes feed on deer. They also needed to have some idea of the effects of overcrowding in a population. Therefore, in planning the problem the teacher must design its level of sophistication so that it makes the students "reach" conceptually, but not be so remote from their background that they cannot grasp it.

The second consideration is in the structuring of the problem itself. Our experience suggests that problems most effectively used in inquiry activities have three characteristics: (1) motivational, (2) specific, and (3) usually involve a comparison. Let's look at each of these characteristics now.

Motivation is achieved through the structuring of events to make them appear discrepant. For instance, in the example from psychology, two brothers from the same family behaving in vastly different ways is discrepant, or at odds with our normal expectations. Differing growth rates of cities with similar geographic conditions is discrepant, and the hanging of the innocent men for no apparent reason is also discrepant. Each of these cases arouses the students' curiosity and creates added interest in finding an explanation to the problem.

The teacher can increase the discrepant nature of the problem (and thus its ability to motivate students) by structuring it properly. For example, in a lesson on the effect of altitude on boiling temperature, rather than merely asking why it takes longer to hardboil an egg in the mountains, the teacher might present the event in the following way.

> Two boys were camping at different locations and began preparing their evening meal. Jimmy built a fire, prepared a stew of meat and vegetables and put it on to cook. Tommy did the same. In a short while Jimmy tested his stew and found it ready to eat. Tommy also tested his and found the potatoes and carrots still uncooked. Why should there be a difference?

An event or problem presented in this way arouses the students' curiosity and is more motivational than merely asking why it takes longer to boil an egg in the mountains. Here, as in other areas of teaching, a sense of theatrics, or at least an intuitive feel as to what kind of events intrigue or captivate children, is necessary. Unfortunately, there is no patented prescription for developing such qualities.

As an additional example of this staging, consider an illustration dealing with good health habits. A teacher might ask the class why it is important to adopt good habits in cleanliness by structuring a problem as follows:

> Pat and Jean are from the same family. Pat is a bright girl with a lot of energy who is rarely ill and almost never misses school. On the other hand Jean, who is also a bright girl, is often ill and misses a considerable amount of school. Why should there be so much difference in the health of two girls from the same family?

This example is similar to the previous one in that it is developed in a way that does not seem intuitively sensible. This has the effect of increasing students' curiosity and enhancing motivation.

The second characteristic relates to the scope of the event. The problem should be narrow enough to provide focus for the inquiry activity, but should still be psychologically motivating. For instance, in the social studies example, the students focused on two particular cities rather than on the growth of cities in general. In the hygiene example the students focused on two girls in the same family rather than on the importance of hygiene in general. The example concerning high-altitude cooking focused on the experiences of two boys on camping trips instead of asking why it takes longer to cook at high altitudes in general.

Narrowing the problem provides a better sense of direction for students and makes it easier for them to begin gathering data. For instance, it is easier to begin gathering data about two girls in a family than it is to begin analyzing health habits in general. The narrower focus also increases the chance that the entire class views the problem the same way and reduces misconceptions about the task at hand.

In looking again at the sample problems, we see that there is a comparison made in each case. In Mr. Smith's lesson, the populations of the deer before and after the removal of the predator were compared. Two cities and two brothers were compared in the social studies and psychology examples. The only case not involving a comparison was the literature example. In general, problems that are discrepant, specific, and involve a comparison result in very successful inquiry lessons.

The major function of the problem is to present a simulated portion of the real world for analysis through inquiry. Consequently, the role of the teacher in this phase of the model is to design experiences which will bring students into contact with a problem-evoking situation. Films, audio tapes, demonstrations, graphs, tables, maps and case studies can all be used to start inquiry activity. In addition, if properly planned, all can provide sufficient data to initiate the data-gathering process at the heart of every inquiry session. Actual selection of the medium should be done after the content area and type of event have been chosen. Characteristics of the learner such as conceptual background, facility with different levels of abstraction and skill in data gathering, should be considered in selecting a stimulus event that is thought provoking but not bewildering. In many ways, the considerations the teacher makes in selecting a medium for presenting the event are similar to those necessary for the selection of examples to teach a concept or generalization. With younger students it must be more concrete in order to minimize memory and experiential demands.

For instance, a third grade teacher in planning a Suchman Inquiry lesson with her class planted two plants. After a period of time she brought the plants to class and displayed them for the children. One obviously had grown much higher and looked much healthier than did the other. The obvious problem was to try and explain why the plants should look so different. Her activity with the young children was very successful, largely because the children could see the actual plants in front of them. With older students drawings would probably have been appropriate, but with the younger children the actual plants were important to the success of the lesson.

In summary, the characteristics of a problem that must be considered in preparing for inquiry can be outlined as follows:

1. The level of the problem must be appropriately matched with the level of sophistication of the learner.
2. The curiosity and motivation of the student are enhanced if the problem is prepared in a way which makes it appear discrepant.
3. The problem focuses the student on a specific problem rather than on a set of problems in general.
4. The presentation of the event accommodates background and developmental characteristics of the learners.

This completes the discussion of the planning phase of Suchman Inquiry activities. Turn now to the exercises which follow and answer the questions based on the information in the anecdote.

EXERCISES

1. Examine the folllowing content objectives. Identify those that are not appropriate for Suchman Inquiry and explain why they are inappropriate.

a. A social studies teacher wants students to know the time span of the Civil War.

b. A science teacher wants students to know the difference between the processes of observation and inference.

c. A humanities teacher wants students to know why the work of Van Gogh changed in emphasis over the period of his productive life.

d. A middle school teacher wants students to learn to cooperate in group activities.

e. A math teacher wants students to understand closure.

f. A science teacher wants students to know why dew forms.

2.   Select from the following list one or more objectives appropriate to your teaching area. Describe an event which would allow the objective to be met using a Suchman Inquiry activity.

a. A music teacher wants students to understand the reasons why some sounds are considered music and others are considered noise.

b. A teacher of literature wants to study the nature of traditions and has chosen the story *The Lottery* as a vehicle for study.

c. A social studies teacher wants students to know factors affecting the decsion to drop the first atomic bomb on Hiroshima.

d. A social studies teacher wants students to understand the factors involved in the astounding victory of Truman over Dewey in 1948.

e. A science teacher wants students to understand that objects will float on a fluid if they are less dense than the fluid.

f. An art teacher wants students to understand the factors which will affect the price of a commercial painting.

3.   Read the following problems prepared for Suchman Inquiry activities. After reading each, decide which one is most appropriate according to the characteristics described in the previous section.

a. Two countries have a common border. Their natural resources are similar, both possessing considerable wealth in minerals and timber. They are of approximately the same size. Country A is a thriving dynamic society with a sound economy, while Country B is struggling for its economic existence and is on the brink of bankruptcy. Why should there be such a difference between the two?

b. Animals have many different ways of protecting themselves. Some animals are small and can hide, others have long legs so they can run. Still others have a form of protection called protective coloration. What do we mean by protective coloration?

c. Students in classes are asked to write themes. Some get high scores while others are low. Why should we see such a difference?

FEEDBACK

The following is a brief analysis of each objective:

1.   a. This objective involves teaching factual information and is not amenable to inquiry.

b. The science teacher wanting students to know the difference between the processes of observation and inference actually wants his students to learn concepts. The concepts could be taught with a Concept Attainment or an Inductive Model.

c. A humanities teacher wanting his students to know why the work of Van Gogh changed in emphasis requires an explanation and is appropriate for inquiry.

d. This objective is not within the scope of information processing models and is not appropriate for any of the models described in this book. While teachers using the information processing models are also interested in group processes and the development of the student as a person, the primary focus is helping students learn to gather and relate information.

e. A math teacher wanting students to understand closure again has an objective which is essentially concept learning and therefore more appropriate to the models designed for this goal.

f. This objective is appropriate to Suchman Inquiry. However, merely asking the students why dew forms does not narrow the phenomenon sufficiently to allow the student to deal with it, nor does it give them concrete information to work with. One of the functions of the event is to focus students' atention on a specific portion of the environment. A more appropriate stimulus event might be:

> Mr. Anderson went out of his house on Monday morning and found that the windshield of his car was all wet. Before he left for work he wiped all the windows of his car with a towel. Tuesday morning as Mr. Anderson prepared to go to work he noted that the car windows were all dry. Why should they be wet on Monday and dry on Tuesday?

The students, in explaining this phenomenon, would actually be explaining the conditions under which dew forms. This description narrows the scope for students and allows them to focus directly on the problem.

2.   a. The event that the teacher could present might appear as follows;

> He could play excerpts of sounds considered to be musical and excerpts of sounds considered to be noise. After playing the excerpts, the teacher might say something such as "Why was the first selection considered to be music and the second selection noise?"

b. The teacher might begin the description of the event in either verbal or written form in this way:

> Mrs. Jones was a typical housewife in the town of Stevensville. She was married to a respected citizen, was the mother of three children, was active in civic groups, and she attended church regularly. However, on Saturday, June 17, the day of the annual community picnic, Mrs. Jones was taken aside and stoned to death by the rest of the people in the town. Mrs. Jones had done nothing to deserve this execution and yet it was performed by most of the townspeople in front of the rest of the citizens who did nothing to prevent it. Why would this happen?

c. The teacher's description of the event might be as follows:

> Hiroshima, a city of approximately 250,000 people, was located at the end of the main island of the Japanese chain. Hiroshma was not the largest city, nor was it the city with the bulk of the military supplies on the Japanese mainland. It was not the main cultural center of Japan. Yet, this city was selected as the target for the dropping of the first atomic bomb in World War II. Why was Hiroshima selected as the first target when other places would seem to be more desirable?

d. A description of the event could be:

> Prior to the 1948 presidential election which pitted Truman against Dewey, public polls favored Dewey by a wide margin. In fact, on the night of the election, one prominent newspaper's headlines reported a victory for Dewey. According to the preelection polls, Dewey was more popular, was felt to be better qualified for the presidency, and had powerful people on his side. Yet, when the final tally was taken, Truman had won a tremendous upset victory. How could this have happened?

e. One description of an event is the following:

> The teacher places two beakers of colorless liquid (water and alcohol) on a demonstration table for the children to observe. The teacher then puts an ice cube into each of the containers of fluid. The ice cube floats on one of the fluids and sinks in the other. The two fluids appear to be the same, and the ice cubes are the same or nearly identical. The teacher would then ask why the object floats on one of the fluids and sinks in the other.

f. In this case the teacher might show the students pictures of apparently similar paintings. They could be similar in style, coloring and framing. The teacher might say something on the order of the following: "The painting on the right sold for $5,000 while the painting on the left sold for $25. When the paintings appear to be similar, why should the one be so much more valuable than the other?"

3.   a. This event has all the characteristics required of an appropriate inquiry problem and is probably the best designed of the three. It poses a problem to be solved, provides students with starting points for data gathering, and yet is limited enough in scope to provide focus for the inquiry process.
b. This problem is inappropriate in that it actually is designed to teach the concept *protective coloration* rather than an explanation. It also is general as opposed to being narrow in focus and shows no apparent discrepancy.
c. This problem is essentially appropriate for an inquiry activity. It could be improved by making it appear more discrepant and narrower in focus. For instance, the event could be described as follows:

> Jim and Susan are two students in Mr. Jones' tenth-grade English class. They each wrote an essay on the same topic, and the length of the essay was almost the same in each case. Both had typed their final product. However, Susan received an A, while Jim got a C. Why should there have been such a dramatic difference in their grades?

This event narrows the focus of the problem and increases its discrepant nature. In addition, the information provided would facilitate the data-gathering process and arouse the curiosity of the students to seek an explanation for this discrepancy.

IMPLEMENTING SUCHMAN INQUIRY ACTIVITIES

After reading the following section you should be able to meet the following objectives:

1. You will know the procedural rules with inquiry activities so that when given a list you will identify those that apply to Suchman Inquiry activities.
2. You will understand acceptable data-gathering questions so that when given a problem and a list of questions, you will identify the appropriate questions.
3. You will understand how a lesson arrives at closure so that when given a description of an activity, you will describe how the lesson arrived at closure.
4. You will understand the Hypothesizing—Data Gathering—Hypothesizing (H-DG-H) cycle so that when given a description of an everyday situation, you will identify the parts of the cycle in the situation.

Presentation of the Problem

The first step in the implementation phase of the Suchman Inquiry model is the presentation of the problem.

In presenting the problem, the teacher's main goal is to insure that all students understand it. The form the presentation occurs in will depend on the kind of problem and type of students involved. Maps, graphs, diagrams or written scenarios are often used. When the focusing event is complex, or the memory spans of students are short, it is often helpful to place the focusing event on an overhead, blackboard or handout. This prevents having to memorize the details and allows students instead to focus on solving the problem.

Hypothesizing and Data Gathering

In presenting the problem the teacher should make a special effort to insure that all students clearly understand the question to be answered or the problem to be solved. When this is not done, inefficient data gathering results.

Technically, according to the General Inquiry procedure, hypothesizing a possible explanation precedes data gathering and serves as a focus for the data-gathering process. In the classroom, the task of explaining the event often begins with the gathering of data. What this often indicates is that the problem is perplexing to students, offering no immediate opportunity to make explanatory inferences.

Beginning with data gathering is perhaps not as pure philosophically but the goal of inquiry is the development of thinking skills, and this goal can be accomplished either way. In Mr. Smith's activity the students began by gathering data, but the activity could have begun with students hypothesizing possible explanations.

Let's turn now to a more complete discussion of the hypothesizing—data gathering—hypothesizing cycle. In an attempt to bring the real world into the classroom for the purposes of examination through inquiry, one constraint is placed on the activity, the method of data collection.

Outside the classroom, inquiry occurs with students observing, handling and manipulating objects and events as they naturally occur in the world. However, in an educational setting, this is impractical because of limitations of time, location and expense. An on-site visit to the location of a city or an animal population generally would not be possible. Having students gather data through written references and other sources often is a slow, tedious process which may discourage many students. In addition, the process of inquiry when spread over a long period of time is not as visible for study by the student. With these limitations in mind, Suchman devised a method of data collecting in which the students ask questions and the teacher acts as an information source and answers these questions. Basic rules guide the interaction. These rules structure the inquiry session and place the responsibility for forming explanations and gathering data on the students. One of the ways that the inquiry model does this is by requiring students to *gather data by asking questions which are answerable yes or no.* This places the responsibility for forming the explanation on the students and promotes the development of thinking skills.

To illustrate this, consider the following problem:

> Jim, in comparing his gas mileage with a neighbor, finds that he gets five less miles to the gallon than his neighbor, even though their cars are approximately the same size. In investigating this problem, an inquirer could ask Jim the question "What's wrong with *your* car?" Doing so, though, places the responsibility of finding the explanation on Jim rather than the inquirer.

There is a parallel in the classroom. Allowing students to ask questions such as "Why did this happen?" takes the responsibility for solving the problem *away* from students and places it on the teacher. One way to prevent this is to stipulate that students in their attempt to solve the problem only ask questions that can be answered with a yes or no. Examples of such questions from the previous problem might include:

> Is your neighbor's car newer than yours?
> Does he keep it tuned?
> (Do you keep yours tuned?)
> Do both of you use your cars for commuting to work?
> Does your neighbor's car have radial tires?

Note how questions framed in this manner require the student to search for possible answers and ultimately to piece the explanation together himself.

As data are gathered, an hypothesis or several hypotheses may begin to form. For example, in the previous situation, some possible hypotheses are:

1. One car is in better running shape than the other and, therefore, uses *less* gas.
2. One car is used more for stop-and-go driving and, therefore, uses more gas.

Once formed and formally stated, these hypotheses aid inquiry efforts by giving direction to the data-gathering questions. With an hypothesis in mind students no longer have to hunt for possible avenues of explanation but instead can proceed with either proving or disproving their hypothesis.

In the inquiry activity at the beginning of the chapter, data gathering occurred in the following questions:

"Have other animals been seen killing deer?"

"Were more bobcats seen in the deer's habitat after the wolves were eliminated?"

"Were numerous barkless dead trees found in the region after the wolves were eliminated?"

"Were deer carcasses found in the region after the wolves were eliminated?"

In each case the questions could be answered with a yes or no. In the event that a student asks a question that is not answerable yes or no, the teacher asks the student to rephrase the question in the proper manner. The teacher should encourage the student to rephrase the question rather than merely note that the form is not according to procedure and leave it at that. If the student is unable to do this, it is advisable to show the student how the question could be rephrased. This type of help may be necessary when students are first introduced to the model.

A second procedural rule for the data-gathering process is that *students must ask questions in such a way that the answer could be obtained through the process of observation alone.* For example, in Mr. Smith's activity the students asked, "Were deer carcasses found in the region after the wolves were eliminated?" The answer to this question can be found through observation alone. On the other hand, Steve's first question in Mr. Smith's activity, "Does prey-predator balance have anything to do with the problem?" cannot be answered with an observation, and Mr. Smith asked Steve to rephrase the question. A primary purpose in Suchman Inquiry activities is to help students learn to make explanatory inferences based on observable information, and Mr. Smith, by answering Steve's question, would have removed from Steve the responsibility for making the inference.

Consider as a second example the question about barkless dead trees in the area. The answer could be obtained through observation (barkless trees are observable), and students could infer that the deer were starving because they stripped the trees of bark. The inference would be further supported by the observation that emaciated carcasses were found. Note that the question "Were the deer starving?" even though it is answerable by a yes or no, would need to be rephrased because *starving* must be inferred.

Let's turn now to some additional illustrations of the data-gathering process with some of the problems described earlier.

Consider first the problem of the two cities with differing growth rates. The following are a list of acceptable questions which could be asked.

1. Is there a large mountain range around Y?
2. Is there a large mountain range around X?
3. Is the highest peak of the mountains around Y more than 5,000 feet in elevation?
4. Is the highest peak of the mountains around X more than 5,000 feet in elevation?

The first two questions indicate that the student is attempting to establish if there are mountains around each city and, if there are, whether or not there is a difference in the ruggedness of the mountains. If the third and fourth questions are asked before the first two, the teacher may want to suggest that it hasn't been established that there are mountains around either or both cities and perhaps the students should gather this information. By contrast, note the following questions.

1. Are the mountains in the area a factor in the cities' different growth rates?
2. Are the mountains related to the growth rate?
3. Are the mountians in the area significant to the growth of the cities?
4. How big are the mountains around Y?

The first three questions are answerable yes or no, but the information cannot be obtained through observation alone. The last question would be unacceptable because it requires something other than a yes/no answer.

A possible hypothesis behind these questions might be that the mountains around Y are too rugged to allow access to the interior of the country, so they hamper travel and commerce and thus impair the growth of the city.

Consider a second set of questions designed to test the following hypothesis: The river near X has a greater capability than the river near Y for carrying goods and people to and from the interior, and therefore, city X grows more than Y.

Acceptable questions to test this hypothesis might include:

1. Is Y on the mouth of a large river?
2. Is X on the mouth of a large river?
3. Is the river near Y capable of carrying ocean liners?
4. Is the river near X capable of carrying ocean liners?

Some unacceptable questions which would have to be rephrased by students are:

1. Are the rivers near the cities significant to their growth?
2. Is the access to the country's interior a factor?
3. Is it important to know about the rivers?

Again, the students who ask unacceptable questions should be encouraged to rephrase their questions. The teacher should be sensitive to the possibility of discouraging students who ask "unacceptable questions." Often, a compliment about the thought or the opportunity to ask the rephrased question is all that is needed to prevent students from becoming discouraged.

Another procedural rule for inquiry activities is: *Once called on, the student may ask as many questions as he or she wishes before yielding the floor.* The rationale for this rule is that it allows a student to plan an orderly sequence of questions. In doing so, the student need not worry about formulating one complex question to gain more than one piece of information but rather can obtain this information in an unhurried manner. Mr. Smith followed this rule when he asked Pam to wait until Steve was finished.

Note also that Mr. Smith encouraged Jim and Pam when they worked on the problem cooperatively. This relates to a final procedural rule of the inquiry model which is: *Students should be encouraged to work together whenever possible.* This facilitates cooperation among students and helps simulate the way in which problem-solving in the "real world" takes place.

This concludes our discussion of the data gathering and hypothesizing phase of the model. Key points in this phase can be summarized as follows:

1. The students are presented with a problem and begin trying to explain it by gathering data or forming an hypothesis.
2. Students gather data by asking the teacher questions which can be answered by yes or no responses, with the teacher acting as an information source.
3. The information gathered through the questions should be obtainable through observation alone. This allows students to gain competence in constructing their own inferences.
4. As hypotheses are formed they may be combined to form the final explanation.
5. The hypothesizing and data gathering continue in a cycle until the final explanation is reached.

Understanding the cyclical nature of the data-gathering—hypothesizing process is central to understanding the Suchman Inquiry Model. In its most typical form the cycle begins with the formulation of an hypothesis. This hypothesis determines the direction of the data gathering. If the data gathered support the hypothesis, then the hypothesis is retained as part of the explanation. If the hypothesis is rejected because of the data collected, then alternate hypotheses are formed and the cycle continues. This process is illustrated in Figure 7.1.

These two alternate paths that the hypothesizing—data-gathering—hypothesizing cycle can take were illustrated in the anecdote at the beginning of the chapter. At one point in the lesson Steve suggested the hypothesis that the reduction in the deer population was due to increased pressure from other predators. However, data gathered failed to support this hypothesis as none of the natural predators of deer increased in number when the deer population was declining. Alternate hypotheses concerning starvation and disease were then offered, and being supported by data, they were ultimately included as part of the explanation.

One way a teacher has to evaluate the inquiry skills of students is to examine the hypothesis-forming—data-gathering cycles which occur. Typically during the first few sessions, students gather data almost at random or without a sense of direction. They may also propose explanations which don't relate to the data, or after an explanation is proposed, they may gather data which do not relate to the explanation. However, after the students acquire experience with inquiry, they become more efficient. Their data gathering becomes directed toward consciously testing an hypothesis, and explanations are developed to consciously account for the available data. Not all data are of equal worth in that some are irrelevant to an hypothesis and therefore do not aid in the formation of explanations. With experience, the students gather less irrelevant data and become more efficient inquirers.

Look again at Mr. Smith's activity as an illustration. His students were quite efficient in analyzing the problem he presented because most of the data related directly to an hypothesis. However, some of the questions gathered

FIGURE 7.1   The Cyclical Nature of Inquiry

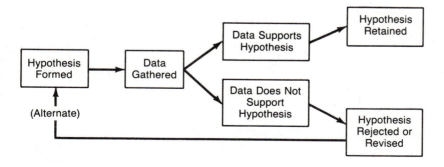

irrelevant data. For example, the question concerning the species of deer was irrelevant to the hypothesis being tested at the time. The severity of the winters was also irrelevant in that they presumably hadn't changed appreciably before or after the wolves were eliminated. The ability to separate relevant from irrelevant data is acquired with practice, and students become more efficient inquirers as they gain experience.

Closure

An intrinsic feature of the hypothesizing—data-gathering—hypothesizing cycle is that its completion provides closure. In the Suchman Inquiry Model, closure occurs when the explanation adequately accounts for all existing data with no further revision necessary. As such, closure is the last part of the implementation phase of the model.

During this phase, students are primarily responsible for reaching and establishing closure. Having formed hypotheses and gathered data, students concern themselves with wrapping up loose ends, relating data to hypotheses, combining confirmed hypotheses, and rejecting unconfirmed ones. Often, closure occurs spontaneously, with students feeling the need to tie things together. At other times the teacher can precipitate closure by asking students to review the work at hand. The teacher in the beginning episode did this when he suggested, "Let's look at the hypotheses you've suggested and see how they fit the data." However, two contingencies may arise. First, the students may be satisfied that an explanation accounts for all the data when it actually does not, or significant factors have not been isolated. In this case, the teacher will find it necessary to prompt the students to gather more data or further analyze the existing data. A second possibility is that the students may be dissatisfied with the form of closure described above and may demand a confirmation of their explanations from the teacher. This second possibility can occur particularly with small children who may initially be frustrated by the absence of a teacher's confirmation of their explanation.

While advocates of inquiry would consider teacher confirmation of an explanation as a detraction from the true spirit of independent inquiry, teachers may have to make pedagogical and affective considerations in keeping with their professional judgment. It is preferable for the students to have a positive affective experience with the inquiry process, which will leave them eager to pursue inquiry again rather than have them leave an inquiry session unsettled and frustrated. If the teacher must confirm their explanations in order for this to happen, then so be it. As the students gain experience and confidence in their ability to form and analyze explanations, they will be more willing to accept their own results and will have moved an additional step toward becoming truly independent inquirers.

Please complete the following exercises which cover the implementation phase of the Suchman Inquiry Model.

EXERCISES

1.   Consider the problem cited earlier which described two girls from the same family named Pat and Jean. Pat was rarely ill but Jean often was. The question was why should there be such a difference between the two girls? From the list below identify the questions which do not satisfy the rules of the inquiry model and would consequently need to be rephrased.

    a. How old are the girls?

    b. Is Jean heavier than Pat?

    c. Are their cleanliness habits a factor in the difference in their health?

    d. Does Pat take vitamins every day?

    e. Does Jean get enough exercise?

    f. Does Pat eat from the basic four food groups every day? Does Jean?

2.   From the following list identify all the statements that *do not* describe Suchman's rules.

    a. Students gather data by asking questions answerable yes or no.

    b. The teacher never clarifies a point, which places the responsibility for inquiry on the students.

    c. Students are allowed to collaborate on the solution to problems.

    d. Students may hypothesize a possible explanation for the problem at any time in the activity.

    e. Students are asked not to make inferences in an inquiry activity.

    f. The information from the data-gathering process should be obtainable through observation.

3.   Consider Mr. Smith's activity described at the beginning of the chapter. Describe how the lesson came to closure.

4.   Read the following short anecdote and describe how the H-DG-H cycle is illustrated.

Two teachers, Susan and Bill, were sitting in the lounge one day discussing an incident between two other teachers.

"I've never seen Joan flare up that way," Susan said to Bill.

"Why do you suppose she jumped all over Mary that way?"

"I don't know for sure," Bill responded. "But I think she's having some trouble at home. I notice that she's edgy when she first comes in in the morning but settles down as the day goes on. Also, she made some snide remark about her husband yesterday morning."

"Yes, I heard that too," Susan nodded. "But I think it was all in fun. Also, she commented only last week how happy she was and how well things were going both at home and at school. I really don't think her home life would cause her to jump on Mary that way."

Joe had also been in the lounge, had seen the incident, and had been listening to Susan and Bill talking. "I think," he said, "that she's simply exhausted and her nerves are on edge. She's taking two classes at the university in addition to teaching, she's the annual and school paper advisor, and now that it's spring she's trying to help with the girls' tennis team. It's just too much."

"That's probably it," Susan agreed.

"She commented that she's averaged five hours of sleep since she started with the coaching. That's been three weeks, and she's probably exhausted."

"Also, her husband sells," Bill added, "and they do an awful lot of entertaining of prospective buyers."

FEEDBACK

1.   The following questions would require rephrasing.
a. This question is not answerable yes or no and is therefore inappropriate.
c. This question is answerable yes or no but the answer to the question cannot be obtained through observation. To answer either yes or no to the question requires the teacher to make an inference and denies students practice in making inferences.
e. This question also cannot be answered through observation. The question could be rephrased in the following way: "Does Jean get over five hours of exercise a week?" or "Does Jean get more exercise than Pat?" These two questions—both answerable through observation—would allow the inquirer to infer whether she got enough exercise.

2.   The following statements *do not* describe Suchman's rules.
b. "The teacher never clarifies a point" is not one of Suchman's rules for inquiry. The decision as to when to clarify a point requires careful judgment on the part of the teacher. The basic guideline is that the teacher should not remove the responsibility for the inquiry from the students. However, if the investigation is leading the students down a blind alley, the teacher may choose to clarify a point in the activity to allow the students to gather more fruitful results.
e. Students not being asked to make inferences in the activity is the direct antithesis of inquiry activities. In these activities students are asked to gather observational data and are then asked to practice making inferences based on these observations.

3.   Mr. Smith's activity came to closure when the class was satisfied that the final explanation (hypothesis) accounted for the data, and the data supported the hypothesis. This occurred when Jackie asked the final question regarding the age of animals and then noted that Bill's hypothesis accounted for the data.

4.   The anecdote illustrated an inquiry problem as well as the H-DG-H cycle. The problem needing explanation was why Joan flared up at another teacher. The first hypothesis suggested to explain this phenomenon was that Joan was having marital problems. However, this hypothesis was not supported by the data which indicated that Joan was happy both at home and at school. Having rejected this hypothesis, our inquirers then formed an hypothesis suggesting fatigue as a cause for Joan's behavior. Subsequent data seem to support this hypothesis but the reader should note that no formal closure was reached.

Developmental Considerations in Implementation

Teachers when first using Suchman Inquiry activities often experience difficulties. These difficulties center around the problem, "My students don't know how to do inquiry." Of course not; if they did, then they would not have to be taught. Both kinds of inquiry activities described in this chapter need active teacher support when first introduced. In addition, as they proceed the teacher needs to insure that all students understand the activity and how to participate in it.

An analogy with learning to play a game might be helpful. When first encountering a new game, two things need to be learned: how the game is played and how to play the game. This is not a "play on words." The first type of knowledge is structural and relates to the rules and goals of the game; in essence this type of knowledge relates to understanding how the game operates. The second is more personal and relates to how skilled they become.

The parallel with learning in inquiry activities is clear. First, students need to understand how the game is played. If students are accustomed to teacher-centered, expository learning activities, they need help in understanding the structure of the activity and their role in it. Once this is understood, provisions need to be made to help students understand the thinking skills involved and how they can become better at them.

Let's address the structural problem first. When first introducing inquiry activities, it is necessary to spend some time and effort to help students understand how the activity works. A sample lesson on a simple topic is an effective way to introduce the structure. Researchers have found that background knowledge has a powerful effect on the student's ability to implement thinking skills (Chi, 1983; Chi and Glaser, 1983). Lack of sufficient background can have a powerful negative effect on students' efforts to develop new thinking skills. Doing a demonstration inquiry activity on a familiar topic minimizes the effect of prior knowledge and allows students to focus all of their energies on the task at hand, that is, learning how the activity works.

For example, the teacher might begin an inquiry lesson on one of the following topics: (1) Why is watching TV Billy's favorite leisure time activity while reading is Joe's? or (2) Why does Nikki like one TV show, and Megan like another? or (3) Why does one group of students like a particular rock star and another group prefer a different star?

In introducing these topics to students, the teacher should explain that a different type of activity is taking place and that a demonstration lesson is being used to introduce them to its structure.

As the teacher walks through the demonstration activity, new terms such as *hypothesis* should be explained and the functionality of the various subcomponents should be stressed (Voss, 1986). For example, if hypothesis were a new term for students, the teacher could provide a simple definition with several examples and explain how hypotheses help to focus our data-gathering procedures.

In both the demonstration lesson and the actual inquiry lesson itself, modeling is one of the most effective teaching strategies (Beyer, 1984). The teacher can do this by "thinking out loud" while proceeding through an aspect of inquiry or promoting this in students by asking them to think aloud or explain how they produced a given idea.

One strategy to build effective questioning techniques in Suchman Inquiry activities focuses on numbers or letters of the alphabet. In this activity students are told that the teacher is thinking of a number from 1 to 100 (or letter of the alphabet), and the class has to find out what it is by asking yes/no questions. The teacher should write questions on the board for analysis later. In addition, displaying the alphabet or the numbers on an overhead helps not only in the data-gathering process but also in the analysis of questions at the conclusion of the activity.

As the activity is done several times, student questions will proceed from "Is it 19?" or "Is it a C?" to "Is it an odd number?" or "Is it in the first half of the alphabet?" Discussing and comparing the quality of different questioning strategies allows all students access to the thinking of the more effective question askers.

Similar types of analysis can be done with the questions asked within an actual Suchman lesson. To do this the teacher needs to write the questions in the sequence they were asked. Then after the lesson is completed, the class can return to the questions on the board and discuss the strategies involved. Asking students to think aloud and explain the questions they asked allows other students to examine the thinking of participants and provides models for the thinking skills involved.

Other developmental strategies to help students learn the process of inquiry relate to grouping. Suchman (1966a) suggested conducting initial inquiry sessions with a smaller target group as participants while the remaining students act as observers. The observers can then focus on the process of inquiry rather than the content. When using this approach, the teacher needs to take an active role in explaining and translating the thinking skills being used to those students. This can occur during the lesson itself or in a postlesson analysis.

Another grouping strategy involves the use of learning teams. Researchers have found peer tutors to be an effective means of teaching both content and skills (Slavin, 1980). When using learning teams in inquiry lessons, the teacher pairs students who understand the process and are proficient at the skills with other students who are not. The skilled student is then responsible for explaining to the other student the strategies and skills involved in the course of the lesson.

As a final note on developmental aspects of using inquiry, some teachers express concern over the ability of young children to participate in inquiry and developmental psychologists have noted that children below the stage of formal operations have trouble controlling variables (Flavel, 1985; Klausmeier, 1985; Lefrancois, 1982). Our experience has been that children as young as kindergarten students can profit from General Inquiry activities if they deal with comprehensible content areas that are properly structured by the teacher.

For example, we have observed kindergarten teachers using the Inquiry Model to teach students about seeds and plants. Students were able to understand the process of inquiry and to interpret the relationship between variables such as watering and sunlight on subsequent plant growth.

The same may not be true for Suchman Inquiry. Our experience suggests that the cognitive strains of dealing with both content and the task of asking yes/no questions is difficult for lower elementary students. A quick way to test for developmental readiness is to use the number or alphabet game mentioned earlier. If they can strategically ask questions in this activity, then they are ready to begin Suchman Inquiry in content areas familiar to them.

EVALUATION OF INQUIRY ACTIVITIES

After reading this section you should be able to meet the following objective:

> You will recognize appropriately written evaluation items for measuring inquiry process skills so that when given several items, you will select the ones appropriate for evaluating inquiry process skills.

The preceding sections of this chapter have described how Suchman Inquiry activities are planned and implemented. In this section the final phase of the general teaching process—evaluation—will be discussed.

Evaluation for Content Acquisition and Process Skills

As in the other information processing teaching models, the two primary goals of content and process are so intertwined that it is difficult to either teach or test only one. Because of this interrelationship, all evaluation techniques must be described as having an emphasis rather than being a separate evaluation. Content measures are not process-free nor are process measures content-free.

The evaluation phase of the model is an essential one in that it provides the teacher with information about an individual's progress, something which can often become masked in the group inquiry process. Students don't all participate equally in an inquiry activity, and the teacher informally observing the class may evaluate the class as a whole on the basis of those who participate rather than on the basis of each individual. The only way to evaluate each student is to obtain information from each student.

Let's turn now to the evaluation process itself. The most critical form of evaluation is the determination of the students' ability to relate data to explanations and to form hypotheses. An excellent way of doing this is with case studies. In this approach students are given an event and are asked to provide relevant hypotheses, data-gathering questions, and observations or data from the focusing event itself. As an example, consider the following items.

For the following situation, develop an hypothesis for Joe's behavior, write two data-gathering questions that could be used to test this hypothesis, and list three observations that can be made from reading the passage.

Two boys had been good friends throughout their childhood. One day the boys were diving from a tree into a swimming hole. As Jimmy crawled out to the end of the tree branch and prepared to dive, Joe shook the branch and Jimmy fell to the ground, suffering a permanent injury to his hip. Why did this happen?[1]

a. Hypothesis: _____

b. Data-gathering questions:

    1. _____

    2. _____

c. Observations:

    1. _____

    2. _____

    3. _____

The following might be responses to the questions.

a. Hypothesis: Joe was jealous of Jimmy's athletic ability.

b. Data-gathering questions:

    1. Is Joe the smaller of the two boys?

    2. Are Jimmy and Joe on an athletic team together?

c. Observations:

    1. The boys were good friends.

    2. The boys went swimming together.

    3. Joe shook the branch.

An alternate way of measuring students' inquiry skills is to provide them with the script from an inquiry session together with a possible explanation

[1]This incident was adapted from John Knowles' novel, *A Separate Peace.*

and ask them to determine the relationship of data to that explanation. As an example of this measurement format, consider the following example based on the social studies problem concerning the two cities.

Both cities are on the coast and exist at the mouth of rivers. However, Metropolis is large and a busy transportation center while Podunk is small and insignificant.

The following is a proposed explanation for why there should be so much difference in size and significance:

> While both Podunk and Metropolis are on the coast and are at the mouth of rivers, the entrance to Podunk's harbor is quite small, and the prevailing winds and tricky currents made entrance dangerous in the early years when sailing ships were used. Further, the coast range of mountains isolated Podunk by land but became foothills by the time they reached Metropolis, leaving it freely accessible to overland shipping.

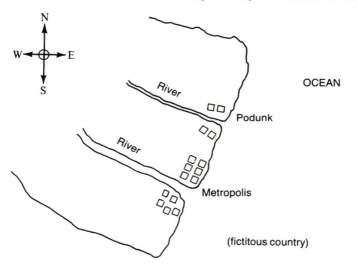

The following data were gathered in the form of questions with the responding answer in parentheses. In the blank by each question write Support (S), Not Support (NS), or Unrelated (U) if the data respectively support the explanation, do not support the explanation, or aren't related to the explanation.

_____ a. Does the current along the coast run from north to south? (Yes)

_____ b. Is Metropolis' harbor larger than Podunk's? (Yes)

_____ c. Are Metropolis and Podunk over 100 miles apart? (Yes)

_____ d. Did approximately as many ships run aground near Metropolis as near Podunk in the sailing days? (Yes)

————— e. Is the river near Metropolis capable of carrying heavier ships than the river near Podunk? (Yes)

————— f. Are the mountains around Podunk more rugged than the mountains around Metropolis? (Yes)

————— g. Are Metropolis and Podunk both in the meteorological belt of the prevailing westerly winds? (Yes)

————— h. Are the local winds more variable around Podunk than they are around Metropolis? (Yes)

As an additional measure of students' inquiry skills, the teacher may also choose to expand the measurement process by asking the students to rewrite the explanation (hypothesis) in keeping with the additional data.

With any type of format for measuring process the teacher should be certain that the situation used in the measurement is one not previously presented. Otherwise, the students may be merely recalling previous information rather than being involved in the process of analysis.

The preceding discussion centered primarily on measurement of the process aspects of inquiry. The teacher can, of course, evaluate the acquisition of content in the same way that content is measured in the other models.

This concludes the section on evaluating Suchman Inquiry activities.

EXERCISES

Mr. Smith, our teacher in the introductory anecdote, wanted to measure his students' process inquiry skills, so he prepared a case study for the students. The case study was composed of (a) a problem, (b) hypotheses suggested as an explanation for the problem, and (c) data gathered to test the hypotheses. He then prepared several questions for his students. Your task is to analyze the quality and appropriateness of Mr. Smith's questions. The case study appeared as follows:

There is a country which is shaped as it appears on the map below. This country is unusual in that most of the population lives on the eastern coast. Why did this unequal distribution of population occur?

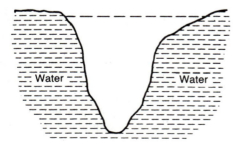

The following hypotheses were included with the case study.

1. There are more natural seaports on the east coast which promote shipping to that area, thus leading to a buildup in population.
2. A mountain range exists on the west coast, preventing the area from being developed.
3. A railroad extended from the country to the north down the east coast, promoting immigration and commerce between the two countries and leading to a buildup in the population in the east.

The data relating to the problem are as follows:

1. The number of seaports on the east and west coasts are approximately the same.
2. The country is flat throughout its area.
3. The climate conditions in all parts of the country are similar.
4. The ocean currents along the east coast run from south to north.
5. Railroads run north and south in the country on both coasts.
6. The first railroad was built on the east coast.
7. A mountain range runs from north to south in the country above the country in question, about 200 miles in from the coast.

Mr. Smith then prepared the three questions which follow. Your task as a reader is to analyze each question and determine if each is appropriate for measuring the process abilities of Mr. Smith's students.

Question 1. Which of the following factors can influence the location of cities?

_____   1. Rail lines

_____   2. Currents

_____   3. Mountains

_____   4. Harbors

Question 2. On the basis of the data, decide which of the three hypotheses can be accepted and which must be rejected, and explain the basis for the decision.

Question 3. On the basis of the data, revise the hypotheses to form a final explanation for the problem.

FEEDBACK

Question 1 would be inappropriate for measuring process skills because it primarily covers content which has already been discussed in class. Consequently, what is being measured here is recall of information rather than process skills.

An important factor in measuring for process is uniqueness, i.e., the students are asked to analyze a problem *not* previously discussed. If the problem is previously unfamiliar, the students' ability to analyze is being measured. If the problem has been discussed, the problem measures recall or comprehension of content rather than process abilities.

Question 2 is appropriate and directly measures the students' ability to relate explanations and data. The question could probably have been described more specifically to provide better directions to the students. For example, the illustrated item with the two cities is clearer and more specific. Again, however, the reader is reminded that the explanation and the data regarding the cities must be unfamiliar to the students or the teacher will be measuring recall of previously covered content.

Question 3 is also appropriate and measures the students' ability to apply the information they've analyzed to develop a revised explanation. A combination of Questions 2 and 3 would be excellent for measuring students' process abilities.

DISCUSSION QUESTIONS

1.   Are there some areas of the curriculum that are ideally suited to inquiry activities? Are there some areas of the curriculum in which it is difficult to implement inquiry activities? What do your responses to the first two questions say about the academic disciplines undergirding the curriculum areas?

2.   Are inquiry activities better at the beginning or end of a unit? Why?

3.   From a developmental perspective, what would be an optimal sequence for introducing the Inquiry Model, Suchman Inquiry, and Concept Attainment I, II, and III?

4.   What would be the advantages and disadvantages of asking students to independently pursue a research topic using the Inquiry Model? If you did this, what would have to precede individual inquiry?

5.   Brainstorm. How many primary data sources can you list in your area of the curriculum? Secondary data sources? Compare your answers with others in your class.

6.   The Suchman Inquiry Model has been erroneously compared to a game of 20 questions. In reality it is very different. Identify the key characteristics that make it different.

7.   How are the planning processes for the Inquiry Model similar to those in Suchman Inquiry? How are they different?

8.   Using concept learning as a perspective, what can the teacher do to improve the quality of questions in Suchman Inquiry?

REFERENCES

BEYER, B. (1984). Improving thinking skills—Practical approaches. *Phi Delta Kappan, 65*, pp. 556–560.
BROWN, S., FAUVEL, J., & FINNEGAN, R., eds. (1981). *Conceptions of inquiry* (New York: Methuen).
CHI, M. (1983). *Interactive roles of knowledge and strategies in the development of organized sorting and recall* (Pittsburgh: University of Pittsburgh, Learning Research and Development Center).

CHI, M. & GLASER, R. (1983). *Problem-solving abilities* (Pittsburgh: University of Pittsburgh, Learning Research and Development Center).

CLARK, W. (1942). *The Oxbow Incident* (New York: The Press of the Readers Club).

DOYLE, W. (1983). Academic work. *Review of Educational Research, 53,* 159–199.

DRIVER, R. (1983). *The pupil as scientist?* (Milton Keynes, England: Open University Press).

FLAVELL, J. (1985). *Cognitive development,* 2nd ed. (Englewood Cliffs, N.J.: Prentice-Hall, Inc.).

GOODLAD, J. (1984). *A place called school* (New York: McGraw Hill).

KLAUSMEIER, H. (1985). *Educational psychology,* 5th ed. (New York: Harper and Row).

LEFRANCOIS, G. (1982). *Psychological theories and human learning,* 2nd ed (Monterey, Cal.: Brooks/Cole).

MCCOLLUM, J. (1978). *Ah hah! The inquiry process of generating and testing knowledge* (Santa Monica, Cal.: Goodyear).

SLAVIN, R. (1980). Cooperative learning. *Review of Educational Research, 50,* 317–343.

SUCHMAN, R. (1966a). *Inquiry development program: developing inquiry* (Chicago: Science Research Associates).

SUCHMAN, R. (1966b). *Teacher's guide: inquiry development program in physical science* (Chicago: Science Research Associates).

VOSS, J. (1986). Problem-solving and the educational process. In R. Glaser and A. Lesgold, eds., *Handbook of psychology and education* (Hillsdale, N.J.: Erlbaum).

8

THE DEDUCTIVE MODEL

INTRODUCTION

The Deductive Model is the Inductive Model's close counterpart. In many ways they are identical; both are designed to teach concepts and generalizations, both rely on examples, and both depend on the active involvement of the teacher in guiding the students' learning. There are significant differences, however, in the sequence of events during the lesson, the thinking skills involved in the processing, the motivational features of the procedure, and the time involved. We discuss each of these features in later sections of the chapter, but let's first examine a lesson that illustrates the model in action.

Miss Lake began her language arts class with, "Today, class, we're going to talk about a different kind of word pair. Who remembers what other word pairs we've been studying? John?"

"Yesterday we were talking about synonyms," answered John.

"Good, and who knows what a synonym is? Mary?"

"Synonyms are word pairs that mean the same thing, like big and large."

"Very good, Mary. How about another example? Toni?"

" . . . Fast and speedy."

"Super! And one more? Bob?"

"How about skinny and thin?"

"Yes, very good example, Bob. Well, today we're going to study a different kind of word pair called antonyms. When we are all done with the lesson today, you will be able to give me some examples of antonyms. Also, when I give you a word you will be able to give me an antonym for it."

She then wrote the following on the board.

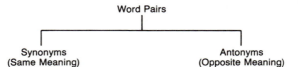

Word Pairs

Synonyms
(Same Meaning)

Antonyms
(Opposite Meaning)

"Antonyms are word pairs that have opposite meaning. What do we mean by word pairs?" Miss Lake asked.

Susan hesitated and then said, "I think pair means two."

"Good, Susan," Miss Lake said with a smile. "So word pair means two words. Now, what does opposite mean?"

"It sort of means different or not the same, I think," Joe volunteered.

"That's very close, Joe," Miss Lake said. She continued, "Let me give you an example. Big and small have opposite meanings and they're two words, so they're antonyms. Opposite means having a different or almost a reversed meaning like big and small."

With that, she wrote big and small under the term, *antonym*.

"Another example of antonyms is up and down. They are antonyms because they're pairs of words whose meanings are opposite. So let's put them up here under the antonym column. Let me try another one. Are happy and glad antonyms? Andy?"

"No," replied Andy.

"Why not?" asked Miss Lake.

"Because the words don't have opposite meanings. They mean the same thing."

"So what are they, Andy?"

"Synonyms."

"Fine, Andy. Let's put them under the synonym column. Now let's try another one. Are cold and hot antonyms? Ted?"

"Yes, because they're a word pair, and the words have opposite meanings."

"So, let's put them over here on the board. And what about alive and dead? Pat?"

"Those are antonyms, too, because they mean the opposite."

"Fine. Now I want to see if you can give me some examples of antonyms. Think real hard. Anyone? Lynne?"

"How about in and out?"

"Good. Anyone else? Alta?"

"How about high and low?"

"And why are those antonyms?" asked Miss Lake.

"Because they are word pairs that have opposite meanings."

"Real fine. Now one last test. Remember we had the word pair *happy* and *glad* and you said that they weren't antonyms? Can anyone make antonyms from these words? Jim?"

"How about happy and sad?"

"Good, Sam, do you have another one?"

"Glad and upset."

"Those are both excellent antonyms. I think you've all done a good job today in learning about this new kind of word pair. Now someone tell me what we learned today. Susan?"

" . . . Well, we learned about antonyms."

"Good. Go on," Miss Lake smiled.

"Antonyms mean the opposite."

"Yes, excellent! And one more thing. Brad?"

"They're word pairs."

"Exactly. Very good, Brad."

She then closed the lesson by saying, "Remember, word pairs that mean the same are . . . class?"

"Synonyms!" they all shouted in unison.

"Fine, and word pairs that are opposite are . . . ?"

"Antonyms!" they again shouted.

"Excellent. Now I have some exercises that I would like you to do individually." She then distributed a worksheet among the students and the lesson was completed.

Let's look at the example and use it to introduce the structure of the Deductive Model. There are four steps or phases to be followed in using this procedure. The first is the *presentation of the abstraction.* In this phase, the teacher defines the concept or states the generalization, links the new material to content previously covered, clarifies terms within the abstraction and explains the objective(s) for the lesson. Miss Lake was in the first phase when she defined antonym, compared it to the concept *synonym* which had been previously covered, clarified the terms *word pairs* and *opposite,* and described what students would be able to do when the lesson was completed.

In the second phase, the abstraction is *illustrated with examples.* Initially, the teacher classifies these examples as belonging or not belonging to the concept, and then she asks the students to do the same. In each case the basis for the classification is explained by relating the examples to the characteristics identified in the definition. Miss Lake gave the students the examples *big* and *small* and *up* and *down* and told them why they were examples when she said, "They're antonyms because they're pairs of words whose meanings are opposite." She then went on to ask the students for examples and a basis for their selection.

Phase 3 in the Deductive Model is identical to the application phase in the Inductive Model. In each case the students are asked to provide additional examples of a concept or apply a generalization to a unique situation. Miss Lake began the application phase when she asked Lynne to give an example, and Lynne responded with *in* and *out.* This phase continued with examples elicited from Alta, Jim, and Sam.

Miss Lake then completed the lesson by coming to closure, the final phase, as she asked Susan and Brad to restate what they had learned in the lesson and had the class identify the label for both synonyms and antonyms.

We will return to these four phases when we discuss the implementation phase of the model. Now let's turn to the decisions teachers make when planning lessons using the Deductive Model.

PLANNING DEDUCTIVE MODEL LESSONS

After reading this section of the chapter, you will be able to meet the following objectives:

1. You will understand the types of content appropriate for Deductive lessons so when provided with a list of topics, you will identify those most effectively taught with the model.
2. You will understand the role of examples and illustrations with the Deductive Model so that when using a topic of your choice, you will prepare examples that can be used to effectively teach the topic.

As the number of options available to us in any situation expands, so do the number of decisions that must be made. So it is with the choice of models. The number of considerations you must make in choosing a procedure increases with the options available. To help you structure your thinking as you consider instructional goals, we will discuss separately considerations of *content, thinking skills, motivation,* and *time.* Each of these will impact your choice of procedure as you plan your learning activities. Let's turn to them now.

Content Goals

Content goals appropriately reached with the Deductive Model are essentially the same as those for the Inductive Model. If learning a specific concept or generalization is the goal, you have either as an option. Identifying the specific characteristics of the concept or the precise relationship in the generalization is identical with both models, and we would encourage you to review the section "Planning Lessons with the Inductive Model" in Chapter 4 to review your understanding of the goal-setting process.

Choosing the number and quality of examples needed to illustrate the concept or generalization is also the same for both models. In each case the specificity in the goal helps the teacher select examples that will be most effective for illustration. The observability of the characteristics in the case of concepts and the relationship in the case of generalizations is no less critical with the Deductive Model than it is with the Inductive Model. A common misconception among teachers is that deductive activities can be effectively implemented with abstract examples, such as words, whereas real objects and pictures are necessary for inductive activities. Nothing could be farther from the truth. Students will sometimes appear to understand the concept from abstract examples because they quickly learn to repeat the definition or generalization and the accompanying examples. However, their learning is primarily at a memory level which does not transfer to new situations, and when asked to generalize they usually encounter great difficulty.

Thinking Skills

The development of thinking skills is a goal that is less overt and explicit with the Deductive Model than with the Inductive Model. While learners are asked to compare and generalize when they classify examples and generate their own, they do not look at a series of examples or a body of data and formally search for patterns. In selecting the Deductive Model, the teacher is making a conscious choice to compromise the focus on thinking skills in favor of emphasis on other aspects of the lesson. In addition, the Deductive Model also sacrifices some of the motivational features inherent in an inductive approach.

Motivation

Because the Deductive Model is less open ended than the Inductive or Integrative Models, less opportunity for students to respond without the uncertainty of giving a "wrong" answer exists, and the possibility of enhanced motivation through this process is reduced. Also the opportunities for incidental learning that often result from open-endedness are somewhat lessened. In addition, the attraction that learners have to a sense of the unknown, inherent within inductive and inquiry-oriented lessons, is lost. As a result it is more difficult for a teacher to recapture the attention of a student who has momentarily "drifted off" using the Deductive Model than would be the case with an inductive approach. This does not mean that a teacher selecting a deductive activity is not concerned with student involvement, success, or self-concept. It means, instead, that a less explicit emphasis is placed on these goals than in inductive activities. Teachers who are more content-oriented or who have a limited amount of time to teach a concept or generalization may opt to use this model. Further, while compromises in thinking skills and motivation are made, advantages can be gained in efficiency.

Time

Because the processing of information in a Deductive Model lesson is less open ended and does not diverge in the same way that an inductive lesson might, it can be used to teach concepts and generalizations more quickly than might be possible with the Inductive Model. This efficiency might cause a teacher to choose the Deductive Model to teach simple abstractions which students quickly learn without much difficulty. For example, consider the concept *quadrilateral*. It is any four-sided plane figure bounded by straight lines. It can quickly and easily be illustrated with examples such as the following:

Nonexamples such as those following can also be readily presented.

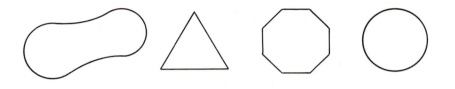

This concept can be taught in a matter of minutes, and teachers may choose to save the time open-endedness would take and spend it on a more substantive concept or generalization.

At the other end of the spectrum, some concepts are difficult to illustrate and students must be coached as to what should be seen in the examples. For instance, in teaching the phases of the moon which is generally a rather difficult concept for learners, teachers often use a flashlight or slide projector as the sun, a globe, and a small ball as the moon. Students then look for the illuminated and shadowed portions of the small ball as it revolves around the globe. This is virtually impossible to illustrate in a large group because all the students must see the light and dark portions of the ball for themselves. A concept such as this may be most effectively taught by having the teacher initially describe and illustrate the process and then coach small groups in what they are supposed to see in the examples. The Inductive Model would be a difficult and uncertain approach to teaching this concept.

This discussion serves to reinforce the position that there is no one best way to teach, and that the most effective teachers have a repertoire of strategies to choose from in helping their students learn. This also allows variety, a factor related to a teacher's effectiveness (Rosenshine, 1971), and it further helps a teacher to match a teaching model to the goals of a particular lesson with a given class. If a teacher has been using primarily a deductive approach with a group of low achieving, poorly motivated students, perhaps an inductive approach with pronounced emphasis on observation would help. With highly motivated students, the mere variety might help maintain their motivation (Brophy, 1983).

In considering the goals appropriately reached with either the Inductive or the Deductive Model, the difference is primarily a matter of emphasis, which can be represented on a continuum as follows:

FIGURE 8.1 A Comparison of the Inductive and Deductive Models

DEDUCTIVE MODEL	INDUCTIVE MODEL
Strong content orientation	Emphasis on thinking skills and affective goals
High structure	Less structure
More time efficient	Less time efficient
Less opportunity for incidental learning	Greater opportunity for incidental learning

This completes our discussion of planning for lessons using the Deductive Model. Before continuing, consider the following exercises.

EXERCISES

1.   Consider the following list of topics. Identify those most appropriately taught with the Deductive Model.
   a. The concept *prime number.*
   b. The rule "In simplifying arithmetic expressions, you always multiply, divide, add, and subtract in that order."
   c. The concept *square.*
   d. The concept *major scale.*
   e. The principle, "For nonmixing substances, less dense materials float on more dense materials."
   f. The concept *gerund.*
2.   Select a topic in your teaching area. Then prepare a set of examples that could be used to effectively teach the topic.

FEEDBACK

The exercises in this section do not have clear-cut answers, and the responses will partially be a matter of professional judgment. The feedback is presented not as the "correct" answer, but rather as information designed to further stimulate your consideration and analysis of the material in this section. Please read the feedback with this idea in mind.

1.   The concepts *prime number, square,* and *gerund* are each straightforward and could be readily taught with either the Inductive or Deductive Model. The choice of one over the other would depend on the teacher's goals related to motivation, thinking skills, or time rather than content.

   The concept *major scale,* on the other hand, is more difficult to process. It can be defined as a scale that proceeds in the sequence of whole step, whole step, half step, whole step, whole step, whole step, half step.

First, some students initially have difficulty perceiving the difference between a whole and half step in music. Second, it might be difficult for the students to hear the notes played and recall the sequence as they tried to describe their observations. A concept such as this might be more effectively taught with the Deductive Model.

In discussing this topic with music teachers, we have found that about 75 percent of them would agree with this analysis and would favor a deductive approach. The remainder view an inductive approach as a viable and exciting approach to teaching the concept.

The principle relating density and flotation is readily conducive to either approach. The major advantage an inductive procedure would have is related to motivation, thinking skills, and the role of observation, which is fundamental in learning science topics.

The rule regarding order of operations could be taught inductively, but a deductive sequence would be more efficient and perhaps less confusing. Students might have problems processing examples inductively without significant uncertainty. For example consider the following:

$$2 + 4 \times 6 - 9/3 = 23$$
$$2 + 4 \times 6 - 9/3 = 9$$

Students who did not know the rule in advance would have an extremely difficult time trying to determine why the first example is correct and the second one is not. As a result an inductive approach might better serve a different topic.

2.   The responses to this item will vary widely. Select the topic and discuss the examples with your instructor or a colleague. The criteria for good examples are the same for the Deductive Model as they would be for the Inductive or Concept Attainment Models.

IMPLEMENTING DEDUCTIVE MODEL LESSONS

After reading this section of the chapter, you will be able to meet the following objective:

> You will understand the four phases of the Deductive Model so that when provided with a teaching episode where the model is used, you will identify each phase.

Phase 1: Presenting the Abstraction

Phase 1 serves as the introduction to the lesson. In it the teacher presents a definition or generalization, links the statement to previously covered content and clarifies any uncertain terms for the students. This phase is the umbrella under which the remainder of the lesson is sheltered.

It begins when the teacher presents an abstraction to the students. This is usually as simple as writing a definition or generalization on the board or displaying it on the overhead to focus the students' attention and begin the

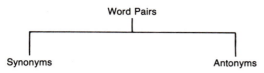

lesson. Miss Lake began Phase 1 when she presented the short structural outline on the board and defined antonyms as " . . . word pairs that have opposite meaning." An outline such as she used, while not absolutely required in every case, provides the students with a link to previously learned content which accomplishes several functions (Bloom, 1984; Brophy & Good, 1986; Rosenshine & Stevens, 1986). First, it provides an opportunity for the teacher to diagnose the students' understanding of the previously learned content; second, it allows for additional practice and overlearning; and finally, it insures that the new material will be connected to their cognitive structure. Miss Lake did this by relating antonyms to the previously learned concept *synonyms.* She simply asked the students to define synonyms and had them give her examples. This allowed her to move naturally to *antonyms* as a new word pair.

After presenting the definition of *antonyms* and linking it to *synonyms,* Miss Lake went on to insure that the definition would be meaningful by clarifying terms such as *word pair* and *opposite.* If the students had not understood the terms, Miss Lake would have taken time to teach or reteach them before moving on to the concept itself. Obviously, students are not able to understand *antonyms* if they do not know what *opposite* means. This process may not only familiarize the students with the key attributes of the concept but also help to channel their attention. In a sense it tells them what to look for in the examples (Klausmeier, 1985; Klausmeier, Ghatala, & Frayer, 1974).

In the case of a generalization, the teacher would check to see if the students understand the concepts within it. For instance, a teacher wanting students to learn the generalization, "If demand stays constant, price is inversely related to supply" would first display the statement, then identify terms such as *supply, demand, price,* and *inversely,* and finally check students' understanding of each. There are several ways to assess students' understanding of concepts, but probably the safest is to ask them to provide new or unique examples. Asking for a definition in their own words is often used, but it is sometimes hard to determine if the definition really comes from the student's understanding or if it is a mere paraphrase of a memorized statement.

Having determined that students understand key concepts, the teacher can concentrate on helping students understand the relationship between the concepts, that is, the generalization. As with learning concepts, this is accomplished by presenting illustrations of the generalization.

A final task in Phase 1 of a Deductive Model lesson is the sharing of the objectives for the lesson. This not only provides a clear content focus but also tells students what knowledge and skills they are to learn and how their learning will be evaluated. A number of studies have shown that stating or sharing objectives with students can have a positive effect on learning (Brophy & Good, 1986; Rosenshine & Stevens, 1986).

Phase 2: Presentation of Illustrations

After the abstraction is presented and clarified, it is illustrated with examples. Their function in learning abstractions was discussed thoroughly in Chapter 2, and their importance was reinforced in Chapters 4 and 5. At this point we want to further underscore the value of examples in learning concepts and generalizations by outlining several additional functions they serve.

In addition to being a primary factor in student learning, illustrations also provide feedback to both teacher and students. If students can correctly identify or supply them, the teacher has a reliable, yet informal, measure of student comprehension, and the students themselves can easily determine if they are correctly interpreting the illustrations. In addition, they provide each student with an opportunity to become actively involved in the lesson, a factor that increases student interest and student engagement rates.

A common misconception about teaching in general and about deductive activities in particular is that abstractions alone are enough for students to understand the concept or generalization. This misconception is reinforced when the students are able to restate the original abstraction. For example, consider again the case with *supply and demand*. A teacher could ask the question, "In a case of constant demand, how are price and supply related?" The student's response, "They're inversely related," could be considered as evidence that he or she understands the generalization. Too often this type of questioning sequence determines little more than students' ability to memorize a string of words. Obviously, the ability to remember the words in a generalization does not insure students' understanding nor their ability to apply it to a real-life situation.

This inability to apply the abstraction is a problem of transfer (Good & Brophy, 1980; Klausmeier, 1985), and the best solution to the problem is the liberal use of carefully chosen examples. In some instances (Miss Lake's lesson for example), the selection of examples is very easy. In others, such as the case with supply and demand, they are not so easy to identify or select, and teachers may have to create their own. This process is further illustrated in the exercises at the end of the chapter. To reinforce your understanding of the different types of examples, you may want to review the discussion of concepts and generalizations in Chapter 2 at this time.

In discussing examples with the class, the teacher provides and explains the first one or two and presents the remainder for the students to analyze and classify. This latter task places the responsibility on the students for linking the examples to the abstraction and provides them with valuable practice.

Miss Lake gave the students *big* and *small* and *up* and *down* and then moved on to having the students classify additional examples.

In presenting examples for student response or reaction, an effective sequence is to present the example, call for hands and then call on a student to explain or respond. Presenting the example to the whole class allows the teacher to see how many hands are raised and how quickly which indicates the breadth and depth of student learning (Rosenshine & Stevens, 1986).

To prevent "call-outs," the teacher may wish to say something such as, "Now on this one I want the whole class to think about it and respond before I call on an individual student. Then I want to see the hands of all the people that think this is an example."

This procedure gets all students to actively respond which allows both teacher and students to see if the new material is being learned. A large proportion of hands raised quickly indicates a generally high level of understanding. A large number of hands raised slowly indicates that students are understanding the material but do not yet feel confident, which means additional examples are needed. Few or no hands with long pauses or latencies may be a sign to go back to the original abstraction to reteach the material (Rosenshine & Stevens, 1986). When students seem comfortable with analyzing and classifying teacher generated examples, the lesson is ready to progress to having students generate their own examples.

Phase 3: Student Created Examples

Having students generate their own examples is valuable for several reasons. It provides them with the opportunity to relate the new material to their own world, and seeing examples that relate directly to their experiences will help reinforce their understanding of the abstraction. It also helps the teacher diagnose the students' ability to transfer their understanding to new situations. If students are able to classify but not generate their own examples, they have not generalized to the most optimal extent and their transfer is not as complete as possible. In this case, additional teacher examples may be needed.

In asking students for examples, the teacher should encourage students to explain and defend their illustrations in terms of the concept or generalization. This insures that there is a link between the words in the abstraction and the experience of the students. Once the teacher is satisfied that students understand the relationship between the abstraction and the examples, the teacher is ready to bring the interactive part of the lesson to closure.

Phase 4: Closure

Closure in a deductive lesson comes through a summary of the major ideas covered in the lesson. This includes not only a restatement of the abstraction but also any important ideas that surfaced in the analyses of the examples. During this phase the teacher should also directly address any problems or misconceptions that arose during the lesson. The summary also sets the stage for homework or seatwork. Miss Lake came to closure when she asked the students what they learned that day, had them restate the definition, and repeat the concept name *antonym* and its coordinate *synonym*.

A critical reader trying to identify the similarities and differences between the Inductive and Deductive Models might wonder why *closure* is identified as Phase 3, followed by the application phase, for both the Inductive and Concept Attainment Models, but is specified as the final phase for the Deductive Model. The reason lies in the sequence for each and the requirements made of the students.

In an inductive sequence, which both the Inductive and Concept Attainment Models follow, a formal statement of the definition or generalization is made by the *students* after examples have been presented and analyzed. On the other hand, in a deductive sequence, the abstraction is stated by the *teacher* at the beginning of the lesson. As a lesson progresses, it is easy for students to lose their focus on the abstraction, and the emphasis on closure can help prevent the potential problem.

This concludes our discussion of the implementation phase of the Deductive Model. Let's continue now by considering how deductive activities are evaluated.

EVALUATING DEDUCTIVE ACTIVITIES

After reading this section of the chapter, you will be able to meet the following objective:

> You will understand the evaluation of Deductive Model lessons so that when provided with a lesson topic, you will describe different ways of measuring the content goal for that lesson.

The evaluation of content outcomes in a Deductive Model lesson is identical to the process with the Inductive Model. This process was discussed in detail in Chapter 3 and reinforced in Chapter 4. You may wish to review those sections at this time.

To further reinforce the evaluation process, let's look again at Miss Lake's lesson. She has several options to choose from in assessing her students. For example she could do one or more of the following:

1. Have the students define antonyms.
2. Give them a list of word pairs and ask them to identify the atonyms.
3. Give them a word and ask them to provide an antonym for it.
4. Give them a paragraph and have them identify all the antonyms in the paragraph.

5. Have them write a paragraph including several antonyms and identify the antonyms in each case.

We can readily see that having the students define antonyms is a very superficial measure of their understanding of the concept unless used in conjunction with another measure. However, each of the others would be a valid indicator of their understanding, with the demands on the students being progressively greater in each case.

An efficient measure of concept learning in general is to have the students classify examples and nonexamples of the concept. In this case Miss Lake could present the students with an item such as the following:

Circle each of the following word pairs that are antonyms.

a. heard   herd
b. too   two
c. hard   soft
d. pretty   beautiful
e. came   went
f. fast   slow
g. big   large

An item such as this not only is a valid measure of student understanding, but it is also easy to prepare and score. With the ever increasing demands on teacher time, classifying examples is a very efficient measure that can be readily implemented.

Obviously, several other measurement procedures could also be effectively used. We have presented the previous example for sake of reinforcement and understanding, and we do not intend to suggest that it is the only appropriate format. We would strongly encourage teachers to use their professional judgment in making decisions about the most appropriate way to measure student outcomes.

Because the Deductive Model is strongly content oriented in its format, a discussion of measuring for thinking skills would not be appropriate in this section. Instead, turn now to the exercises designed to reinforce your understanding of the material in the chapter.

EXERCISES

Let's look again at the generalization relating supply and demand. Read the anecdote that illustrates a social studies teacher using the Deductive Model to teach the generalization, and answer the questions that follow.

Mrs. Evans wanted to teach her students the generalization "If demand stays constant, price is inversely related to supply."

She began her lesson by stating, "We have been studying the economics of different countries for several lessons, so let's review what we've done so far. What do we mean by economics? Jerry?"

"Economics sort of deals with money," he responded.

"Good, and what particular aspects of money? Tim?"

" . . . Well, it tells how money is made and how it is spread around," Tim answered.

"Excellent, Tim!" Mrs. Evans exclaimed. "Now everyone, today we're going to deal with a particular law in economics. This law states that 'When demand stays constant, price and supply are inversely related,'" and as she stated the generalization, she wrote it on the chalkboard.

"Now how does this relate to economics? Cheryl?"

"Price relates to money and how someone would make money," Cheryl answered after hesitating briefly.

"Yes! Very good, Cheryl. Now let's look at the terms *supply, demand, price,* and *inversely.* What does the word inversely mean? Mike?"

"It means something like when one thing gets bigger, another gets smaller," Mike responded.

Mrs. Evans continued the discussion of each term until she was satisfied that the students' conception of each was valid. At that point she went on with the lesson. Let's return to it now.

Mrs. Evans then said to the students, "Let's look now at the overhead. The paragraph on it illustrates the generalization." With that she showed the students the following example.

> As I drove into a city of approximately a half million people in August of 1972, I filled my car with gas at an independent station for 24.9 cents per gallon.
>
> In March of 1974, I made a trip into the same city. I could hardly get across some streets because cars were lined up so close together at stations. I looked at a pump which said 62.9 cents for regular. I recalled the Arab embargo was on at that time.

After allowing the students time to read the anecdote she asked, "How does the example relate to our generalization? Judy?"

After hesitating Judy answered, "The embargo would mean that the supply was reduced."

"Yes, you've identified a key variable in the example, Judy. What else? David?"

"The price shot way up," David answered quickly.

"And what do we call that kind of relationship?"

" . . . Oh. That's what inversely means," David answered after thinking a moment.

"And the amount people wanted to buy stayed about the same," Anna volunteered.

"Very well done," Mrs. Evans smiled. "We see how the example illustrates that the price and supply are inversely related if the demand stays the same."

"Now look at the following example and tell me if it illustrates the law," she went on. She then showed them the following example.

> Jimmy decided to put up a lemonade stand. He charged four cents a cup, and people were buying lemonade at the corner of his father's lot faster than he could make it. Jimmy decided, "I'll bet they'll still buy my lemonade if I charge five cents a glass." So he did.
>
> Two days later Joey, who saw how well Jimmy was making out, decided to open up his own lemonade stand across the street from Jimmy's. He charged three cents a glass, and soon most of the people who had been stopping at Jimmy's stand were going to Joey's instead. Jimmy then lowered his price to three cents a glass, and both the boys sold lemonade.

"Does this example illustrate the principle we've been discussing?" Mrs. Evans wondered.

"..."

"How is the demand affected by Joey opening his stand? Jason?"

"I guess it isn't. It should be about the same."

"Very good, Jason. There is no reason to think that Joey's stand would have any effect on the amount people wanted to buy."

"Yes, Kristy," Mrs. Evans smiled in response to Kristy's waving hand.

"I've got it," Kristy said excitedly. "Since the demand was the same and Joey's stand increased the supply, the price had to go down, which is an inverse relationship."

"Excellent analysis, Kristy. So does the example illustrate the principle?"

"Yes," Kristy replied confidently.

"Let me show you one more," Mrs. Evans said, and she displayed the following example on the screen.

> In the years immediately following the launch of the Soviet Sputnik (1957), the United States felt that they were at a technological disadvantage with respect to the Soviet Union. They then launched a campaign to prepare and train more scientists and engineers to make up the gap they felt. At that time, a Ph.D. in some science areas could virtually name his salary at most universities.
>
> Later years showed increased good relations with the Soviet Union and detente as a political reality. This, together with concerns for the environment, caused a reduced emphasis on the "pure" sciences. Still the pendulum had not totally shifted, and approximately the same number of people were still taking degrees in the sciences and engineering.
>
> In 1977, if some scientists could get a job at all, they would receive salaries lower than those commanded in many other professional areas.

"Does this example illustrate the law we're discussing?" Mrs. Evans queried. "Karen?"

"I'm not sure," Karen answered.

"Let's look carefully," Mrs. Evans suggested. "What has happened to the price?"

"Their salaries were lower," Karen tentatively suggested.

"Yes they were. That's good Karen. Now, how about the supply? Jan?"

"It doesn't look to me as if it's changed that much."

"Aha! But the demand has gone down!" John added with a look of insightfulness on his face. "The example doesn't illustrate the idea we're discussing, because our generalization says the demand stays constant."

"Bravo, everyone!" Mrs. Evans gushed. "That is an excellent analysis. Since you've done so well, think now and see if you can create some examples that illustrate the generalization."

The students with Mrs. Evans's help then generated some additional examples which they analyzed as they had the first three. She then continued,

"Let's look at what we've done so far. What have we been discussing? Toni?"

" . . . We're studying a law or generalization in economics."

"Good. And what is the law? Kim?"

"If the supply goes up the price goes down." Kim answered.

"Good, Kim. But under what conditions?"

"The demand stays the same," Kim answered quickly.

"And what would be a case of that? Bob?"

"When Joey opened his lemonade stand, the supply was increased, so the price had to go down," Bob responded.

"Excellent, everyone. You've done a superior job with this idea."

Look now at the following questions.

1.   Identify each of the phases of the Deductive Model in Mrs. Evans's lesson.
2.   Consider evaluating the abstraction that Mrs. Evans taught. Prepare a test item that could be used to evaluate the principle.

FEEDBACK

1.   Mrs. Evans opened the lesson by reviewing the topic *economics* with the class. This provided the link between the work in the previous class period and what they were to do that day. She then went on to present the generalization and clarify the terms *supply, demand, price,* and *inversely.* This part of the lesson made up Phase 1.

Phase 2 began when she presented the example with gas prices and told the students it illustrated the law. She then showed the students two more examples, asking them to determine if they illustrated the generalization.

Mrs. Evans only used three examples in Phase 2. There could be two possible reasons for this. First, in terms of preparation, creating examples of a principle such as the one in her lesson is more demanding than might be the case for some other concepts or generalizations. Second, and more importantly, the students seemed to analyze the examples with facility, which would allow the lesson to smoothly progress to Phase 3.

Phase 3 began when Mrs. Evans asked the students to create some examples of their own, and she began Phase 4 when she said, "Let's look at what we've done so far. What have we been discussing?" . . .

2.   Mrs. Evans could evaluate the students' understanding of the generalization by

presenting some additional examples and having them classify the examples as illustrating or not illustrating the generalization. This should be done in a formal setting where she would get information from each individual. She informally measured the students' understanding in Phases 2 and 3 of the lesson.

An excellent additional measure would be a seatwork or homework assignment in which the students would be asked to create in writing some additional examples.

DISCUSSION QUESTIONS

1.   Compare the Deductive Model to the Inductive and Concept Attainment Models. What are the primary similarities and differences? What are relative advantages and disadvantages of each?

2.   How does the Deductive Model differ from typical lecture procedures? What are its advantages and disadvantages compared to the lecture method?

3.   We encouraged in the exercises an analysis of content that would be effectively taught with the Deductive Model. Consider now other circumstances that might make a Deductive Model lesson more effective than an Inductive Model lesson. How do the type of students to be taught and goals of the lesson affect this decision?

4.   Consider content goals again. How do these goals affect the decision to select the Inductive or Deductive Model? Discuss this question in terms of the abstractness of the concept or generalization, vagueness of the abstraction, and background familiarity to students.

5.   What alternative does the teacher have if he or she reaches the end of a Deductive lesson and the students still do not understand the abstraction? How would this compare to an Inductive lesson?

6.   Compare the amount of teacher talk and student talk in a Deductive compared to an Inductive lesson. What conditions could cause these amounts to vary?

7.   We have suggested that the emphasis in thinking skills with the Deductive Model is less than it would be with the Inductive Model. Consider again Mrs. Evans's lesson. How did she promote thinking skills on the part of her students even though her approach was Deductive?

8.   Consider again Mrs. Evans's lesson in terms of questioning skills, such as prompting and repetition. How did she employ the skills in the lesson?

REFERENCES

BLOOM, B. (1984). The search for methods of group instruction as effective as one to one tutoring. *Educational Leadership, 41* (8), 4–17.

BROPHY, J. (1983). *Conceptualizing Student Motivation* (East Lansing, Michigan: Institute for Research on Teaching, Michigan State University).

BROPHY, J. & T. GOOD. (1986). Teacher behavior and student achievement. In M. Wittrock, ed., *Handbook of Research on Teaching,* 3rd ed. (New York: Macmillan) pp. 328–375.

GOOD, T & J. BROPHY. (1980). *Educational Psychology: A Realistic Approach,* 2nd ed. (New York: Holt, Rinehart & Winston).

KLAUSMEIER, H., E. GHATALA, & D. FRAYER. (1974). *Conceptual Learning and Development* (New York: Academic Press).

KLAUSMEIER, H. (1985). *Educational Psychology,* 5th ed. (New York: Harper and Row).

ROSENSHINE, B. (1971). *Teaching Behaviors and Student Achievement* (London: National Foundation for Educational Research).

ROSENSHINE, B. & R. STEVENS. (1986). Teaching functions. In M. Wittrock, *Handbook of Research on Teaching,* 3rd ed. (New York: Macmillan), pp. 376–391.

9

THE INTERACTIVE MODEL

INTRODUCTION

"The most important factor influencing present learning is what students already know."

The focus of this chapter is the Interactive Model which is designed to teach organized bodies of knowledge for long-term retention. While all the models presented in this text are strongly interactive, we are calling this one the Interactive Model to emphasize the importance of the process with a model that is deductive in its approach and more expository in orientation than the others we have described. Also, interaction in this context means more than the exchanges that take place between teacher and students. In addition to teacher-student communication, there is the interaction of students with new content, plus the connections made in the activity between what students already know and the content to be learned. To illustrate these processes, let's look now at the model in use with a group of psychology students.

Miss Martello began her class by saying, "Class, today we are going to continue our discussion of operant conditioning by looking at different reinforcement schedules. But before we do that, let's return to some points that we made yesterday. Who can give me an example of operant conditioning and explain how it differs from classical conditioning? Jack?"

"Well, in classical conditioning the response that the organism makes can be involuntary, like the dog salivating. In operant conditioning the response is voluntary."

"Can you give me an example of that?" Miss Martello probed.

" ... Well, my mother always thanks my dad when he helps pick up the kitchen and living room, so he does it all the time now," Sherry responded hesitantly.

"Also, in classical conditioning the behavior follows the environmental factor which we called the stimulus, that influences it, and in operant conditioning the behavior precedes the environmental influence, which in this case we called reinforcement or punishment," Carol volunteered.

"Very good! Now we're going to focus on one aspect of operant conditioning which is the system of rewards that can be provided for desired behaviors."

With that she displayed the following statement on the overhead.

> Reinforcement schedules are a description of the frequency or intervals of rewards provided an organism for a desired response.

She then put the following outline on the board.

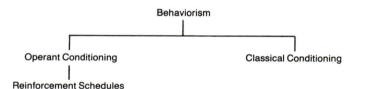

"Now, what can you conclude based on the outline? Jim?"

"Well, apparently reinforcement schedules only go with operant conditioning," Jim responded, "because we only see them under it and not under classical conditioning."

"Excellent, Jim. That's exactly right. Now look at the statement on the overhead again. It talks about rewards for desired behavior. This means that the reward comes after the organism has responded, so it's an operant kind of conditioning."

"Now, let's proceed on with our discussion of operant conditioning and focus on the rewards," Miss Martello went on. "What does the statement suggest about reinforcement schedules? Joel?"

"They describe how often the person or I guess even other animals get rewarded."

"Good, Joel, and what would continuous reinforcement mean? Sandy?"

"Apparently that would be when every desired behavior got a reward," Sandy replied after thinking a moment.

"Excellent, Sandy. Now give me an example of that ... Susan."

"One example would be like in a Skinner box where every time the rat pushes a bar he gets some food. If he doesn't press the bar, he doesn't get rewarded."

"Fine, Susan, and so now you can draw in your notes this outline:

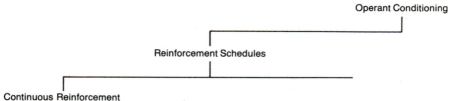

"And what do we have at the other end of the continuum? What happens when a behavior is never reinforced? Sharon?"

"The organism would stop the behavior after awhile."

"Excellent, Sharon. That's called extinction. Let's put that up on our outline too."

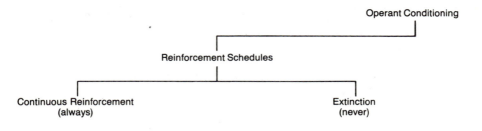

"How do continuous reinforcement and extinction compare?" Miss Martello continued.

"They're at the opposite extremes," Judy volunteered.

"At one end you get reinforced for every desired behavior, and at the other, you never get reinforced."

"Let's look again at our statement," Miss Martello went on. "It said that a reinforcement schedule is the frequency or interval of rewards. How do the two items on our outline relate to the statement? Nikki?"

"In the first case the frequency is very high and in the second, it's low. Actually nonexistent," Nikki responded.

"Excellent, Nikki. So we see that both are forms of reinforcement schedules because they both describe a frequency of rewards. Now let's add partial reinforcement to our outline and define it as a schedule in which behavior is reinforced some of the time."

After writing the definition on the board, she continued, "There are two main kinds of partial reinforcement schedules that depend upon how the reinforcement is delivered. These are called ratio or interval schedules. Let's talk about ratio schedule first. In a ratio schedule the organism has to produce a fixed number of responses before he is reinforced. It's like piecework in a factory. Who knows how that works? Gerry?"

"Well, my dad works in a factory that has piecework, and he gets paid in terms of how many cars they make in a day."

"Good, Gerry. That would be an example of a ratio schedule. Who can give me an example from the Skinner box that we saw in the lab? Jill?"

"It would be like having a cat get rewarded for every third press of the bar."

"Now let's compare the partial and continuous reinforcement. Kathy?"

"It's actually simple," Kathy answered. "Every desired behavior is rewarded with continuous reinforcement, but only a certain number are with partial reinforcement."

"Good, Kathy. And, class, how does this type of reinforcement influence behavior? Bruce?"

"Hmmm."

"Let's compare it to continuous," Miss Martello prompted. "Do you think the rate of response would be greater or less?"

"Greater."

"Why?"

"Because the rat would have to press faster or more times to get the reward and wouldn't take as much time off to eat it."

"Good answer, and what would happen if we stopped reinforcing in an interval schedule? Would the behavior stop quicker or slower than continuous reinforcement and why? Dan?"

"I think faster because the behavior isn't as firmly established."

"Sarah?"

"I think slower because the cat is used to not being reinforced."

"Interesting. We have two different predictions. What about our work with classical conditioning? Does that help us out any?"

The lesson contiued with a resolution of the problem, and then moved to a discussion of variable and fixed ratio partial reinforcement schedules and finally ended with a discussion of interval schedules. The period ended with the following outline having been developed.

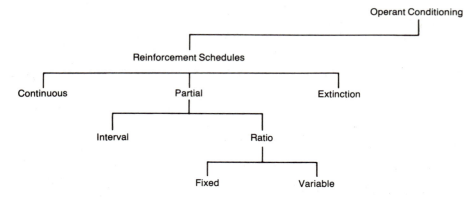

The preceding lesson was an example of a teacher using the Interactive Model. The model is conceptually based on the idea of schemata, a concept we introduced in Chapter 1. Schemata were described as one way of thinking about the organization of knowledge in the brain. We now want to review and expand the discussion of schema theory and discuss its implications for future learning.

Schema Theory

The beginnings of schema theory have been traced to the 18th century when the philosopher, Kant, talked about the process of "productive imagination" in the application of categories to make sense out of new knowledge and experiences (Rumelhart, 1980). He viewed the mind as actively using schemata, or mental organizing structures, to guide perception and to categorize objects. Contemporary interest in the idea of schema goes back to the 1920s and the work of the psychologist, Bartlett (1932). Bartlett was interested in the process of remembering as it applied to written passages. In this sense he was a true forerunner of the information processing school of psychology with its emphasis on meaningful learning in real-life situations.

To investigate this phenomena, Bartlett asked subjects to read folklore passages about Indians and to recall the passages at different time intervals. His outcomes were not as expected, however. First, he found that even with immediate recall, individuals remembered different aspects of the stories. In addition, through the process of interpreting the stories from their own frame of reference, they changed the facts to make them fit into the framework they had established. Furthermore, as time went on, subjects' distortions of the stories increased; but these distortions, though incorrect in terms of the tests, invariably were linked together so as to make them meaningful to the subjects themselves.

From the results Bartlett concluded that there exists a strong drive in people to make sense of what they encounter. (This is related to the need for structure we discussed in Chapter 2.) In addition, he accounted for the personal and idiosyncratic nature of the distortions through the idea of individual schemata. Each person was making sense of the passages on the basis of their prior experiences stored in the form of schemata. Let's see how this works. Read the following passage and answer the questions that follow.

Rocky slowly got up from the mat, planning his escape. He hesitated a moment and thought. Things were not going well. What bothered him most was being held, especially since the charge against him had been weak. He considered his present situation. The lock that held him was strong but he thought he could break it. He knew, however, that his timing would have to be perfect. Rocky was aware that it was because of his early roughness that he had been penalized so severely—much too severely from his point of view. The situation was becoming frustrating; the pressure had been grinding on him for too long. He was being ridden unmercifully. Rocky was getting angry now. He felt he was ready to make his move. He knew that his success or failure would depend on what he did in the next few seconds.

What is happening here? Do we have an imprisoned criminal planning his escape, or a wrestler attempting to get out of a precarious position? Actually, the passage was written so it could be interpreted either way. When researchers gave it to physical education and music students, they found that 64 percent of the physical education majors interpreted it as a wrestling story while only 28 percent of the music majors viewed it this way. How did you interpret the passage, and what does this say about your background?

A parallel situation exists in every classroom. As students enter classes with diverse beliefs, attitudes, and knowledge structures, they bring with them diverse schemata. They read the same account of the Viet Nam War and some go away convinced of the need at that time for a strong stand against communism while others interpret the passage as an example of a super power trying to exercise external control over a basically internal struggle involving two warring factions in a distant country.

As another example, consider students viewing two different sized metal balls falling in a vacuum. The fact that they appear to hit at the same time is viewed by one as a measurement error and by the other as a demonstration of the generalization that "The mass of an object does not influence the falling speed of two objects in a vacuum." In each case students' preexisting schemas influence the interpretation and retention of new information.

Before continuing, let's define the idea of schemas more systematically. Rumelhart (1980) described schemata as the building blocks of cognition. He emphasized that within each schema are elaborated networks of interconnected ideas. Cornbleth (1985) described these networks as maps consisting of nodes (concepts, objects or events) that are linked by relationships among the nodes.

For example, let's take the schema for the process of learning. Embedded within each person's schema for learning in general is a more specific one for learning in school. This school schema typically has nodes within it for how to dress, when to go to school, what to do when you get there, and how to act toward the teacher. Within it, even more specific schemas for specific learning modes such as lecture, discussion, or group work are embedded.

From this example we can see that schemata have three major characteristics (Rumelhart & Ortony, 1977). First, each is composed of variables whose content is determined by the person's past experience. What do you know about soccer or dog shows? Your response to this question provides some indication of the quality of your schemata for these two areas of knowledge and your past experiences with them. Second, each schema is typically embedded within another larger schema and in a similar way has other schemata embedded within it. This embeddedness allows us to link schemas together in some coherent fashion.

A third characteristic of schemata is that they vary in abstraction, and the information within each schema also varies in degree of abstraction. This characteristic has special meaning for both teaching and learning; the emphasis the teacher places on the level of the schema influences student learning behaviors. For example, how do you study differently for a multiple-choice, fill-in-the-blanks test versus an essay exam? Students tend to memorize more facts for an objective test and focus on more relationships in an essay exam. The type of evaluation instrument influences the amount of stress the learner puts on various levels of abstraction. In a similar way, a teacher who announces at the beginning of a class "Don't worry about specific facts. I want you to understand the big picture" communicates to students that one level of abstraction is being stressed rather than another.

At this point it would be helpful to differentiate between two types of schemata, descriptive and procedural. Descriptive schemata help us organize our knowledge about a body of knowledge. For example, what you know about the animal world is probably organized into a schema containing the inter-related concepts of vertebrates, invertebrates, mammals, reptiles, and so on.

Procedural schemata guide our actions and help us perform in an effective manner. Rumelhart (1980) described procedural schemata in terms of a play with scripts that actors perform. For example, when we go into a store to buy something, our store schema helps to define the actions of the buyer (e.g., give item to clerk plus money, then wait) as well as the seller. Procedural schemata are especially important in the areas of problem solving and skill learning, where the particular schema determines the actions of the problem solver (e.g., invert the divisor and multiply).

Two other related characteristics of schemata are also important: Schemata are active processes and are constantly being re-evaluated in terms of their fit and utility. First, we use our schemas to make sense of the world; when the world makes sense, the schemata do not need to change. Second, however, when they do not fit the data, then dissonance occurs and we are motivated to make our world make sense. Sometimes we do this by rejecting information from the outside. At one level we call this being stubborn, bull headed, and dogmatic. At another, more serious, level we call this behavior schizophrenic.

The process of learning can be thought of as the development of schemata that allow individuals to understand and function in their world. Using this line of thinking, we can view teaching as a deliberate attempt to influence the content and structure of student schemata. In doing so we must keep in mind that the students' preexisting schemata can either be liabilities or assets; they can either assist or hinder the new learning.

Let's turn our attention now to the dynamic nature of schemata and examine more closely what occurs when new information is introduced to the learner. When the learner encounters new information, three qualitatively different modes of learning can occur: *accretion, tuning* and *restructuring*. Accretion is the simplest of these processes and involves the incorporation of new facts or instances to an existing schema. Cornbleth (1985) gave the example of learning that a basenji, and African breed similar to a terrier, is a dog. The schema for dog would remain essentially unchanged. This is similar to Piaget's notion of assimilation in which present cognitive structures are strengthened or exercised through encountering new instances but remain relatively unchanged (Flavell, 1985). Rumelhart & Norman (1981) observed that most models of the memory process are accretionary; the material to be remembered is attached to old structures without changing these structures.

By contrast, tuning involves the modification of a schema to accommodate new information. When an elementary student learns that a dolphin is a mammal, then the previous structure for mammal being four legged and living on land must change. In a similar way, language arts students learning that many of Dickens's novels were first produced as serials for mass consumption in popular tabloids of the times gives new meaning to the concept *novel*.

A more radical, and sometimes more painful and disquieting kind of learning occurs when restructuring takes place. Restructuring involves the creation of new schemata to make sense of situations that cannot be interpreted with existing schemata, even after some tuning. This can occur when the new learning occurs in a relative void where the learner has had little or no contact with the area. Taking a class in nuclear physics or eastern mystical religions are potential examples. A more typical instance of restructuring occurs when students are forced (induced?) to make their old schemas compatible with new information or vice versa. Science students, comfortable with a creationist view of the world, having to integrate evolution into this view might be an example.

One explanation of how this occurs is through the process of analogy (Rumelhart & Norman, 1981). Through this mechanism schemata are not created anew but are modeled or based upon previously learned schemas. Teachers take advantage of this process when they actively employ analogies in their teaching. Two examples might be helpful here. When teaching chemistry students about the molecular structure of atoms, an analogy is often made with the solar system, with the nucleus corresponding to the sun and the electrons to the planets. In a similar way tennis instructors attempting to teach students how to put topspin on the ball often recommend hitting the ball like "spanking a baby on its bottom." In both instances, previously familiar schemata are used to aid in the formation of new schemata. Further discussion of the use of analogies in the Interactive Model occur in the next section which focuses on the work of David Ausubel and his applications of schema theory to educational settings.

Let's see how Miss Martello applied the theory in her lesson on reinforcement schedules. She was attempting to aid the students in their development of a schema by systematically introducing the subordinate concepts related to reinforcement schedules and displaying them on a hierarchical outline. She began by having them compare operant and classical conditioning to take advantage of a larger schema into which the present one would fit.

Seeing *reinforcement schedules* under *operant conditioning* helped the students to avoid confusing operant and classical conditioning concepts. Further, she called for and got examples of classical and operant conditioning to insure to the extent possible that the background of the learners was consistent enough to allow the lesson to proceed.

As she introduced the concepts, she helped the students link them to the developing schema through the outline and additional examples. She also compared each concept to the others to insure that they were properly accommodated. This process takes into account the accretion and tuning processes that occur when new material is introduced. We turn now to a discussion of verbal learning as originally presented by David Ausubel.

Meaningful Verbal Learning: The Work of David Ausubel

One of the most influential psychologists in bringing the ideas behind schema theory to bear on the classroom is David Ausubel. Beginning with studies done in the early 1960s and captured in his book, *The Psychology of Meaningful Verbal Learning* (1963), Ausubel has continued to stress the importance of cognitive structures on learning. He would wholeheartedly agree with the statement introducing the chapter that the most important factor influencing present learning is what students already know. In our discussion of his theory we will explain how teachers can take advantage of this in their interactions with students.

As can be seen from the title of his first major work in the area, Ausubel also places heavy emphasis on meaningful verbal learning, that is, the acquisition of information that has several links to other ideas. By contrast, rote learning places heavy emphasis on the memorization of specific items of information at the expense of students exploring relationships within the material. Meaningful learning occurs when the ideas in a new schema are connected not only to each other but also to previously established schemata in a logical manner.

Ausubel also contrasts his view of teaching and learning with discovery learning. He feels that discovery learning has a place in the curriculum for teaching thinking skills but that most of the time teachers should use a deductive approach which is highly structured and which allows students to explore relationships in the content.

One other general characteristic of Ausubel's theory should be stressed. Though he favors teacher centered, deductively sequenced teaching sessions, he is adamantly opposed to passive learning on the part of students. Though the teacher is the central figure in the lesson, a major task facing the teacher is encouraging and requiring students to actively think about the new material to be learned, and helping them to find relationships not only within the new content itself but also with content previously learned. To help students in this process Ausubel suggests that teachers employ three concepts: *advance organizers, progressive differentiation* and *integrative reconciliation.*

Advance organizers.   Advance organizers are a teacher's conscious attempt to preview and structure the new material to be learned and to link it to content already existing in students' preexisting schemata. In this sense advance organizers are like cognitive road maps; they allow students to see where they have been and where they are going. Effective advance organizers connect new information to existing schemata and provide students with a means to create new schemata. They are at a higher level of abstraction than the content they organize and they subsume this information (Luiton, Ames, & Ackerson, 1980).

The idea of advance organizers is a powerful one with broad applicability across grade levels and subject matter areas and has been interpreted by researchers and practitioners in a variety of ways (Dinnel & Glover, 1985). Good & Brophy (1980) emphasized the forward effects of advanced organizers when they stressed their ability to cue students to key ideas and to organize these ideas in relationship to one another. They included teacher modeling and the presentation of objectives at the beginning of the lesson as examples of advance organizers. Other researchers have used schematic diagrams as a prelude to a lesson on radar (Mayer, 1984).

In a review of research in this area Mayer (1984) listed a number of characteristics of advance organizers: (1) They are typically a short set of verbal or visual information; (2) they are presented prior to learning a larger body of information; (3) they contain no specific content from the new information to be learned, instead being at a higher level of abstraction; (4) they provide a means of generating logical relationships in the new material; and (5) they influence the learner's encoding process.

To illustrate these characteristics, let's look at two advance organizers that have been used to influence learning. The first is from an elementary social studies lesson on governments.

> The organization of a government is like a family. Different people in the government have different responsibilities and roles. When all the people work together effectively, both families and governments operate efficiently.

The second is from a study conducted with college students who were learning about linguistics.

> We all use language every day. And yet, unless we are writing papers for a course or completing an assignment in English class, we generally give language very little thought. There are people who study language, much as there are scholars who study other important areas of life. These students of language analyze our language in ways that are far more complex than the sentence diagramming most of us have done. Not only do they study how the written language works, they

also examine how it is generated. These language scholars also study spoken language—how it is learned, how people use it to share meaning with other people, and what the various parts of the spoken language are. In addition, the study of language relates what is known about spoken and written language.

Another point of interest in the study of language comes from comparing different languages (e.g., English and Spanish). Just as sociologists compare life in different cultures and anthropologists study the origin of cultures, the scholars of language compare different languages in terms of how they evolved and how they are now written and spoken. The scholars you will read about believe that the study of language can shed light on how people think and how human ideas have evolved. As is the case in any field such as law, education, or science, there are some basic conventions or rules that all who study language agree on. The chapter you are about to read explains the study of language and the rules followed by people in this profession (Dinnel & Glover, 1985, p. 521).

Both of these advance organizers attempted to provide a cognitive framework for new content to be learned. The second one is obviously not short, but it is designed for college students, and it illustrates the other characteristics of advance organizers that Mayer identified.

Differences between these advance organizers illustrate one other important feature: They must be tailored to the learning situation to be effective (Ausubel, 1978). The exact form that an advance organizer takes is dependent upon: (1) the nature of the learning material, (2) the age of the learner, and (3) the degree of prior familiarity with the learning material. Ways of constructing advance organizers based on these three principles are discussed in the planning section of this chapter.

Progressive differentiation. Advance organizers are presented prior to a lesson and are designed to provide scaffolding for the ideas to follow. Once an advance organizer is presented, progressive differentiation and integrative reconciliation are processes the teacher uses to help students explore relationships within the new content and between new evolving schemata and previously established ones.

In the process of progressive differentiation, the more general and inclusive ideas of a discipline are presented first and then broken down into smaller component parts. This can occur in a number of ways. One of the most common forms of progressive differentiation is the breaking down of superordinate into subordinate concepts. For example, Miss Martello broke the concept *reinforcement schedules* into the subordinate ideas as follows:

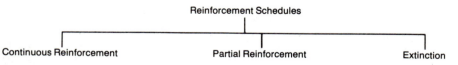

The differentiation progressed when partial reinforcement was further differentiated into *interval schedules* and *ratio schedules* as was shown in the outline. Finally, ratio schedules were differentiated into *fixed* and *variable* schedules.

Another form of progressive differentiation involves the breaking down of a concept into its constituent parts. For example, a unit on birds might examine the following concepts:

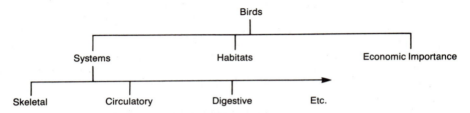

FIGURE 9.1   Progressive Differentiation Through Component Concepts

Bird systems, bird habitats, and the economic importance of birds are not strictly subordinate concepts but are topics that the teacher would pursue after first introducing and discussing the main topic.

A third form that progressive differentiation can take is the breaking down of broader generalizations into more specific ones. This type of progressive differentiation can often involve the use of examples to illustrate the generalization being discussed. For example, an outline using generalizations based on Miss Martello's lesson might appear as follows:

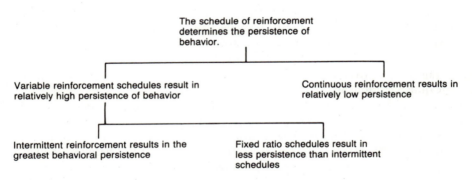

FIGURE 9.2   Structure Utilizing Generalizations

Notice that in each of the examples the ideas in the new schemata were systematically linked to previous ideas in an organized fashion. Evidence for this organization can be seen in the fact that the process of progressive differentiation could be schematically diagrammed. This organization is important because it influences not only the initial encoding of information but also its subsequent storage and retrieval.

Integrative reconciliation. Integrative reconciliation refers to the teacher's conscious attempts to make the logical relationships between ideas in the developing schema apparent to students. Ausubel explained the purpose of integrative reconciliation as being " . . . to explore relationships between ideas and to point out significant similarities and differences and to reconcile real or apparent inconsistencies" (1963, p. 80). Another function of integrative reconciliation is to combat compartmentalization, a special case of rote learning. By the active exploration of relations between ideas, the teacher insures that the developing schema is connected to older, established schemas and that ideas within the new schema are interrelated.

There are two basic types of integrative reconciliation. Vertical reconciliation explores relationships between more and less abstract ideas (e.g., a superordinate concept and a subordinate concept) and is designed to insure that new ideas become attached to old in a hierarchical fashion. Horizontal reconciliation, as the name implies, investigates similarities and differences between coordinate concepts and other ideas at a similar level of abstraction. The uses of both forms of reconciliation are explored further when we discuss the implementation phase of the Interactive Model.

This concludes our discussion of schema theory and Ausubel's application of that theory to the area of meaningful verbal learning. The next section of the chapter deals with planning issues related to the Interactive Model.

PLANNING LESSONS USING THE INTERACTIVE MODEL

In the previous sections we discussed schema theory and the implications of this theory for teaching. In addition, we discussed the work of David Ausubel and his work in the area of meaningful verbal learning. In this work Ausubel stressed the importance of advance organizers in structuring new schemata and connecting new schemata to old. The processes of progressive differentiation and integrative reconciliation insure that newly formed schemas are learned in a systematic and organized fashion.

In this section of the chapter we discuss how the teacher can plan for individual lessons, incorporating the content of that lesson into previously established schemata. In addition, we will discuss how to construct advance organizers, structure content and plan for the use of progressive differentiation and integrative reconciliation in the lesson.

After reading this section you should be able to meet the following objectives:

1. You will understand different uses of the Interactive Model in planning so that when given an illustration, you will identify the scope of the teacher's planning.
2. You will understand hierarchical organization of content so when given a brief classroom scenario, you will describe the content organization according to the example.
3. You will understand the types of advance organizers so that from a list, you will identify each as being a definition, a generalization, or an analogy.

Identifying Goals

In beginning the planning phase of an Interactive activity as with any other activity, the teacher first considers the goals of the lesson. The Interactive Model differs from the Inductive, Concept Attainment, and Deductive Models in that it is not designed to teach a specific concept or generalization. It differs from the Integrative Model in that it is not designed to teach systems of generalizations. Instead the goal of the model is to help students develop schematas, or in other words, to structure knowledge. Rather than teaching one particular concept or generalization, it is designed to teach organized bodies of content (schemata), or to help learners organize already understood concepts and generalizations into an overall schema.

At the classroom level, the model can very effectively serve two primary functions. First, it can be used as a means for organizing content to be taught in an entire course, a unit within a course, or a single lesson. It is an aid for the teacher in helping him or her decide on the scope and sequence of the content, and it can aid the students as a guide in their progress throughout the material. We used the model as an organizing scheme for the content of the text and presented the information at the end of Chapter 1. Note that you did not learn the content of each model at that point. Instead the advance organizer and structural outline served as a means to organize the content, the specifics of which were presented separately in each of the succeeding chapters.

The second function the model serves is to help learners structure previously learned concepts and generalizations into comprehensible schemata. To illustrate this process let's consider again Miss Martello's lesson. The students understood the concepts of continuous reinforcement, extinction, and partial reinforcement as evidenced by their ability to explain the concepts and provide examples of them. However, when asked which of the schedules would result in the quicker reduction of behavior, the students were uncertain. The Interactive Model can be a powerful aid in helping to eliminate this uncertainty and structuring the concepts into interrelated schemata.

Miss Martello was very clear and organized in her planning process. She first planned to teach the individual concepts, and in a second lesson teach the relationships among the concepts that would result in the students forming valid schemata.

The same process would apply in your classrooms. At the course level the teacher would outline the content and determine relationships for the entire year. Then, at the unit level the teacher's planning task would be to relate the content to both the year's work and to the specific lessons within the unit. Finally, at the lesson level the teacher plans so that schemata learned previously are activated and linked to the new material. How this might look in a geography class is shown in Figure 9.3

From the diagram we see the model's two functions illustrated. First, it was used as a guide for long-range planning for the year's work on geography and a particular unit on elements of the physical environment. This is similar to the guide we presented in Chapter 1. Second, it was used to relate concepts in a single lesson focusing on landforms. The focus of the lesson was to compare the characteristics of the landforms and form an overall structure rather than introduce the landforms for the first time. The first use of the model was organizational and the second was instructional.

In planning for an interactive lesson it is essential that background knowledge is considered. Let's look again at the lesson on landforms. Remember that the Interactive Model is not designed to teach the individual concepts per se, but rather is designed to help students structure or form a schema for the relationship among the landforms. However, the model would be completely ineffective if the students did not already know what mountains, plateaus, hills, and plains are.

From this discussion we see that using the Interactive Model effectively depends more on student background than any of the other models presented. For this reason, accurate diagnosis of their existing schemata is very important. We address this topic in the next section.

FIGURE 9.3   Three Complementary Uses Of The Interactive Model

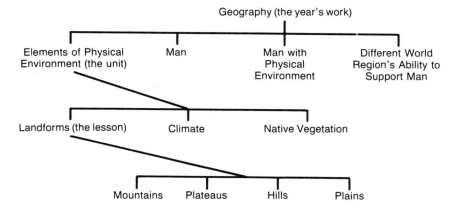

Diagnosing Students' Backgrounds

One simple way to determine how much students know about the new content to be learned is to present the ideas in an overview, and ask for a show of hands if students think they understand each of the concepts. For example, a teacher in the lesson on landforms might list the concepts on the board asking for a show of hands after each is written to see how many students think they understand them.

One disadvantage to this approach is that some students may be reluctant to share with others their ignorance of—or knowledge of—the topic. Stallings (1983) suggests as a partial solution to this potential problem, rather than having students raise their hands, that students put their hands on their chest with a thumbs-up if they think they know the answer, and a thumbs-down if they do not.

A second way of assessing students' background knowledge is to ask students to list, group and label ideas related to a concept (Taba, 1966, 1967). Using this strategy the teacher would first ask, "What comes to mind when I say the word _____?" This word would be the central focus of an upcoming unit or lesson (e.g., landforms, reptiles, novels, and so on). The teacher then writes on the board all the ideas that the class can brainstorm. The quantity and quality of these responses give the teacher one assessment of students' knowledge in the area.

After the students are through brainstorming, the teacher then asks students to group the ideas together, with the teacher putting a number or letter by all the terms that go in group 1. When group 1 is exhausted, the class would turn to the second group and continue doing this until all the terms are grouped. Finally, the teacher would ask the class to supply names for the categories formed.

Finally, the simplest and best form of diagnosis is to ask the students to explain the concepts in their own words and to provide examples of them. The process takes little time and is the most accurate assessment of the students' background knowledge. This is the process Miss Martello employed in her lesson.

One disadvantage of these interactive ways of assessing knowledge is that the more knowledgeable and outspoken students may dominate the lessons, giving the teacher a false impression of the overall knowledge of the class. An alternative is the use of a diagnostic pretest. This may be as simple as listing key concepts on the board and asking students to define them on a sheet of paper.

A slightly more complicated process which provides the teacher with a look at not only the content but organization of students' schemata asks students to first define as many of the terms on the board that they can (Champagne, Klopfor, Solomon, & Cahn, 1980). Then students are asked to take the terms they know and explain the relationship between the terms. This measures the organizational structure of student existing schemata. The combination of the two tasks provides a fairly accurate description of the students' backgrounds.

Teachers can use the results of their diagnostic efforts in several ways. The most important is as a guide to which concepts and ideas need increased development and which can be discussed more quickly. The diagnostic information can also be used to determine pace and coverage. Finally, thorough knowledge of students' preexisting schemata allows the teacher to design organizers and structure content in a way that is compatible with their background. These are the topics of the next sections.

Structuring Content

After the background of the students has been determined and the goals for the lesson, unit or course have been identified, the next planning step for the teacher is to structure the content in a systematic way. Some topics already hierarchically organized into superordinate and subordinate concepts lend themselves naturally to this type of organization. For example, a lesson on mammals could be organized according to taxonomic description. The organization of such a lesson might appear as follows:

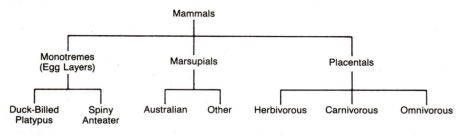

FIGURE 9.4   A Hierarchical Structure In Biology

The real number system is also hierarchically organized.

FIGURE 9.5   A Hierarchical Structure In Math

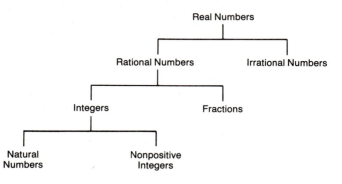

On the other hand, there are many situations in which the teacher will have to impose structure on previously unstructured material. In the absence of unifying themes, there are several ways in which this can be done. One is to arbitrarily impose a structure on the content using your best judgment. For example, a social studies topic on community helpers might be organized as follows:

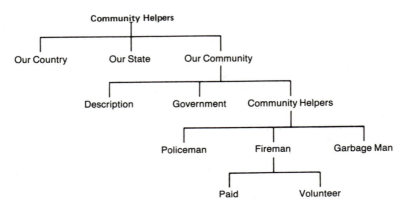

FIGURE 9.6   Community Helper Outline

The organization of this content allows students to see the relationship of community helpers to each other as well as their relationship to the larger picture.

Another way of organizing content is through the use of interrelated generalizations. An example of this would be to structure an Interactive lesson around the following generalization: America has expanded because of natural resources, form of government and a unique mixture of people. The structure which evolved from this generalization might appear as follows:

FIGURE 9.7   Hierarchical Structure Based on Generalization

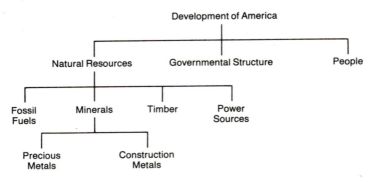

Again, in this form of organization, the generalization is broken down into topical areas, and these are either illustrated with examples or further broken down into subordinate concepts.

A third way of organizing a large body of content for an Interactive lesson is through the use of an extended analogy. The use of an analogy allows students to relate the new knowledge they are learning to schemata already acquired. For example, the structure for a lesson using the solar system as an analogy for the structure of an atom might look like this:

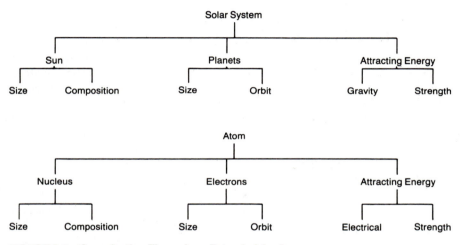

FIGURE 9.8   Organization Through an Extended Analogy

We discuss the use of analogies in more detail when we discuss the construction of advance organizers.

Note that in the cases where structure is imposed on material that lacks a natural structure, one organizational scheme is not necessarily better than another, and the decision is a matter of teacher judgment. It should be emphasized that the purpose of structural outlines, as with all the other techniques presented in this text, is to increase student learning. A structural outline, whether derived from a discipline or imposed by the teacher, is designed to enhance learning. Therefore, an arbitrary structure, unless it is obviously inconsistent with recognized views of the content, is completely legitimate. The value of such structural organizations is measured by the degree to which they help students learn and retain material. The examples presented in the previous paragraphs are just possible ways to structure content.

In the previous paragraphs we have discussed content organization based primarily upon the internal logic of the content itself. In other words, subordinate concepts are subsumed by superordinate concepts, and broader, more inclusive generalizations are related to those narrower and less inclusive. A second major factor, however, is the cognitive structure of each individual student. For example, it makes no sense to talk about "modern capitalist democratic countries" if the learner does not understand terms such as capitalist and democratic. Lefrancais (1982) cited a vivid example of this problem in teaching Eskimo children sentences such as "Use your handkerchief when you sneeze" (handkerchief?) and "Little Jack Horner sat in a corner" (corner?). In organizing the topic, the developing schema is anchored to a general, subsuming generalization, definition, or analogy which serves as an advance organizer. Let's consider this topic now.

Preparing the Advance Organizer

The teacher's final task in the planning phase is to create an advance organizer. We discussed the concept of advance organizers as they relate to Ausubel's theory of meaningful verbal learning. We now want to describe advance organizers in a bit more detail and apply their use to the classroom.

An advance organizer is a statement preceding a lesson that is designed to preview the material to be learned and link it to content already existing in learners' schemata. It is more general and abstract than the content to be organized and subsumes the subsequent material.

For example, Miss Martello's advance organizer was:

> Reinforcement schedules are applications of operant conditioning in which the frequency of rewards provided an organism for a desired response is described.

By preparing the organizer as it appears, Miss Martello helped link the impending lesson to an already existing schema for operant conditioning and to a larger schema that had operant and classical conditioning "in tune" with each other. Also, we can see that the statement " . . . frequency of rewards provided an organism for a desired response . . . " is more general and abstract than "continuous reinforcement," "partial reinforcement," and "extinction," which were the specific topics of the lesson.

Consider again the advance organizer we used in Chapter 1 to initiate the organizational structure of the text. It appeared as follows:

> Information processing models are teaching strategies based on information processing theory that are designed to help students learn content at the same time as they practice thinking skills under the guidance and direction of an active teacher.

Notice again that this organizer is more general, abstract and inclusive than any of the succeeding material in the text. As the content has evolved, we have identified the characteristics of each model, the specific thinking skills involved, and the behaviors an active teacher demonstrates when using the models. All this information has been subsumed by the advance organizer.

There are three basic types of organizers: *concept definitions, generalizations* and *analogies.* Let's turn now to a discussion of each.

Concept Definition

Definitions can be valuable organizers of content when the material is new or unfamiliar. Ideally, the defining statement should possess the characteristics of a good concept definition, in that it states the concept, a superordinate concept, and characteristics of the concept. The superordinate concept helps link the concept to existing schemata, and the characteristics differentiate the concept from other similar ones. The organizer Miss Martello used in her lesson and the one we presented at the end of Chapter 1 were both definitions.

The preparation of the organizer, while not extremely difficult, requires clear thinking on the part of the teacher. It is general, abstract, and inclusive, but it does not include totally unfamiliar language or ideas. For example, when the students in Miss Martello's class read her definition, they were familiar with concepts such as *operant conditioning, frequency,* and *reward.* On the other hand, the organizer did not identify specific reinforcement schedules or how they were applied. This information followed the organizer and was anchored to it.

Organizers that are too abstract or unfamiliar lose their ability to link the succeeding structure to the students' existing schemata. For example, in a physiology class, to define active reabsorption as "the transport of a substance through the tubular epithelial cells into the interstitial spaces by means of special chemical transport mechanisms" would be futile unless the learner knew the meaning of concepts such as *tubular epithelial cells, interstitial spaces,* and *special chemical transport mechanisms.* An unhappy chain of events such as this is often seen in the classroom where students look up one word in the dictionary only to find that they must look up others as well. A perceptive teacher can avoid this type of cognitive tail-chasing by carefully developing the necessary background and choosing language carefully.

Generalizations

Because of their ability to summarize large amounts of information, generalizations can also be effectively used as advance organizers. As with the use of definitions, teachers must be certain that each of the concepts in the generalization is understood by the students when using generalizations as advance organizers. If they are not, these concepts cannot serve as anchors for the new material or links to previously learned content.

In the Introduction we saw how a generalization could be used as an organizer to subsume narrower generalizations. As another example consider the following generalization taken from a unit in geography:

> The climate and natural resources of a cultural region will determine its economy in large part.

This generalization would then be linked to specific cultural regions, and the climate, natural resources, and economy of each would be investigated. In this case, the generalization would not be used to subsume narrower generalizations, but rather would be used to anchor specific information about different geographical and cultural areas.

Analogy

Perhaps the most effective type of advance organizer is the analogy, or what Ausubel calls a *comparative advance organizer*. Analogies work well because they can be customized to fit the background of a particular student population. Rumelhart & Norman (1981) used the analogy of a play with a script to describe procedural schemata. Analogies can also be useful in organizing school content. For example, the following analogy has been used to teach students about the functionings of a river system.

> A river system is as important to the other elements of the physical environment as the circulatory system is to the human body. It also has some of the same features. A main river, such as the Mississippi, provides the "life blood"—water—for plants and animals as well as the agriculture and hydroelectric industries, just as the aorta as a major artery carries blood to the parts of the body. Besides water, it also carries many sources of food for plants and animals. The rivers and streams resemble the arteries, veins, and capillaries of our body. They carry the nutrients and wastes of the area they serve.
> Just as humans can misuse the circulatory system, they can also misuse a river system. When too much waste is carried by either one, they can get clogged. Factory pollutants, insecticides, and other chemicals spoil rivers just as cholesterol, smoking, and other substances clog our circulatory system. As with the circulatory system, this damage sometimes is irreversible.

Using this analogy assumes that the students understand the workings of the circulatory system. Other analogies could have been used, such as the flow of students in a school building or the flow of traffic around a city. The choice depends on the students' interest and familiarity.

In general, the value of an analogy as an advance organizer depends on two factors. The first is the familiarity of the analogous element to the students. The power of analogies comes from their ability to connect new ideas with old. If the old ideas are not clear, they cannot provide any firm points for connections.

The second factor is the degree of overlap between the analogy and the ideas to be taught. As an example consider the river/circulatory system analogy again. It had the potential for the following areas of overlap: function, composition, abuses, and problems if overused. In general, the greater the overlap the more effective the organizer.

Let's consider now some additional analogies which could be used as organizers. In each of these, note the way in which the new material is linked to something familiar to the student and the number of possible similarities between the two concepts being compared.

1. A tree can be thought of as a city of cells in which each type of cell has a job to do and depends on the jobs of other cells.
2. A schema is like a computer program; the content and the relations between the content are dependent upon the learner (programmer).
3. Birds are reptiles with feathers; except for flight, their bodies work primarily the same way.
4. Outer space is the last frontier. The same dangers and hardships faced by the pioneers are encountered by the astronauts.

In summary, advance organizers are statements which are introduced in advance of the learning material itself and are designed to help students learn and retain new material. Other educational concept labels that describe a similar function are *instructional set,* which is designed to provide the students with an understanding of what the lesson is about, and *frame of reference,* which gives students a conceptual framework into which the lesson, ideas, concepts and facts can be placed in an organized fashion. The advance organizer links the new material to more abstract ideas which already exist in the learner's mind. The function of the organizer is to provide ideational scaffolding for the stable incorporation and retention of the differentiated material that will follow in the lesson.

EXERCISES

Read the case study below and answer the questions that follow.

Mr. Brown was teaching his English class about parts of speech. He wanted them to understand the function of different parts of speech in the total communication process. He also wanted them to understand the relationship between the different parts of speech. He began his class with a review of previously discussed material.

"Who can remember how we started our unit on communication and parts of speech?" asked Mr. Brown.

Steve responded, "We defined communication as the two-way transmission of information that typically takes place through language, and said that parts of speech and punctuation were components of the communication process."

"And what did we say about parts of speech yesterday?" Mr. Brown continued.

Steve replied, "We said that parts of speech are like building blocks in a house. The parts of speech function as the building blocks of written communication and the arrangement of blocks determines the structure of the message as well as the meaning."

"We also said words could be divided into naming words, action words, describing words and other words," Evelyn added.

"That's good," Mr. Brown smiled. "Now how did we describe these groups?"

The lesson continued with a discussion of each of these parts of speech.

1. Describe the scope of the teacher's planning for the lesson.
2. Identify and describe the two organizers in the illustration.
3. Diagram the organization of the material illustrated in the anecdote.

Identify each of the following advance organizers as a definition, a generalization, or an analogy.

4. A Spanish verb is like a good mystery story. It tells who did it and when.
5. A community is a group of people in geographic proximity who have interrelated functions. Certain groups provide services to the community and are called community helpers.
6. People's concept of work and play is influenced by the type of world they live in.
7. The circulatory system is like the sanitary system of a city. In both there is a pumping station, pipelines with varying sized pipes, a filtration plant, an exchange terminal, and a capacity for disposal of waste.
8. Economics is the study of the distribution of desired commodities.
9. An inductive lesson is like a good mystery novel. It presents a problem to be solved. It gives clues to the reader (learner) and there is closure when the mystery is solved (abstraction is derived).
10. A mammal is an animal that has warm blood, gives live birth to its young, and nurses its babies.

FEEDBACK

1.   The Ausubel model was used to plan in two ways. The first was to organize a unit of study on communication, and the second was to organize the lesson on parts of speech.

2.   There were two advance organizers illustrated in the anecdote. The first advance organizer was used to organize the unit on communication and was a definition ("com-

munication is the two-way transmission of information that typically takes place through language''). The second advance organizer was an analogy comparing parts of speech to building blocks and was used to organize the lesson on parts of speech.

3.   The organization for the unit as well as the lesson can be diagrammed as follows:

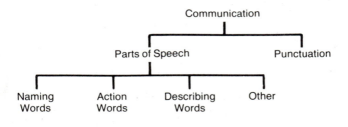

4.   Analogy
5.   Concept definition
6.   Generalization
7.   Analogy
8.   Concept definition
9.   Analogy
10.   Concept definition

IMPLEMENTING INTERACTIVE MODEL LESSONS

''Learning . . . is the process of constructing meaning, a representation, a model, or an explanation, for example, of words, sentences, paragraphs and texts that agrees with our knowledge, logic and experience and that makes sense to us'' (Wittrock, 1983, p. 602).

The quote epitomizes the goals of the Interactive Model. As we discussed in the Introduction, the model is designed to help students make previously existing concepts and generalizations more meaningful by increasing the number of associations that can be made with each. This is accomplished by direct application of Ausubel's concepts: advance organizers, progressive differentiation, and integrative reconciliation. As we discuss each in implementing the model, you will also see that the procedures are very similar to those discussed in other chapters.

Presenting the Advance Organizer

Having prepared the advance organizer and structured the content in the planning phase of the model, the lesson simply begins by displaying the advance organizer on the board or screen. The organizer serves as the lesson's focus and the point of reference for each of the subsequent ideas. Miss Martello followed this procedure by reviewing the previous day's discussion and then displaying her statement:

> Reinforcement schedules are a description of the frequency or intervals of rewards provided an organism for a desired response.

She then continued the lesson by displaying her structural outline for the students. It is from this point that the essence of the learning process begins.

Progressive Differentiation

Progressive differentiation is the separating of general and abstract concepts or generalizations into more specific and concrete subsets. This has been demonstrated to be effective as an instructional aid (Eggen, Kauchak, & Kirk, 1978) and usually exists in the form of hierarchies or structural outlines. For example, consider again the structural outline Miss Martello used in her lesson.

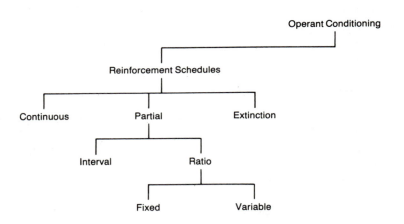

From the outline we see that *reinforcement schedules* is differentiated into *continuous reinforcement, partial reinforcement,* and *extinction.* The differentiation progressed when partial reinforcement was further differentiated into *interval* and *ratio* schedules. The progression further continued with *fixed* and *variable* ratio schedules. As the differentiation progressed, the concepts became increasingly specific, and with this specificity the potential to relate each concept to others, thereby increasing its meaningfulness.

As another example consider the following topic taken from an English class.

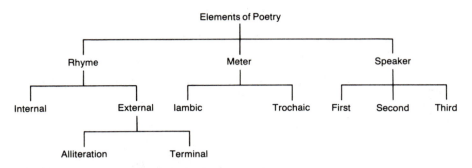

FIGURE 9.9   Progressive Differentiation of Poetry Concepts

In differentiating this content, the teacher has several options. The concept elements of poetry could be discussed and then proceed on to the topic of rhyme, exploring each of the subjects under it. Or, as an alternative, the teacher could briefly discuss each of the major topics—rhyme, meter and speaker—before differentiating these further.

The teacher also has the option of presenting the entire hierarchy at once, as is implied with the poetry example, or an initial component can be displayed and the outline is developed as it is discussed. The second option was the procedure Miss Martello used in her lesson.

To this point, our discussion of progressive differentiation has focused on concepts. It can also involve breaking a generalization down into less inclusive and more specific generalizations. An example of this would be to break the generalization "The price of a product is determined by supply and demand" into the two related generalizations "If demand stays constant, the price is inversely related to the supply of a product," and "If supply stays constant, the price is directly related to the demand." The outline of this process would appear as:

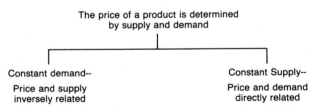

FIGURE 9.10   Progressive Differentiation Involving a Generalization

Another form of progressive differentiation is the illustration of concepts and generalizations with examples. For example, an art lesson on Impressionist painters might appear as follows:

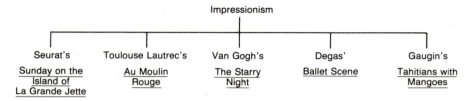

FIGURE 9.11   **Progressive Differentiation Through Examples**

A third form of progressive differentiation involves the identification and discussion of characteristics in a concept such as can be seen in Figure 9.12.

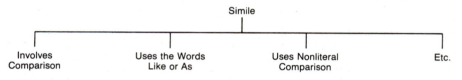

FIGURE 9.12   **Progressive Differentiation Involving Characteristics**

In summary, progressive differentiation is the setting apart of separate ideas as discrete entities. This is important so that the major ideas in the lesson are learned in a clear, discrete manner. Effective progressive differentiation insures that the new schemata being formed by students are organized in a systematic fashion.

Integrative Reconciliation

The goal of the Interactive Model is to help learners form new schemata and relate them to existing schemata. The advance organizer forms the focal point in the process and progressive differentiation creates the potential for its occurrence. It is actually accomplished through integrative reconciliation. Integrative reconciliation is an explicit attempt by the teacher to help students determine significant similarities and differences between facts, concepts and generalizations and to reconcile real or apparent inconsistencies between ideas. In some ways the process of integrative reconciliation is reciprocal to the process of progressive differentiation. In progressive differentiation, the main emphasis is on breaking major ideas down into their components, while integrative reconciliation emphasizes the relationship between major ideas as well as their relationship with the advance organizer. The purpose of progressive differentiation is to help students discriminate new or additional information from the old. The purpose of integrative reconciliation is to insure that new ideas are learned as part of a coherent whole rather than as single, disjointed ideas.

Integrative reconciliation exists at two instructional levels. For teachers it consists of all the questions they ask to help students make connections in the new content. For the students it is the mental effort required to form relationships. Sometimes this process occurs naturally. The teacher's role in an Interactive lesson is to insure that it occurs with all the topics in the lesson.

Integrative reconciliation can take a number of forms. The most common is teacher questions that ask students to find similarities and differences between ideas. For example, in Miss Martello's lesson she asked the students the following questions, all of which called for integrative reconciliation.

> "How do continuous reinforcement and extinction compare?"
> "How do continuous and partial reinforcement compare?"
> "Now let's look again at the statement. It said that a reinforcement schedule describes the frequency of rewards. How do these two forms relate to the statement?"
> " . . . and what would happen if we stopped reinforcing in an interval schedule? Would the behavior stop quicker or slower than continuous reinforcement . . . ?"

Three forms of integrative reconciliation were illustrated in Miss Martello's lesson. The first involves simple comparisons as demonstrated by her first two questions. This process is often called horizontal reconciliation because it involves finding relationships among coordinate ideas.

The second form is called vertical reconciliation and is the process of relating the subordinate ideas to the advance organizer. This process is critical because in addition to making the succeeding content more meaningful, it reinforces the organizer and makes it better able to anchor the content and relate it to existing schemata.

With the last question, Miss Martello asked the students to go beyond simple comparisons to make inferences in the form of an hypothesis about the potential effects of each reinforcement schedule. This is an important form of integrative reconciliation because the students then see how the concepts relate both in terms of their characteristics and in terms of their potential effects. This is an advanced form of association which significantly increases the meaningfulness of each concept. It can be either horizontal or vertical.

This process has been demonstrated to increase learning. In a review of research Anderson & Armbruster (1984) concluded that asking students to create mental images of new material, draw inferences, and to draw networks of relationships all increased learning. Miss Martello applied this research to her lesson through her questioning.

Other forms of advanced reconciliation can be accomplished as well. For example, asking students to paraphrase and summarize information is also effective and is an aid in helping students apply the information to new situations (Annes, 1985). This process forces the students to organize the information so they can describe it in their own words, which helps reinforce the development of their schemata.

Another type of reconciliation is an extension of traditional note taking. As the material is developed, the students can be asked to avoid writing notes taken verbatim from the discussion, and instead improve the meaningfulness of the content by describing relationships based on the information. Peper & Mayer (1986) found that students increased their ability to recall principles and solve problems when they applied this improved form of note taking.

What do these various forms of integrative reconciliation have in common? First, they are all accomplished through student involvement which places the major responsibility for processing on the learner under the watchful eye of an active teacher. In the course of this processing, students are helped to analyze the new information to find relationships in it. Finally, the goal of each of the forms of integrative reconciliation is the generation of schemata that are logically organized in students' minds.

This completes our discussion of integrative reconciliation. We would now like to summarize the implementation phase of the Interactive Model with an example taken from a lesson on theatre.

An English teacher was teaching a unit on the theatre. The sequence of steps followed in implementing the model would be:

1. Having prepared an advance organizer during the planning stage of the model, the teacher would present the organizer on the board or an overhead.
2. She would present the first elements of the structural outline in hierarchical form. Along with the advance organizer, it might appear as follows. Analyzing theatre is much like analyzing a novel; though each novel (and form of theatre) will differ in significant ways, there are common elements such as subject matter, plot, staging and characterizations.

FIGURE 9.13   Initial Structural Outline With Advance Organizer

This represents the initial progressive differentiation.

3. She would ask for examples and characteristics of Greek and Italian plays to check the students' concept of each.
4. The teacher at this point would begin integrative reconciliation by comparing the two theatre forms, discussing the examples, characteristics, similarities, and differences and relating the information to the advance organizer.
5. The teacher now has an option. She may choose to develop the structure horizontally so it would appear as follows:

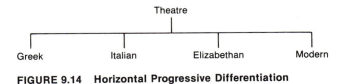

FIGURE 9.14 **Horizontal Progressive Differentiation**

On the other hand, she could continue it vertically so it would appear as:

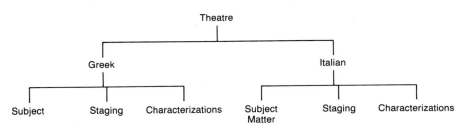

FIGURE 9.15 **Vertical Progressive Differentiation**

With either option the next task for the teacher is to explore the relationships among the differentiated concepts. In the first case, the class would discuss the ways in which the different theatres were related. In the second example, the integrative reconciliation would focus upon the subject matter of the Greek and Italian theatres and how these different subject matters influenced staging and characterizations. The teacher would then continue with progressive differentiation, integrating and reconciling topics until all the content was covered and the lesson completed.

From the discussion in this section we see that the processes of progressive differentiation and integrative reconciliation are reciprocal and complementary. Both are required in order for schemata to be properly developed. For example, if Greek and Italian theatre are not properly differentiated, they are seen by the learner as the same concept. On the other hand, if the concepts are not properly reconciled, the students see them as isolated items of information that are reduced to the level of fact learning. When the two processes are properly employed, students are able to develop well-defined schemata to fit an overall structure that continues to grow and develop.

This concludes our discussion of the implementation phase of the Interactive Model. In our discussion the Interactive Model was described as a procedure designed to teach organized bodies of content in a single lesson. As mentioned previously, another use of the model is as an organizational guide for curriculum development. This use and other variations of the model will be discussed in the next section.

VARIATIONS OF THE MODEL

In the preceding sections we described the Interactive Model as serving two primary purposes. First, it could be used to organize a lesson, unit, or course, and second, it serves to help learners form schemata by finding relationships among concepts and generalizations. Within this general framework, however, a variety of options exist. One of these is the use of "mini" hierarchies to supplement other models. For example, consider Mr. Jaurez's lesson on arthropods from Chapter 4. At some point in the lesson a hierarchy identifying the relationships among his examples would make the material more meaningful for the students. The hierarchy might appear as follows:

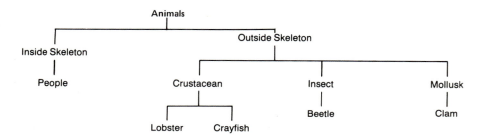

Using the hierarchy would help the students better see the relationships among the animals. It suggests that the lobster and crayfish are the most closely related, which they could verify from the appearance of the animals. They could then continue the discussion identifying the similarities and differences among each of the groups.

As another example, consider a teacher discussing the topic of closure in mathematics. (An operation is considered to be closed if the outcome of the operation produces a number that belongs to the same set as the numbers combined in the operation.) A discussion of the topic could be supplemented with a brief hierarchy such as the following:

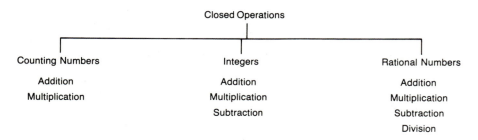

This outline is additionally interesting in that it implies a pattern. The students could then be encouraged to hypothesize on the basis of the pattern and then test their hypotheses with other numbers and sets. In this way the hierarchy, in addition to helping make the concepts more meaningful, could provide an avenue for promoting student thinking skills.

As teachers get used to using hierarchies to supplement other lessons, they uncover a variety of opportunities to enhance their students' learning. We are presenting these examples in the hope that they might further stimulate your thinking about the uses of the Interactive Model.

A second option you might consider would be the use of hierarchies in conjunction with modified data retrieval charts, such as those we discussed in Chapter 6.

Charts describing salient aspects of closely related concepts can do much to help students organize similarities and differences in their minds. As an example of a chart being used to supplement a hierarchy, consider the following outline of material covering a unit of study on the novel.

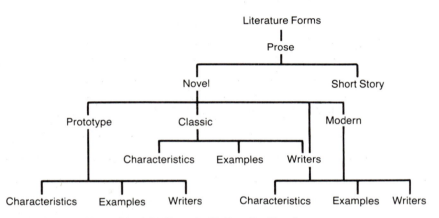

FIGURE 9.16   Hierarchical Outline of a Unit on the Novel

The advantage of an outline such as this is that it shows at a glance the superordinate, coordinate and subordinate relationships contained in the content. However, diagrams can become cluttered, and when they do, the information contained in them is harder to use. One solution to this problem is the use of supplementary data retrieval charts as shown in Figure 9.17.

The use of a data retrieval chart as a supplement to a hierarchical diagram has two advantages. One is that a chart allows the teacher to include and organize data for a lesson, and second, it insures a thorough process of integrative reconciliation. The structural outline graphically illustrates how the concepts are differentiated; the chart, in turn, insures their reconciliation through an analysis of the data in it.

Let's consider another example of a chart used to organize content for

TYPES OF NOVELS

	Characteristics	Examples	Writers
Prototypes			
Classic			
Modern			

FIGURE 9.17   Supplementary Data Retrieval Chart

an interactive lesson. Here protozoans (one-celled animals) and metazoans (many-celled animals) are compared.

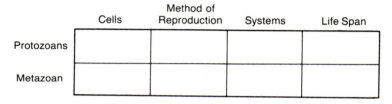

	Cells	Method of Reproduction	Systems	Life Span
Protozoans				
Metazoan				

FIGURE 9.18   Supplementary Data Retrieval Chart in Biology

A chart such as this could be used to supplement the following hierarchy:

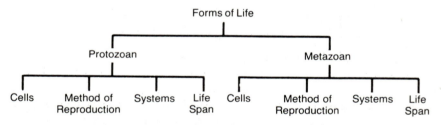

FIGURE 9.19   Organizational Hierarchy in Biology

An additional advantage of charts is that they are easy to use in a classroom setting, in that information can be conveniently organized and stored in cells. This allows the teacher to present data rather than processed conclusions to students and thus encourages the processing of information during the class.

In using either charts or outlines, it should be remembered that both are means toward an end: the transmission of stable organized bodies of information. The value of the charts and diagrams lies in their ability to organize material for teaching and learning.

This ends our discussion of the implementation phase of the Interactive Model. The final section of this chapter discusses problems and issues in the evaluation of Interactive learning activities.

EVALUATING INTERACTIVE MODEL LESSONS

The Interactive Model as described in previous sections of this chapter is designed to teach the relationships among interrelated concepts. This is somewhat different from the previous models which had specific forms of content as the content goals rather than a series of generalizations. In addition, little mention has been made of the thinking skills involved in the model. Though the model is largely content oriented, thinking skills can be taught. One of the most distinctive of these processes is the ability to structure content hierarchically. Measuring for this skill as well as for the content outcomes of the Interactive Model will be discussed in the following paragraphs.

As described in the previous sections, the Ausubel model can be used to teach concepts and generalizations as well as the relationship between these abstractions. Evaluating the acquisition of concepts and generalizations has already been discussed in Chapter 3 and will not be discussed further here. What will be described are considerations teachers need to make in evaluating students' knowledge of the relationship between these abstractions.

The ability to relate concepts and generalizations depends on an understanding of the abstractions themselves. Thus, failure on an item designed to measure student understanding of these relationships may be due to a lack of such knowledge or to a failure to understand the concepts or generalizations themselves. Consequently, in evaluating student understanding of the relationship between ideas, teachers should also measure for student understanding of the ideas themselves. Doing so allows the teacher to decide whether failure on an item measuring relational knowledge resulted from a lack of this knowledge or a lack of understanding of the abstractions themselves.

In the evaluation of relationships between abstractions the teacher can measure at the knowledge level or higher. Measuring at the knowledge level would tap students' ability to remember or recall the relationships discussed in class. For example, the teacher in the lesson on theatre might measure students' knowledge of the relationship between the different types of theatre in the following manner:

List as many similarities and differences as you can between Greek and Elizabethan theatre.

This same information could be measured with a multiple choice item:

Which of the following characteristics are shared by both Greek and Elizabethan theatre?

1. Elaborate staging with complex sets.
2. Simple costumes with masks.
3. Complex plot lines with intricate subplots.
4. Absence of musical scores or backgrounds.

An alternate way of measuring students' knowledge of relationships is to ask them to identify superordinate, subordinate, and coordinate relationships within the developed hierarchy. For example, the following is an item designed to measure such relationships in the lesson on parts of speech.

1. Circle those items that are subordinate to naming words.

    a. adjective
    b. pronouns
    c. gerund
    d. noun

Again, the emphasis in items such as these is on the remembering of information previously discussed in class.

An alternate way of measuring students' understanding of subordinate, coordinate and superordinate relationships is to provide them with a list of previously learned terms and ask them to arrange them hierarchically. As an example, consider a lesson on vertebrates in a high school biology class. As a review of previously learned concepts and as a measure of whether students understand the relationships between concepts, the teacher could list the following concepts on the board and ask students to organize them hierarchically.

Reptile	Birds	Vertebrates
Fish	Warm-blooded	Mammals
Snake	Monotremes	Mammals
Frog	Salamander	Placentals
Marsupial	Turtle	Cold-blooded
Amphibian		Lizard

The hierarchy might then appear as follows:

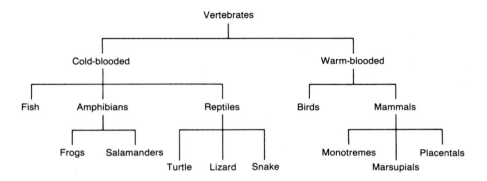

Note that this item is very similar to the diagnostic exercise described in the planning section. The major difference between the two is that this item would be used after the concepts had been covered and is explicitly designed to measure relationships between concepts.

Information attained at the knowledge level is an important part of information processing in that it can become the foundation for further information processing. In addition, it is a content goal in and of itself. However, stopping at this point both in teaching and evaluation severely handicaps development of the learner's ability to process information. One way to insure this capability is to design and use items which evaluate the learning of information at levels higher than knowledge.

One way of evaluating students' understanding of relationships at a level higher than knowledge is to ask them to apply the information learned in class to a new situation. The following example illustrates this type of item.

Briefly describe how the staging for the Greek play, *Oedipus Rex,* would be different if it were done in an Elizabethan theater.

In order to answer this question correctly, the students must know the characteristics of Elizabethan theatre and apply them to a Greek play. This process would provide the teacher with a good measure of the extent to which the schema for theatre had been assimilated in an integrated and organized fashion.

Let's turn now to a consideration of measuring for process. One implicit goal in the Interactive Model is that students can organize or structure previously unstructured information. This amounts to structuring a list of familiar but unorganized concepts into a hierarchy. One way of measuring this skill is to ask students to take a new chapter in their text and either outline the new material or structure it hierarchically. This could also be done with other information sources such as reference books, articles, or movies where the information has not been previously organized for the student.

This concludes our discussion of the evaluation phase of the Interactive Model. The examples and techniques provided here are not meant to be exhaustive but rather are illustrative of ways to measure the learning that occurs in an interactive lesson. The imaginative teacher will develop other equally valid ways of measuring for the learning which occurs in this model.

This completes the contents of this text. It is our sincere hope that the information contained within it has stimulated your thinking about teaching in general and teaching procedure in particular. If this has occurred, our goals in writing the material will have been met. As a way of summarizing the content, we have devised an exercise designed to reinforce your understanding of the topics presented.

EXERCISES

1.   The following is a description of a college class involved in a discussion of information processing models. This is the last day of a three-day presentation. In the blanks in front of each statement mark CD if the statement is a concept definition used as an advance organizer, G if the statement is a generalization used as an advance organizer, and A for an analogy. In addition, identify statements that illustrate progressive differentiation with PD and others that illustrate integrative reconciliation with IR. If the statements are none of these, leave the statement blank.

_____ 1. Mr. Peebles, the instructor, began his Friday class with a review of his Monday and Wednesday class.

_____ 2. "How did we begin the Monday session?" he asked.

_____ 3. "Well," Ron began, "you said a teaching model is like a conceptual blueprint in that both are used to achieve some purpose. A blueprint is used as a guide for an engineering objective, while a teaching model is a guide to achieving content and process objectives.

_____ 4. Arlene added, "You noted that models can be grouped according to whether they emphasize cognitive, affective, psychomotor, or a special kind of cognitive goal called information processing."

_____ 5. "You said that our emphasis in here would be on information processing," Mary added.

_____ 6. "Wednesday you began to deal with the information processing family," Bob interjected.

_____ 7. "And you said you wanted to deal with each of the models separately so that they would remain clear and distinct in our minds," Martha added.

_____ 8. George then said, "You began the lesson on information processing models by stating that they are designed to help students handle stimuli and input from the environment and transform it into more meaningful output."

_____ 9. "You then went on to say that the models are grouped according to whether they are primarily deductive, primarily inductive, or inquiry," Kay noted.

_____ 10. "You further broke the inductive models into the Integrative Model, the Inductive Model, and the Concept Attainment Model, and the deductive models into the Deductive and Interactive Models," Russ added.

_____ 11. "You also noted that while the Interactive Model is primarily expository and deductive and the Integrative Model is inductive, they aren't as unrelated as you would expect because they can be used to process large amounts of information, but the way in which this is done differs."

_____ 12. "We also added that the Integrative Model is much more process oriented than is the Interactive Model," Carol commented.

_____ 13. "You also suggested," Linda noted, "that Ausubel sees the nervous system as an information processing mechanism analogous to a discipline which organizes concepts hierarchically."

_____ 14. "Excellent," commented Mr. Peebles. "You seem to have formed stable concepts of the ideas that we've discussed so far. Today, I want to consider a new model. This information processing model is the Inquiry Model designed to help students develop their ability to form causal explanations for events which occur in people's environments."

_____ 15. "This model combines both inductive and deductive modes of thinking. The first part of the model involves identification of some kind of a problem, and the second part of the model involves gathering information to explain the problem."

_____ 16. Wayne interjected, "We have noted that there are primarily three forms of knowledge we try to teach: concepts, generalizations, and facts. Which of these is the Inquiry Model designed to teach?"

_____ 17. "That's a good question," Mr. Peebles noted. "But before I answer that I'd like to show you some examples of the Inquiry Model and see if you can answer that question yourself." (The class then proceeded to analyze the examples presented and ultimately came up with the answer to Wayne's question.)

2.   In the space below, *using only information from the anecdote,* diagram Mr. Peebles' three-day presentation hierarchically.

FEEDBACK

_____   1. Mr. Peebles, the instructor, began his Friday class with a review of his Monday and Wednesday class.

_____   2. "How did we begin the Monday session?" he asked.

___A___   3. "Well," Ron began, "you said a teaching model is like a conceptual blueprint in that both are used to achieve some purpose. A blueprint is used as a guide for an engineering objective, while a teaching model is a guide to achieving content and process objectives."

___PD___   4. Arlene added, "You noted that models can be grouped according to whether they emphasize cognitive, affective, psychomotor, or a special kind of cognitive goal called information processing."

_____   5. "You said that our emphasis in here would be on information processing," Mary added.

_____   6. "Wednesday you began to deal with the information processing family," Bob interjected.

_____   7. "And you said you wanted to deal with each of the models separately so that they would remain clear and distinct in our minds," Martha added.

___CD___   8. George then said, "You began the lesson on information processing models by stating that they are designed to help students handle stimuli and input from the environment and transform it into more meaningful output."

___PD___   9. "You then went on to say that the models are grouped according to whether they are primarily deductive, primarily inductive, or inquiry," Kay noted.

___PD___   10. "You further broke the inductive models into the Integrative Model, the Inductive Model, and the Concept Attainment Model, and the deductive models into the Deductive and Interactive Models," Russ added.

___IR___   11. "You also noted that while the Interactive Model is primarily expository and deductive and the Integrative Model is inductive, they aren't as unrelated as you would expect because they can be used to process large amounts of information, but the way in which this is done differs."

___IR___   12. "We also added that the Integrative Model is much more process oriented than is the Interactive Model," Carol commented.

_____   13. "You also suggested," Linda noted, "that Ausubel sees the nervous system as an information processing mechanism analogous to a discipline which organizes concepts hierarchically."

__CD__   14. "Excellent," commented Mr. Peebles. "You seem to have formed stable concepts of the ideas that we've discussed so far. Today, I want to consider a new model. This information processing model is the Inquiry Model designed to help students develop their ability to form causal explanations for events which occur in people's environments."

__PD__   15. "This model combines both inductive and deductive modes of thinking. The first part of the model involves identification of some kind of a problem, and the second part of the model involves gathering information to explain the problem."

__PD__   16. Wayne interjected, "We have noted that there are primarily three forms of knowledge we try to teach: concepts, generalizations, and facts. Which of these is the Inquiry Model designed to teach?"

_____   17. "That's a good question," Mr. Peebles noted. "But before I answer that I'd like to show you some examples of the Inquiry Model and see if you can answer that question yourself." (The class then proceeded to analyze the examples presented and ultimately came up with the answer to Wayne's question.)

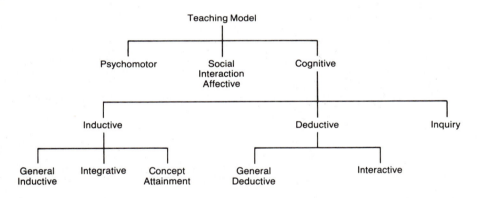

DISCUSSION QUESTIONS

1.   How are procedural schemata typically learned? Give several examples from common experience.

2.   How are procedural schemata and teaching models related? Identify some similarities and differences.

3.   We described three types of learning in this chapter: accretion, tuning, and restructuring. How prevalent or important are these in your content area/grade level? How does the presence of these three forms of learning change: (a) across the K–12 curriculum; (b) within a school year; (c) within a unit?

4.   What conditions might influence the effectiveness of advance organizers? Are they more effective with younger students or older? Are they more effective with new material or old? Are they more effective with abstract or concrete material?

5.   Consider advance organizers in a broad sense. What kinds of aids and/or teacher behaviors can serve as organizers for students? What might be a metaphor for advance organizers in the affective domain? In the psychomotor domain?

6.   The Integrative and Interactive Models appear to be quite different, but in reality have several similarities. Identify some of them.

7.   In what ways is the problem in a Suchman Inquiry activity similar to an advance organizer? How is it different?

8.   We discussed comparison questions in detail in Chapters 4 and 6. How does this questioning technique relate to the theories discussed in Chapter 9?

REFERENCES

ANDERSON, T. & ARMSBURSTER, B. (1984). Studying. In D. Pearson, ed., *Handbook of research in reading* (New York: Longman), pp. 657–679.

ANNES, L. (1985). Student-generated paragraph summaries and the information-processing theory of prose learning. *Journal of Experimental Education, 54,* 4–100.

AUSUBEL, D. (1963). *The psychology of meaningful verbal learning* (New York: Grune and Stratton).

AUSUBEL, D. (1978). In defense of advance organizers: A reply to the critics. *Review of Educational Research, 48,* 251–257.

BARTLETT, F. (1932). *Remembering* (London: Cambridge University Press).

CHAMPAGNE, A., KLOPFOR, L., SOLOMON, C., & CAHN, A. (1980). *Interactions of students' knowledge with their comprehension and design of science experiments.* (Ed 188–950). (Pittsburgh: University of Pittsburgh Learning Research and Development Center).

CORNBLETH, C. (1985). Critical thinking and cognitive processes. In W. Stanley, ed., *Review of research in social studies education 1976–1983* (Washington D.C.: National Council for the Social Studies), pp. 12–64.

DINNEL, D. & GLOVER, J. (1985). Advance organizers: Encoding manipulations. *Journal of Educational Psychology, 77,* 514–521.

EGGEN, P., KAUCHAK, D., & KIRK, S. (1978). Hierarchical cues and the learning of concepts from prose materials. *Journal of Experimental Education, 46,* 7–10.

FLAVELL, J. (1985). *Cognitive development,* 2nd ed. (Englewood Cliffs, NJ: Prentice-Hall, Inc.).

GOOD, T. & BROPHY, J. (1980). *Educational psychology,* 2nd ed. (New York: Holt, Rinehart & Winston).

LEFRANCAIS, G. (1982). *Psychology for teaching,* 4th ed. (Belmont, CA: Wadsworth).

LUITON, J., AMES, W., & ACKERSON, G. (1980). A meta-analysis of the effects of advance organizers on learning and retention. *American Educational Research Journal, 17,* 211–218.

MAYER, R. (1984). Aids to text comprehension. *Educational Psychologist, 19,* 30–42.

PEPER, R. & MAYER, R. (1986). Generative effects of note taking during science lectures. *Journal of Educational Psychology, 78,* 34–38.

RUMELHART, D. & NORMAN, D. (1981). Analogical processes in learning. In J. Anderson (Ed.), *Cognitive skills and their acquisition.* (pp. 335–359) Hillsdale, N.J.: Erlbaum.

RUMELHART, D. & ORTONY, A. (1977). The representation of knowledge in memory. In R. Anderson, R. Spurs, & W. Montague, eds., *Schooling and the acquisition of knowledge* (Hillsdale, NJ: Erlbaum).

RUMELHART, D. (1980). Schemata: The building blocks of cognition. In R. Spiro, B. Bruce, & W. Brewer, eds., *Theoretical issues in reading comprehension* (Hillsdale, NJ: Erlbaum).

STALLINGS, J. (1983). *Findings from the research on teaching: What we have learned* (Vanderbilt University, TN: Peabody Center for Effective teaching).

TABA, H. (1966). *Teaching strategies and cognitive functioning in elementary school children.* Coop. Research Project #2404, Washington, D.C.: USOE.

TABA, H. (1967). *Teachers handbook to elementary social studies.* Reading, MA: Addison Wesley.

WITTROCK, M. (1983). Writing and the teaching of reading. *Language Arts, 60,* 600–606.

INDEX